"Erna Paris has written a sane, helpful, hopeful book about the pitfalls and rewards of remarriage. Her readable style mirrors her advice: gently honest, lively, lucid and utterly free of jargon or condescension. She writes, refreshingly, as an intelligent and perceptive woman who has been there."

Michele Landsberg,
Author of *WOMEN AND CHILDREN FIRST*

"STEPFAMILIES: MAKING THEM WORK provides a wealth of information and 'practical suggestions'...This sensitive and sharp book will be especially useful, not only to reconstructed families, but to counsellors, therapists, and clergy."

Gordon Wolfe, M.S.W.
Executive Director,
Jewish Family and Child Service of Metropolitan Toronto

STEP-FAMILIES:
MAKING THEM WORK

Erna Paris

AVON
PUBLISHERS OF BARD, CAMELOT, DISCUS AND FLARE BOOKS

AVON BOOKS
A division of
The Hearst Corporation
1790 Broadway
New York, New York 10019

Copyright © 1984 by Erna Paris
Published by arrangement with the author
Library of Congress Catalog Card Number: 83-45979
ISBN: 0-380-89670-2

First Avon Printing, March 1985

AVON TRADEMARK REG. U.S. PAT. OFF. AND IN
OTHER COUNTRIES, MARCA REGISTRADA, HECHO EN
U.S.A.

Printed in the U.S.A.

WFH 10 9 8 7 6 5 4 3 2 1

for Tom
for Michelle
for Roland

with love

Contents

Acknowledgments

I AM DEEPLY grateful to the many people who generously offered their time and expertise during the years I spent researching and writing this book. To list them all would require another book-length manuscript, so the best I can do is to name a few and hope that the rest will recognize my important debt to them as they read the text.

My first bouquet must go to Lillian Messinger of the Clarke Institute of Psychiatry in Toronto. Mrs. Messinger is one of the foremost authorities on remarriage and stepparenting in North America. It was through her that I first considered writing about the subject, and she has been consistently helpful throughout. I also wish to thank Dr. Paul Druckman and Dr. Paul Steinhauer of Toronto, both of whom took time from their busy schedules to discuss ideas and, in the case of Dr. Druckman, to read and comment upon transcript material. Penny Gross, a graduate student at the University of Toronto, shared her interesting research on the subject. My friend, Maxine Sidran, helped me gather research; Kathy Vanderlinden offered valuable editorial suggestions, as did David Lewis Stein and my brother, Dr. Peter Newman. Beverley Slopen acted as my sage, practical and always encouraging. Pat Russo typed the manuscript with her usual demon speed and accuracy.

I also wish to extend profound thanks to the many, necessarily anonymous people who agreed to allow their personal stories to appear in this book. I share, along with them, the hope that their successes and their failures will help inform others.

I reserve my deepest gratitude for the last. It goes to my husband, Tom Robinson, for his never-failing commitment, his constant encouragement and for his sharp editorial eye.

Erna Paris
Toronto, Ontario
June, 1983

STEP-
FAMILIES:
MAKING
THEM
WORK

Introduction

DURING THE LAST days of a dying marriage, husbands and wives may dream of the release that awaits them. After the separation, they tell themselves, they will be able to sleep at night again; they will build a sharply different life for themselves and the children; they will—they *hope* they will—meet other men and women easily; and the thought of rediscovering sex, or merely being touched with gentleness after years in a brittle-angry marriage, may flood them with half-forgotten feelings.

The long-awaited day may turn out to be one of the saddest in a lifetime, but sometimes a sense of excitement and euphoria will, indeed, carry them out the door. A middle-aged man may shed a few pounds, buy a set of up-to-date clothes, and surreptitiously pick up a book on how to meet liberated women. His wife is unlikely to have the same access to the sexual marketplace, much as she'd like to, but at first, just having HIM out of the way is happiness enough. The arguing stops. A blessed tranquility descends on the household.

The children, of course, are not euphoric. They are frightened that the remaining parent will also leave them and worried about who will look after their needs. They are confused and shocked because an unlooked-for grenade has exploded at the centre of their lives; and they wonder if it was their fault. . . .

Husband and wife, however, do not stay euphoric for long. The flash of joy so devoutly wished for too often turns out to be a flash in the pan.

The wife (presuming she has the children)[1] must reconstruct a life in which all of them are financially secure;[2] but if she has been a housewife and has no marketable skills, that will be painfully difficult to do. She will have to balance the emotional neediness of her children with her own profound yearning for friendship and affection. She must cope with feelings of rejection and anger if she has been "left." And most important (although she may not see it that way), she must work out an accommodating relationship with her former husband, who, perhaps unfortunately for her but fortunately for her children, is likely to remain connected to all of their lives for a very long time.

Her husband's lot may be easier materially (he doesn't usually have to look for a new job) but painful in other ways. A man who has been looked after in a traditional marriage for so long he can hardly remember otherwise (most marriages now break up after an average of eleven and a half years), who has grown accustomed to finding dinner on the table and his shirts in the cupboard, may now be in an unfurnished apartment wondering how to poach an egg. The silence, free of children's squabbles, may seem ominous and empty. He may feel guilty at having left home, or consumed with rage at his wife for having steered him out the door. And although he is feeling as down as he's ever been, he may not be getting the same emotional support from friends and family that his wife is receiving. They may consider him a despicable cad for having left her even if she kicked him out.

The good news is that at the end of a year's time, both husband and wife will probably have made some sort of initial adjustment to their new lives. Finances may still be a serious problem, but she may have discovered an independent personal strength she didn't know existed. After a period of grief at having "lost" his children, he will ideally have set up regular visiting with them and begun to accept the altered relation-

---

[1] Fathers are getting custody of their children more than they used to, but the majority of orders are still in favour of the mother.

[2] In 1980, in Canada, the U.S., and Britain, working women earned between 60 and 64 percent of what men earned.

ship. And each of them will probably be thinking about finding another mate—in spite of the pain, in spite of the bitterness, in spite of divorce.

If statistics work in their favour, they will probably remarry: 80 percent of men and 70 percent of women do. But almost half of these remarriages currently fail.

Remarriage is a country few people visit as tourists, and it occupies the imagination a little vaguely and a little diffusely. It is a longed-for paradise of peace and love from which the pain of divorce and the suffering of the children have been banished forever. It is a world of eternal happiness where loneliness is cast away and past injustices are rectified. No discordant notes sound on the heavenly lutes. In the fantasy land of remarriage, no one ever cries.

Men and women who have been through a harrowing marriage breakup are as hopeful as people who have never married. They dream that this time the longed-for promise will materialize.

And therein lies the problem. The standard, romantic dream that failed the first time is even less likely to succeed the second time around. Remarriage requires two hard noses and at least a modicum of strategy.

Lots of remarried people are profoundly happy, but some are as miserable as they've ever been in their lives. Their kids may be miserable, too, some even attempting suicide; but, in spite of such serious crises, the problems of second marriage are largely unknown. To be in trouble in this new relationship is not something the participants admit to lightly, and who can blame them? Parents and friends may have been sympathetic during the divorce, but when the remarriage took place they probably heaved a sigh of relief and thanked the Lord that dear Suzie was going to be okay. New problems start to look like carelessness, as Oscar Wilde might have put it—or, worse still, a repetitive neurotic pattern that can be cured only by years on the analyst's couch.

Anyone thinking about hooking up with another mate should know one essential fact: Second marriage is not the same as first marriage. This is not a quantitative statement, as in ''More second marriages are successful than first marriages," or "more second marriages are troubled than first marriages." The difference, rather, is qualitative. Second marriages are quite simply another kettle of fish—especially when children are involved.

The problems of stepfamilies are endemic. Who is in charge of discipline? How can a stepparent relate in an effective way to children he or she cannot possibly "love," at least at the outset? How can the new family function as a unit when there are ex-mates around who may be disruptive and who never, ever, become ex-parents to their children? What can adults do when children are torn by conflicting loyalties and are hostile or sad? Or when they don't like each other? Or when the adults don't like the children? How can blended families blend—i.e., prevent themselves from splitting into hostile camps led by generals who happen to be married to each other? And what about the question of who is and who is not related? Is a stepfamily a "real" family? And if it is, what happens when the natural children of the husband or the wife live somewhere else?

Some of these questions arose first from my own experience in a second marriage. I lived alone as a single parent for five years, and when I met the man I would eventually marry, part of my joy came from the thought that my children would be as delighted as I was. It seemed self-evidently true that if we were happy together, the children would participate in that happiness.

My husband and I were unqualifiedly surprised by the difficulties we encountered, many of which were rooted in our own hitherto-unexplored attitudes. It took time and perseverance before we began to feel even remotely like a family—and there were moments when we doubted the outcome—but I did not discover how universal our experience was until I began to research this book. First I followed up personal contacts by travelling to interview families who were willing to meet me. Then I put ads in the personal columns of several newspapers. I was flooded with replies from people who needed to talk but hesitated to seek help because the problems they were having felt like a second failure. On the other hand, some happily married couples who had thought about their relationships wanted to communicate what had worked for them.

I interviewed just over one hundred people and, whenever possible, talked privately with every member of the family in order to see a whole spectrum. The children were of special interest. Almost without exception, they were open and direct. And very, very moving.

I collected thick file folders of individual case histories. I collated a bibliography and read everything I could on the subject. I interviewed authorities in the social-work and mental-health fields and discussed some of the case histories with them.

But in the final analysis, the words that rang clearest to my ears came from ordinary people who spoke to me about their private lives. While each story was necessarily unique, there emerged a pattern of experience in remarriage. There seemed to be identifiable reasons why some couples were successful and others floundered.

These are their stories. Most people asked for anonymity, and I have changed names, locations, and some occupations, but not so radically as to distort the nature of the person. All the interviews were taped, and no significant contextual details were altered.

The statistical facts tell their own story. In Canada, during the decade of the 1970s, the divorce rate increased by 100 percent;[3] in Britain it increased by 155 percent,[4] and in the United States by 53 percent[5] (although the overall divorce rate in the U.S. was almost double that of the other countries). By 1983 it was being estimated that about 80 percent of divorced men and 70 percent of divorced women remarried and that approximately one out of every three marriages in Canada, the United States, and Britain involved at least one partner who

[3] Divorce: Law and the Family in Canada; Statistics Canada, 1983.

[4] Social Trends, 1982, Government Statistical Service.

[5] Statistical Abstract of the U.S., 1981, U.S. Bureau of the Census.

had been previously married. If trends continue, and they are expected to, it is not outrageous to predict that remarriage will soon become the most common form of coupling in society.

Each year thousands of children who have already lost a parent through death or divorce must adjust to stepparents and stepsiblings in new, uncharted relationships. They, their stepparents, and their natural parents face one of the greatest challenges they are ever likely to undertake. The stepfamily is a second chance at happiness, with high stakes and great rewards, but it is also a hurdle course. And as in the case of all such events, it is the quick and the nimble who survive.

CHAPTER ONE

False Expectations: The Trials of the Renzetti Family

CARLA RENZETTI CAME to the door of her house looking slightly apprehensive. I had come, after all, to ask questions about her marriage, this second experiment in intimacy that so much depended upon. Her self-esteem, for one thing. She had been married for nine years the first time and that had failed. For six years—and they had seemed very long to her—she had been alone. Then she met Anthony, and within weeks she had decided to take both her children with her into a new marriage.

The risk to her children's happiness (and his children's happiness, too) was greater than she had thought. Somehow, both she and Anthony had simply taken it for granted that if they were happy the children would also be happy. But five years later, everyone had gone through what she called "a desperate time." This was a development neither she nor Anthony had anticipated.

Carla was forty, a large-boned woman who had to watch her weight. She was surely never a beauty in any clichéd sense, but she liked to dress well and keep herself in shape. Anthony had a secure job as a middle-level manager in a large corporation, and that was an important motivation for this marriage. Child support from her ex-husband had been sporadic during the six-year hiatus between marriages, and

Carla's salary as an assistant in a day-care centre was so inadequate that she felt constantly in peril. She had been raised in an upper-middle-class professional family. That status had been maintained during her first marriage: Her husband came from a similar background and worked in his father's prosperous grocery business. But as a single parent Carla had found herself living dangerously close to the edge. Like so many divorced women who have been housewives, she had few marketable skills. Indeed, the drop in income had been almost as hard to cope with as the marriage breakup itself.

So, from every practical point of view, Anthony looked like a good bet. He was well off, he was apparently an excellent father to his children, and he was definitely a family man—his wife had left him, not the reverse. He and Carla seemed to have a lot in common, too. They enjoyed the out-of-doors and they enjoyed each other in bed. He was even good-looking. Carla liked to think of herself as realistic, and she asked herself what more any basically penurious woman in her mid-thirties with two dependent children could want or expect. The situation looked ideal.

Carla's house was expensively decorated and immaculately clean, so clean that it was difficult to believe four teenagers lived there. It had bright, spacious rooms and a two-car garage and was situated on what real estate agents call a "prime" street in a "prime" residential area of Hamilton, Ontario. No one on that street earned less than $40,000 a year, and that was important to Carla.

"I'm quite conventional," she admitted happily. "I wanted my kids to go to school in a good area and make friends with other middle-class kids. I'm not ashamed of that either," she added quickly. "I only want the same things for my children that I had as a child."

A yellow enamel coffeepot perked cheerfully on the kitchen stove and an aroma of baking cookies filled the room. This was the ideal, fairy-tale image of the happy housewife, and I wondered whether Carla had "prepared" for our interview, perhaps unconsciously. Conventional expectations had also defined the terms of the marriage.

"When Anthony and I got married, we had a bargain,"

Carla said. "I would stay home and look after all the children and he would earn our living. Since I had worked in a day-care centre and I was already an experienced parent, we both thought that would work out perfectly. I haven't given up on it entirely, but if this marriage is going to continue, some things will have to change. We were so naïve about remarriage and trying to create a relationship with each other's children. Just like ostriches with our heads in the sand. We thought it would be just the same as a first marriage, only this time the Cinderella story would actually continue through to a happy ending."

When Carla and her first husband, John, separated, Carla just assumed that she would remarry, and probably within two or three years, "the way most people do," she said, smiling ironically. But the years began to run into each other and there seemed to be no serious or even interesting men in her life. During the six years between her marriages she had no serious involvement with anyone at all, so her children had never really seen her dating, nor had they come to terms with their mother as an adult with a life of her own apart from them. Still, she did have a job; and she always hoped she would meet someone nice who would also be a good stepfather to her children. That was of major importance in her mind.

The year before Carla met Anthony, several unexpected shocks occurred and they precipitated a mild depression. Carla didn't recognize the signs of depression at the time. She only knew she wasn't functioning as well as usual and that she didn't feel particularly well.

First, her father died. Carla had always been especially close to her dad, and he had been helping her financially as well. When he died of a heart attack, without warning, Carla found herself emotionally bereft. She was also in difficult straits financially. Her mother grew needier, and for a while the two women considered moving in together, but Carla backed down, feeling in her gut that if she made that move she would never leave home again.

She developed allergies that may have been psychosomatic in origin, and at one point she was hospitalized for a suspected blood clot. While she was in hospital, her aunt died in the same building on another floor.

Two months later Carla met Anthony. Psychologically speaking, it was hardly surprising that Prince Charming appeared on the scene just when he was most needed. The time was right; Carla was at her most vulnerable. They dated once, then twice. On date number three, about one month after they had met, they began to talk about marriage. They also agreed to introduce their kids to each other.

"We didn't have to tell the children what we were planning," she said. "The older ones knew. They were about twelve and thirteen, and they understood that we liked each other without our saying anything. I doubt whether telling them would have made any difference at all."

Carla and Anthony were not in a tradition of openness with children, and they were evasive about their sexual relationship. When they planned a couple of days away together they both lied about where they were going. Carla said the kids knew anyway, so they didn't need to be told.

"We're both traditional people," she explained, shrugging her shoulders. "It was really silly, I know, because my ex-husband was living with somebody and Anthony's ex-wife was living with someone. I guess we're from the old school. In any case, we did eventually broach the subject with the kids because Anthony's divorce wasn't through and my lease was up on my apartment and it seemed foolish to renew it. We thought we would ask the kids how they would feel about our living together for a few months until we could get married. Well, they said they didn't want us to. We didn't feel comfortable about it anyway, so we did something a bit unusual, I suppose. I moved into Anthony's place with my two kids and Anthony moved to his brother's, leaving his two kids with me. He just came to the house for meals. And to leave his laundry."

At this she laughed spontaneously. Although they weren't even living together, she was already looking after the children and the household and the laundry—in his house.

Anthony's children were neither grateful nor impressed that their father had left home so that he and his future wife would not have to sleep under the same roof before they were legally married. His daughter, who was twelve, was showing signs of severe emotional stress. She began to invite her boy-friends into the house to "do everything" as Carla quaintly put it. If one were looking for a precise word to describe what these children felt when their dad moved out and this strange woman moved in to become their parent—their single parent, it seemed—that word would be "betrayal." Indeed, they chose it themselves in a conversation with their father some years later.

During the wedding ceremony several months later, Anthony's eight-year-old son was so hostile and upset that he refused to sit down and be quiet until he was rebuked twice by the priest.

"I had expectations about this marriage that you could write a comic book about," Carla laughed as she lit her seventh cigarette of the hour. But her laughter sounded thin. The afternoon winter sun slanted through the kitchen window and she squinted against the light. Patches of triangle-shaped darkness had emerged under her eyes.

"I said I was conventional, and that's precisely what I set out to be in this relationship. One of my kids gave me a SUPER MOM T-shirt for Mother's Day a couple of years ago. It was supposed to be a fun item, sort of a joke, but in truth that's exactly what I tried to be. I came here thinking I was going to be mother to all these children, but not just a caretaker mother. I was going to be their *real* mother and I was going to do everything just the way I had always done it. I had my ideas about discipline and manners and—well, you name it. I figured I had done a good job with my own kids using my methods and I would do the same good job with Anthony's kids. I really thought I was going to give them all the love and all the mothering and all the guidance . . . you know, everything you would do if you started off from birth with your own children. Of course, it never occurred to me that they might have different ideas, or that they weren't babies. They were twelve and eight. My kids were thirteen and eight. It was crazy, and I guess I was a little insensitive, but I have to be honest and say that Anthony and I never talked about child-rearing styles before we decided to marry—not for one short minute.''

Their troubles began almost immediately. ''What happened was that Anthony let me do everything; he *expected* me to look after everything. And then he was unsupportive. I was supposed to do all the disciplining, but then he got very protective of his children and he would take their part against me.'' Carla paused for several long seconds. ''It was impossible,'' she added quietly, looking away.

''I'm telling you all kinds of private things,'' she whispered. ''I gave up so much. He had had a housekeeper, but then we decided we couldn't afford one. And there really wasn't enough room in the house. We were all squeezed together, but Anthony was one hundred percent fastidious about things and I was expected to have the place in perfect order at all times. I did the laundry and the shopping and the cooking for six people, and that was quite an adjustment. But, in fairness to Anthony, you musn't misunderstand. I wanted it. I thought I could do it. I thought we were going about things the right way. But it was impossible. . . .''

Once again Carla looked away. A thin stream of blue smoke rose and circled about her dark hair, and when she spoke again there was an edge of anger in her voice.

''I wasn't used to surly, aggressive kids. My own were well mannered. Anthony said they were passive, and maybe I *had* repressed them, but I just didn't know what to do with kids like his. I felt like a cheap housekeeper—and I felt my husband treated me that way, because he always backed the children in front of me. I hated it. I hated it so much I thought I couldn't stand it. And then I would try to teach the kids one thing and they wouldn't do what I said, then he would back them and say their misbehaviour was okay as far as he was concerned. But everything was still supposed to be my responsibility. I used to cry and I would swear—*me*—I was a person who never used to swear. The words that came out of my mouth were words I didn't like to hear from the children, or anyone. But I couldn't help myself. I felt helpless. I felt as though I had designed a cage, then locked myself in it.

''After three years we separated, though not for long. But

do you know what I did before I walked out? I actually made their supper and left it on the table."

When Cathy Renzetti was just nine years old, her mother left the family to live with another man. Cathy quickly took over the household. As Carla put it, "She had the lead female role and she loved it." During a three-year period, thirteen housekeepers paraded in the front door and out the back. They left because Cathy wouldn't take direction from anyone. She knew who the real mistress of the household was and she did not plan to give up her prerogative. Dad was her special man. She "knew" with fervent, childlike passion that they would always be together.

So when Anthony began to date Carla, Cathy retaliated. She brought boyfriends into the house and slept with them in her own bedroom. The housekeeper of the hour said "No," but the point Cathy was making was far too important for her to take any notice. Sex at age twelve is rarely erotic. It is far more likely to represent comfort to a child—and Cathy needed comfort. She had lost a mother, and it now looked as though she might lose her father too. When Anthony virtually disappeared from the house so that he and Carla wouldn't be living under the same roof before their union had been legitimized, Cathy's worst fears were realized. She *had* lost her dad. And she had lost the important role she had played in the household.

An involuntary grimace crossed Carla's face as she remembered Cathy's behaviour in the early days of the marriage. Cathy was upset, but so was Carla. Cathy didn't listen to anything Carla said—and then Anthony would take her part against Carla. For example, when she was fourteen Cathy moved out to live with her mother. Three months later she was back, and Carla didn't think Anthony ought to take her in so quickly, but Anthony disagreed. He said Carla was rigid and narrow and unyielding and aggressive and cruel in her dealing with his children. "Those were his words," Carla recalled bitterly.

Anthony's younger child, Paul, was also unhappy, and so were Carla's children. But Carla's kids seemed, somehow, to have suffered the least. In spite of the fact that they had moved to someone else's house, the transition was easier for them. Carla had become "mother" to all the children, that was true; but her own children understood her and loved her and were familiar with her demands. They did not lose as much as Anthony's children, who had, in effect, "lost" both their parents and acquired a "wicked stepmother."

"My kids knew they had my love; Anthony's didn't," Carla said sadly. "Anthony was pleasant to my children and they liked him. But since he didn't want to play a parental role in the house, it was easy for him to be nice."

Carla was stubborn. One marriage failure was all she was willing to acknowledge in a lifetime, and she had used up her self-allotted quota. And in spite of their troubles she and Anthony still got along well when they were alone together. Small trips away from the children were warm and happy and intimate (although sex at home was practically nonexistent). But the problems with the children seemed insoluble.

During the third summer of their marriage, a cataclysmic sequence of events took place. Anthony was away on a business trip and Carla had rented a cottage in the country for herself and the children. The day in question began with the usual tensions between Carla and Cathy. Cathy was dieting and Carla was buying and cooking special food. "It was the same old syndrome," Carla said, flicking her cigarette ash. "Cathy was old enough to look after her own diet, but because that was my 'role' I took on all the jobs related to the house, food, and kids. I made a martyr of myself.

"On that morning—it was a Monday morning—I found out she was eating chocolate on the side. I was so angry I almost went to pieces."

Carla's frustration and anger touched off another incident later in the day. "I had to drive into town to get something for dinner. Paul was swimming and I asked him to get out of the water while I was away. I don't know what happened, but I must have said something, or something in my voice must have touched off something in him, and he began to shout at me. It was as though all the hatred he had been storing up came out at once. He was yelling, 'You're a bitch, you're a bitch.' I told him to go into the cottage—there were neighbours and I was very embarrassed—and he said, 'I'm not staying here.' I went to slap him, but he punched me in the face with his fist. He punched me—nobody had ever hit me in my entire life—he punched me and knocked off my glasses.

"I started to cry. I said, 'What has gotten into you? Why are you doing this?' And he said, 'I don't have to talk to you; you're just a stepmother. Anything you do for us is only because you're married to our dad.'

"The next day Anthony came up and I told him what had happened. His punishment was that Paul couldn't use the boat for one day. He had nothing to say, and that was all he did. I felt like garbage.

"I decided to leave, and I told my kids we were going. The next week, after we had returned to the city, I packed my things and left. That was the time I left dinner on the table."

Anthony and Carla had talked about family therapy but never very seriously. Anthony didn't really want it. He felt they ought to work things out for themselves, and he had a favourite expression with which he liked to remind Carla that successfully blended families require hard, slow work. "You can't make instant coffee in a family like this," he used to say. "You have to let it perk."

Carla interrupted her story. She needed a break, and I was taken on a tour of the house. Every room was orderly, the way Anthony liked it.

She motioned me to sit down in the den and closed the door. The children were expected home.

"You may well wonder what I'm doing here, after what I've told you. Sometimes I wonder too. But I'm more hopeful now, and I'll tell you why in a minute.

"Anthony phoned me right away at my mother's. He knew I would go there. He told Cathy to look after Paul while he came to talk to me. And she said to him, 'Go talk to your *wife*.' While he was gone she swallowed a handful of aspirins. He left her to take care of her brother and she tried to O.D. It was awful. Somehow he convinced me to try again. Don't ask me how.

"It's been two years since then, and maybe things have

improved a little and maybe they haven't. Sometimes I feel so tired and defeated I just don't know. I have gone into therapy on my own—just to get some support for myself. And I'm not making any threats anymore. The next time I leave, that will be it.

"But Anthony and I still care about each other; that's the amazing thing. Sometimes I think to myself, the youngest is thirteen and we'll soon have our life to ourselves. But I don't think I could face another five years like the five years we've just come through. Cathy has tried to O.D. three times, though never seriously. She wants her father's attention, but he won't take her seriously enough.

"In a way I guess we've given up. We've decided that we will each look after our own children, but really, I have no idea how that will work. I just told all the kids that I was in an impossible position. They have no respect for me and I have no authority. I said all I'm good for as far as they're concerned is doing the grocery shopping and the laundry and cooking their meals. I said I'm a maid."

No sound broke the stillness. Carla's despair was palpable. Still, she hoped that one tiny change she had insisted upon would improve things. She wanted to work part-time, and Anthony had agreed to change his holidays to make it possible. She said she was sorry to ask him to change his plans, but she had made a firm decision. He went upstairs and got his diary and a calculator and said yes.

"Getting a part-time job will be important. I'll have a little life of my own. I feel I've failed as a stepparent, but I really mustn't fail as a person. With a little job I can be Carla again instead of someone's wife, or someone's mother—or someone's bitch.

"It's not that we have rotten kids," she said suddenly, turning to look me in the eye. "It's the situation. What did we know about how difficult it would be? But if I had to do it again I would definitely go for counselling before we married, so that at least we'd be aware of the pitfalls. I also have to say that if a husband and wife can support each other and be tolerant of each other, they can take a lot. But if there isn't that support, the kids get to know it quickly. Then they play you

one against the other. Maybe I'm crazy to keep hoping our life
will get better. Do you think I am?''

I squeezed her hand. We walked to the front door.

"Goodbye," she said quietly.

A gust of winter air brushed across my face.

"Goodbye," I said.

The heavy oak door clicked solidly behind me.

"I automatically assumed that the children would be
happy if we were happy." Anthony Renzetti sighed audibly.
He was a slim, handsome man of forty-six with a boyish mop
of dark curls. His blue eyes were friendly, although he was
clearly a little apprehensive about our meeting. He already
knew, for example, that I had spoken with his wife, Carla.

We were in his office, a medium-sized room with a large
desk and enough broadloom and standard corporate paint-
ings to signal his status with the firm. Pictures of himself with
his two children smiled at him from his desk, but there were
no visible pictures of his stepchildren. Nor did there appear to
be a picture of Carla.

Although the five years of marriage had been terribly difficult, Anthony continued to care deeply about Carla and to enjoy her company. "We have marvellous times when we're
alone together," he said. "Our biggest problem has been the
children. We learned to our chagrin that we had very different
ideas about child rearing."

Anthony, it turned out, wanted his kids to think independently and not be "patsies," as he put it. This meant he encouraged them to challenge just about everything they heard,
including parental directions. "I taught them to question
everything," he said. "I didn't want them to accept things
just because someone says they are true, or to do things without thinking about them just because someone tells them o.
But Carla had raised her children to be obedient. They were
much more passive than my kids. They never questioned
anything."

Anthony was committed to his children from the time they
were born, but, like many men of his generation, he had
never participated in their day-to-day care. He took them for

walks when they were little and when they got old enough he taught them to play baseball in the park. In his experience—which derived from his own childhood—mothers too often overcontrolled their children, and he believed that his responsibility was to teach aggressive "masculine" values as a sort of counterbalance. Caring fathers trained their children not to be "patsies."

On a Sunday morning in 1973, Anthony and Elena, his first wife, called a family meeting. They had decided to separate and they wanted to tell the children in the most controlled and comfortable way they could. "We did it as civilly as possible," recalled Anthony. "We just told the children we were going to split and that we had decided it would be best for them to stay with me. But the children were angry, especially at their mother. They blamed her for breaking up the family, and for several years they had only sporadic contact with her."

The children both suffered, especially Cathy, who was approaching puberty when the breakup occurred. Paul was only four years old when his mother disappeared from his life. His response was to withdraw emotionally, although he lashed out in anger whenever it seemed safe to do so.

The children understood instinctively that they could not afford to antagonize their father, lest he, too, desert them; so they took out their confusion and their rage on the succession of housekeepers their father hired to look after them. "They refused to relate to the housekeepers," Anthony acknowledged. "They were cruel and insensitive, and, looking back, I think they became quite hardened to things. Thirteen housekeepers passed in and out of our house in three years, and I think those poor relationships really desensitized the children to other people. But perhaps they needed to be hardened," he added. "Perhaps they were too vulnerable to cope with the reality of what was happening in their lives."

Just as Carla had her good reasons for falling in love with Anthony when he happened along in her life, so Anthony had excellent reasons for falling in love with her. His children were angry—he knew that—and needed firmness. In his world view, men were poorly suited to the domestic routines of *Kinder* and *Küche*. Like many fathers contemplating a second marriage, he also thought his kids would actually welcome having someone assume the role of their lost mother. "I thought she was the sort of woman I needed," he said earnestly. "She had been married before, so domesticity would not be new to her. She had raised children, and that was important. She had even worked in a day-care centre, so in a sense her parenting skills had been extended to the work place. But I wasn't consciously looking to remarry—it was the furthest thing from my mind. I just fell in love with her, and marriage seemed like a good idea. Our biggest mistake was not preparing the children. At first the kids thought it would be exciting to have a stepmother or a stepfather in the house— sort of glamourous, I guess. But they didn't realize what the pitfalls would be, and neither did we. Now I know what happened—a bit late, of course. My children actually felt I had betrayed them.

"We had our roles, Carla and I. Carla was the mother—she wanted to play the mother role—and I was the father and the provider. If punishment had to be meted out, I gave her carte blanche to do it. But this was a big stumbling block in our growth as a family. The kids resented her because she was stealing my role, my special relationship with them. When I felt we were drifting apart I held a meeting with them. That was when they used the word 'betrayal.' " He paused a long while.

"My children resented Carla from the very beginning," Anthony added slowly. "I know now that I turned her into the bad guy, a real wicked stepmother, by making her responsible for all the discipline. But there were other factors. Cathy had been the female head of the family, in a way, and she didn't want to give up that role. The kids had trouble getting along with each other, too. Carla's children had moved into our house, and I guess my kids didn't really like that. It was their space. Cathy especially resented Carla's son, Richard, who was a year older than she was."

Anthony had his own emotional reactions to contend

with. He, too, resented—deeply resented—Carla's approach to discipline, and he considered himself more tolerant.

"I always feel I can accomplish more by trying to get to the root of a problem and dealing with it, as opposed to simply making pronouncements. Carla says, 'If you're not home at five P.M. you're banned from going out for three nights.' I'd handle it differently. I'd say, 'You weren't home at five o'clock; well, why weren't you home?' Then I would try to adjust a punishment, if one were needed, to the offence."

But Anthony's solutions were necessarily conditional, because in reality he had stripped himself of his parental authority—to everyone's chagrin.

Carla had left him, he had begged her to come back, and she had. That was two years ago. All in all, five difficult years had passed since they had first linked their private fantasies of remarriage. They were still together, but they had to struggle not to let sex disappear from their relationship and not to let the bitterness and the anger corrode what was left between them. The family had reached an uneasy compromise, a truce of sorts in the ongoing battle.

A wry smile played at the corner of Anthony's mouth.

"My kids tolerate her now—no more, no less," he said. "That's the main difference. I think they're cynical and I don't think they trust people. They don't give of themselves easily. But then again, they won't con her to achieve their own ends," he added with unmistakeable pride. "They're not like that. They weren't brought up to be con artists."

In desperation, Carla and Anthony had decided to discipline only their own children. If things went wrong during the day, Carla would let Anthony handle it when he returned in the evening. Anthony thought this system might work well.

"I'm very pragmatic about this marriage," he said. "I'm much less emotional than I was with my first wife. I try to be as objective as I can about what is possible. Maybe I'm more honest about how I feel. Maybe the truth is I feel less.

"But there are a few things I would do differently if I had the chance. I would definitely hold family meetings before we were married to see how the children felt about the marriage and about my wife-to-be, and how her children felt about me, and how we might best live together. So they couldn't say they had been betrayed. So they could feel, 'My dad is still for me even though he has remarried.' I would also make sure that the woman I wanted to marry and myself shared the same basic philosophy about raising children. I mean, if something is very important to you, you shouldn't be expected to give it up. Neither Carla nor I have wanted to give up an approach to children that worked well for us as individuals before we got together.''

He paused another long moment.

"My children were the first priority in my life—and I guess they still are. I'm not going to make my wife more important than my children. I'm not built that way.''

"Children have supersensitive antennae when it concerns their parents," I said, "and in their minds, Carla took over your role as a parent. Do you think they might have been using you to get back at her?''

"Oh, I don't really think so," replied Anthony. "I think they just wanted my support when things got rough; and I was glad to give it.

"We stay together because we really enjoy each other when we're alone," he went on. "We just didn't expect it to be so hard, so damn hard.''

Carla and Anthony had both wanted this marriage to be wonderful. They were adults when they chose to link their lives and their families. They had both been through difficult times. And even now, after five years in a new kind of hell, they still wanted to be together. With all that good will and experience, why had they had such trouble?

Carla and Anthony had made serious mistakes from the outset because they failed to understand that second and first marriages require a different perspective. For example:

1. They decided to marry for the "wrong" reasons.

2. They were dishonest about the sexual aspect of their early relationship.

3. They did not prepare their children for the remarriage, or discuss their own ideas about child-raising.

4. Carla, in particular, was insensitive to the status of rela-

tionships in Anthony's family and to the fact that she might be displacing her stepdaughter from the "mother-wife" role the girl had adopted.

5. Both Carla and Anthony thought they could impose attitudes and assumptions from the first nuclear family onto the remarriage family—with disastrous results.

Remarriage for the "wrong" reasons

Being a single parent is enormously stressful. There is far too little social and community support for people struggling to maintain their own and their children's equilibrium under such circumstances, and one can appreciate that many single parents feel tempted to remarry for the sheer relief a partner can offer in the daily running of a household. It is, however, a temptation they should avoid.

Anthony Renzetti's household seemed chaotic, with housekeepers marching in and out and a young teen-age daughter who was in a full-blown emotional crisis. He feared, understandably, that he wouldn't cope, but there was another, more ideological basis for the feelings of helplessness. Renzetti believed that only women, or "mothers," were suited to look after children; at the same time, he resented this "fact."

Anthony Renzetti's attitudes to the family stretched so far back that their origins had been lost in the sealed trunk of memory. His own mother had been overcontrolling—he remembered that. But he had extrapolated that "knowledge" and applied it to all women, especially all mothers. A mother was an authority who would overpower you if she could. A mother was a person one ought to challenge. Anthony saw his parental role as a counterbalance to the mother figure in his adult family life. His job was to make sure that his kids literally disobeyed authority—so they wouldn't become "patsies."

Given this background, Anthony's reasons for choosing a wife like Carla seemed more obvious. He was attracted to her because she had already raised children and because she had extra experience as a worker in a day-care centre. But at an unconscious level, Anthony needed a wife who was first and foremost a mother, a *strong* mother, so that he could set himself up as leader of the opposition, so to speak. Like a child, he would side with his own children against her as part of his ancient struggle against a "mother's" authority. (The children were, of course, delighted to have his support in their campaign against their stepmother.)

Anthony's hang-ups about his mother (and consequently all mothers, including his wives) were not really unusual. Mother-hating has been a minor subtext of North American culture for half a century or more. As women emerged from the suffocating drawing rooms of the Victorian world, they met with resistance: Wives and mothers were singled out for special attack as a new generation of male writers railed against the so-called matriarchy of the American Mom.

Mom was the old battleaxe behind the scenes, henpecking her scrawny husband to death and, most important, usurping his gender-ordained role as "head of the family." At the revealing level of popular culture, there was Maggie—so large and imposing—and Jiggs, her wincing, emasculated spouse. And Cora Dithers, Dagwood's boss's wife. Cora dragged her long-suffering husband around by the ear and made his life miserable at home. (He, in turn, made Dagwood's life miserable at the office.)

In 1942 Philip Wylie invented the term "momism" in his astounding book, *A Generation of Vipers*. One might argue that mom-hating reached its apotheosis with Wylie, for no more deadly creature ever walked the earth than "Mom." What she did to her husband was what Delilah did to Samson—she sapped his strength, castrated his masculinity and destroyed him completely.[1]

At age forty-six, Anthony Renzetti was a member of the generation that had been raised on all this—on Dagwood and Blondie, Maggie and Jiggs, and Philip Roth. Indeed, the roots

---

[1] The flip side of this hatred was, of course, the equally absurd idealization of "Mother." Only in recent years has the literary and cultural image of motherhood been somewhat demythologized.

of his behaviour went back so far he was almost entirely unaware of their existence: Only glimmerings of understanding
had worked their way into consciousness. But withdrawing
as an active parent and making his new wife everyone's
"mother" and therefore responsible for disciplining his children had not made his children happy, he now knew that.
Nor had it made him the family "good guy" in their eyes.
They only felt betrayed. That was the word they had chosen,
and it had lodged in their father's heart like a poison-tipped
arrow.

Carla, on the other hand, "needed" this marriage for
practical reasons: She wanted financial security.

A 1967 study in the U.S. indicated that the probability of
remarriage for men was directly related to their income level,
and that poor men were less likely to remarry. Women with
low incomes often remarried quickly, while divorced or widowed women with relatively high personal incomes tended to
delay remarriage.

Today, with up to 50 percent of women in the work force,
there may be fewer people looking to remarriage for reasons
of survival, but working women still earn considerably less
than men, and since most are squeezed into low-paying job
ghettos, in clerical and service work, a single mother and her
children are quite likely to be living in poverty or close to it.

The basic problem with meal-ticket marriages is that
there's an inequality right from the start. If one person needs
the other in order to survive, there is very little room left for
negotiation on any subject. Successful partnerships, including marriage, depend on negotiations in which each party
ends up feeling satisfied with the results; but where the issue
is seen to be survival itself, there's too much power on one
side and too little on the other to provide a climate for the necessary give-and-take.

Carla knew she was at a disadvantage. She wanted
middle-class comforts for her children. She had gone to summer camp when she was young and she wanted her kids to
have the same opportunity. She had had music lessons and
she also wanted them to have that privilege. But none of that
would have been possible on her salary as a day-care worker.

Anthony also knew Carla was at a disadvantage, and the way he allotted his money further reduced her status. Once they were married, she had no earned income; but Anthony didn't believe in joint bank accounts or any other system where Carla might draw money on an independent basis. He liked the old way. He and Carla drew up a budget for household expenses, and every week he gave her an allowance—not a penny less and not a penny more. When she wanted to buy a pair of stockings she had to ask his permission.

Within weeks Carla felt as though she had been stripped of her adulthood. She quickly learned the truth of the old adage: He who pays the piper calls the tune.

Dr. Alan Lyall, a Toronto psychiatrist, in a paper entitled "The Carryover Effects from First to Second Marriage," pointed to the need for equality in any successful marriage, be it a first, second, or tenth. "The business of working out ways of getting along means, ideally, that both parties have to be able to negotiate from a position of strength and without fear," he wrote. "Without this equality, resentment is almost inevitable."

Equality doesn't mean that both parents have to be earning a salary, but it does mean that they recognize that they both have a job to do and deserve access to the family income.

Because they were each preoccupied with their perceived need to remarry, the necessary "bonding" had not taken place between Anthony and Carla Renzetti, and the couple relationship was not primary in their lives. Before either of them had time to raise a glass of champagne to their future together, both sets of children (fine-tuned as children are to such things) had seized the opportunity to divide and conquer.

Being dishonest about sex

Carla and Anthony pretended they weren't involved sexually, and when they did decide to marry, Anthony moved out of his own house so they wouldn't sully their relationship before the ceremony. This was, at the very least, a distortion of priorities. His moving out had a disastrous effect on his children, who felt abandoned and, not surprisingly, hated their wicked new stepmother for "driving him away." A reflex "morality" set the stage for subsequent misery.

Dr. Paul Steinhauer, who is professor and director of training in child psychiatry at the University of Toronto and staff psychiatrist at the renowned Sick Children's Hospital in that city, suggested in an interview that it probably is wise to protect young children from the sexual component of their parent's more casual relationships. "Generally, it's important not to overstimulate a child," he said. "Six- and seven-year-old kids are at the height of sexual fantasy themselves, and I'm not sure what sorts of things get stirred up in them."

But, he added, the other extreme is to distort a child's sense of reality. "When it is determined that a relationship is strong and the partners are moving toward marriage or some strong commitment, the time is probably right to say as unselfconsciously as possible, 'We have decided to marry, or live together; men and women have sexual relationships, and so we're going to sleep together.' That's presenting a reality of life; and the ability to present and accept reality is crucial in remarriage and stepparenting situations."

Preparing the children

Next to divorce itself, the reorganization of the family through remarriage is the most stressful time of all. (Some research suggests the transition from single-parent family to remarriage family may be even harder than divorce.) Like many couples, the Renzettis assumed that if *they* were happy, the children would be happy too. This is common-garden theory for *nuclear* families, but when divorced or widowed parents are planning a remarriage, it may be wise to remember that it is they who are in love, while their children most definitely are not.

The Renzettis also took it for granted that their children "knew" what they had in mind, and consequently they did not discuss their plans with them. The children may have "known," or they may not have, but what they certainly did apprehend was that whatever was going on between the adults would eventually affect their lives. Not knowing how, and to what degree, naturally made them anxious.

Carla and Anthony also assumed that they would agree on methods of child-rearing. It did not occur to either of them that people who have been previously married and have raised children will probably have very *different* methods, and that there will almost certainly be varying rules and expectations from one family to the next.

Family relationships before the remarriage

Before her father's remarriage, Cathy Renzetti had played an important role in the single-parent family. When her mother left, she had quickly moved to fill the gap as first lady of the house. Her possessive feelings for her father went unchallenged—until Carla appeared on the scene.

With the remarriage, Cathy lost her special status in the family. She had always been the older child and the only girl, but now another girl moved in, an unknown person who was supposed to be her sister. Cathy knew she wasn't her sister. She also knew she had somehow lost out on whatever deal had been contracted in her household.

Both Carla and Anthony appeared unaware of the causes of Cathy's turmoil and of the dislocation their union had caused her. The more Cathy "acted out," the angrier Carla grew. Anthony, in turn, became defensive and rationalized Cathy's anger to suit his personal ideology about overpowering mothers and sex roles in the family.

Cathy's pain had a great deal to do with her age at the time of the remarriage. She was twelve years old when her dad married Carla, and at that critical stage in early adolescence when the all-consuming question, "Who am I, apart from my parents?" begins to emerge. This question persists throughout adolescence and well into the twenties (into the thirties for some people), but never is it more acute than during the early years, when anxiety is accompanied by the tumultuous hormonal and physical changes of puberty. The question "Who am I?" begins in reference to our parents, those magical giants who have protected, disciplined, and cared for us, and who have been, as well, the unquestioned font of all knowledge; but in adolescence the magic veneer begins to wear a little thin, the dross appears through the gold, and the awful possibility that one's parents cannot forever remain protector and centre of the universe worms into consciousness.

Anyone who has ever lived with a twelve- or thirteen-year-old girl and lived to tell the tale knows how difficult life can be, even in an intact nuclear family. For one thing, her emerging romantic sexuality is often projected onto her dad, and at an unconscious level, Mom may be seen as competition. At this age, antagonism between mothers and daughters may be more the rule than the exception. A girl must separate from her mother before she can reidentify with her as a role model for adulthood.

When parents are reasonably mature and have a sense of humour, this stage of development is soon passed over, as the young woman transfers her passion for the first-loved male in her life to boys in her own age group and as she learns to reidentify her emerging sense of womanhood with her mother. But a separation or divorce can interfere with the process, especially if a daughter "chooses" her father and identifies with his overt rejection of her mother. Replacing mother in her father's affections may seem like a childhood fantasy come true, but it is also likely to be extremely frightening. It's no mean feat to "oust" Mom. And there is an emotional price to be paid for believing one has actually done it.

When Carla moved in and later married Anthony, Cathy's distress was acute. She had lost her mother, and now it looked as though she would lose her father too. So she did the most obvious, shocking thing she could do. She began to have sex—and to have it in her own house.

Cathy's behaviour would have been recognized and understood by psychiatrist Marc Hollender. In a study involving twenty unmarried women who had repeated unwanted pregnancies, he found that forty percent of the women consciously and specifically wanted tender stroking, which they got in return for intercourse. What they craved, according to Dr. Hollender, was the comfort of being touched and held—like Cathy Renzetti, who had lost her mother and her father and had acquired a stranger who did not love her, who did not even like her, as a sole, active parent.

False assumptions

Most of the mistakes Carla and Anthony Renzetti made were premised on the belief that assumptions and behaviour patterns that underpin first marriages can be neatly transferred to second marriages. They were not alone in their misconceptions. Many of the parents and stepparents whose complex and interesting lives may be glimpsed through the pages of this book have made similar errors.

Whatever one may think about the value of traditional gender-defined roles in the family, one thing is sure: If they work at all, they can only work in the original nuclear family where "Mother" is everyone's mother and "Father" is everyone's father. In remarried families where there is at least one stepparent, such roles can seem false—like an artificial overlay that does not reflect the reality of relationships. Anthony Renzetti actually abdicated his parental responsibilities to Carla on grounds of gender alone. Far from helping the family unite, this action led to a breach of trust between him and his children and set the stage for his children's rejection of his new wife.

Carla was the ideal mate for Anthony because she shared his belief that mothering was a woman's only important role. Carla came into the family with rigidly defined ideas of what her job there would be. She would become mother to all the children by virtue of the fact that she was a woman.

In Carla's mind, being a mother made her the primary parent, and that meant she would have to give up her job. But the job had provided her with whatever self-esteem she had, and when she left it for a predetermined role, she had nothing personal left. She wanted to do the right thing, to mother the children, but that wasn't where her real sense of identity lay. Soon she began to see herself as the family maid.

Carla blamed Anthony and his children for turning her into a "maid," but this was, in fact, the very role she had opted for. What neither she nor Anthony had properly considered was that roles are lived in by real people. No woman can step into a family and become "mother" just because she's female. Anthony and Carla thought that was possible. More to the point, they didn't think at all. They reacted according to old beliefs and assumptions.

Like so many remarried couples with good intentions and little knowledge, Carla and Anthony were floundering. They thought the stepfamily was, or ought to be, another version of the nuclear family, and they acted accordingly. They relied on behaviour that had worked for them in the past but was no longer appropriate for this new mode of family life. It was as counterproductive as trying to fit square pegs into round holes.

SUGGESTIONS

1. Be aware of your reasons for wanting this marriage. If you are primarily motivated by reasons other than affection, think twice. The children will understand the situation before you've finished cutting the wedding cake. The point to remember is that children are likely to view the remarriage of a parent as a loss rather than a gain and that a strong couple bond will help them come to terms with the new reality.

2. Be matter-of-fact about the sexual component of a *serious* relationship. This also helps children accept reality. Avoid moral rigidities. When Anthony Renzetti left the house so he and Carla wouldn't have to "live in sin" he created anxieties in his children that they never recovered from. He also ensured that they would hate Carla from the first moment on.

3. Prepare the children. Be clear at all stages and reassure them that they will be the first to know when you're serious about someone new. Then keep your word. Let them get to know your partner before you move in together. Ideally, he or

she should spend time with each of them in a quiet, let's-get-to-know-each-other kind of activity.

4. Agree on a child-rearing philosophy and how it will be administered.

5. Be sensitive to relationships that already exist in the family. Children who have enjoyed a particular role need help in adjusting.

6. Be sensitive to assumptions and attitudes that have been carried over from the nuclear family. Do not abdicate parental responsibilities just because you have remarried, and do not try to replace a lost parent. Rigid gender roles probably won't work in the remarriage family. Pretending you are "mother" or "father" to stepchildren who know better won't fool them for a minute. In the same vein, if you're a woman who has enjoyed working outside your home, think carefully before you abandon that source of income and emotional fulfillment for full-time domesticity because you think that as a "mother" you ought to.

CHAPTER TWO
Predictable Problems of Second Marriages

WITHOUT KNOWING IT, people like the Renzettis who are marrying for a second time enter a world where mythology prevails. So little is understood about how the remarriage family differs from the nuclear family of a first marriage that most of us unwittingly carry over a value system that no longer applies. Indeed, many of the most common problems remarried couples and their children face stem from the imposition of these old mythologies on a different reality.

The French have a wonderful expression for this and other communication problems. They speak of a *dialogue des sourds* (dialogue of the deaf)—a conversation where neither party actually hears what the other is saying. In remarriage situations people often mishear each other because their expectations appear to be out of sync with their present lives. The confusion about roles and expectations may stretch even further to include grandparents, aunts, uncles, and friends; and the eventual accumulation of so many missed messages may strain even the most solid of relationships.

The ways in which people in stepfamilies relate to each other are as varied as the individuals concerned, but there are certain discernible motifs that recur. Most stepfamilies will have to cope with one or all of the following stumbling blocks to rewedded bliss.

The wicked stepmother

She's been a part of all our lives, this consort of witches and goblins. As children we knew that she banished poor Cinderella to the ash heap and Snow White to the forest; and that she tried her best to get rid of Hansel and Gretel. She was all-powerful and all-controlling; and her weak, emasculated husband was unable to protect his beloved children against her. When *she* entered the family, the children were automatically doomed until further notice.

Childhood stories heard at the knee of a parent or grandparent make deep inroads into the unconscious, and years later, in our supposedly rational adult lives, the word "stepmother" can still raise a tremor in imaginative minds. After all, who ever heard of a nice one? The brothers Grimm hadn't. And neither had Hans Christian Andersen. A stepmother's only function was to supplant a soft, loving mother who had mysteriously succumbed to an untimely death.

However, with close to one out of two marriages ending in divorce and 75 percent of divorced people remarrying, there are more steppeople around than either Grimm or Andersen ever dreamed possible. Some of the professionals who deal with remarried people try to avoid the unfortunate prefix "step" altogether. Anything would seem to be preferable: "reconstituted family," "remarriage family," "second-marriage family". . . But when it comes to describing the relationship of a man or a woman to his or her partner's children from a former marriage, there appears to be no other option available. *Step* it is. And of all the possible step-combinations, mythology has made it hardest to be a stepmother.

Many stepmothers try so hard *not* to be "wicked" that they finish by disappointing themselves and everyone else. Sometimes they come on too strong in order to show they really care—even when they don't. They may give up their careers to prove that they can look after the new family the way a "real" mother would. (Carla Renzetti did that and made herself and everyone else miserable.) They may march into their new husband's home like an army drill sergeant and re-organize bedtimes or redecorate people's rooms in an attempt to demonstrate how sincerely involved they are.

None of these techniques work, for one very simple reason. They do not allow for the tentativeness and the necessary psychological space that must accompany any beginning relationship. The myth of the wicked stepmother who doesn't care about the children, in conjunction with that other myth, that a "family" is an automatic physical and emotional unit just because two adults have agreed to share their lives, makes stepmothers especially vulnerable to disappointment and resentment.

Sometimes a stepmother is so overwhelmed by the role expectations others impose on her (or she imposes on herself) that she does, in fact, take out her frustrations on the children. It's ironic and sad, but not uncommon. In striving to live up to an impossible self-image, she may actually turn herself into a "wicked stepmother."

Take Margaret, for example. I was especially touched by this woman who had answered my newspaper ad for subjects. Her face was taut and lined and she looked a lot older than her thirty-three years.

Like the Renzettis, Margaret and her husband had adopted all the traditional sex roles. Margaret stopped work even before they married because she wanted to prepare herself for motherhood and staying at home. Unfortunately, she became a full-time stepmother in an unexpected way. Once she and her husband were married, his ex-wife "gave" them his eight-year-old son. The boy had problems and his mother couldn't handle him.

Margaret's first response to this unlooked-for development was one of unmitigated delight. Now, she thought, she would be able to put into practice a number of ideas she had about herself, about marriage, and about motherhood. She liked children and she expected to like this child. She had planned to stay home anyway, so had absolutely no objections to looking after him full-time. Most of all, she wanted to help her husband's child.

But reality refused to conform to the blueprint she drew

up. Margaret didn't like the boy and he didn't like her. He felt pushed and pulled between his "mothers." (Margaret insisted, quite wrongly, that he call her "Mom.") But the crux of the problem was that Margaret hadn't counted on his being there at all; and when he turned out to be difficult, she resented him with every fibre of her being. He had, in effect, cut into her honeymoon. Worst of all, he challenged her image of her own maternal qualities. Even the boy's father didn't like him, it seemed. Margaret thought that sad reality was a confirmation of the child's inadequacy.

Margaret and her husband eventually had two children of their own whom Margaret did truly love, but this only made her feel more guilty about her stepson. At the time of our discussion he was twelve years old, and she and her husband were trying to place him in a home for disturbed children.

Not every stepmother will have as many problems liking a stepchild, but it does happen quite frequently, especially if the child is an unexpected addition to the new marriage. We know that a new baby is initially disruptive to the equilibrium of a marriage, so an eight-year-old who has been buffeted around a bit would naturally be that much harder to deal with. However, if Margaret had had fewer set ideas about her function as a "mother" and her sex-related domestic role in the marriage, she might have been able to face the situation with more flexibility. As things stood, she blamed the child for disappointing her. "I feel cheated because I gave him my best and now I have all this trouble," she complained.

The boy had unknowingly challenged her personal mythology of who she was and what her aptitudes were. It was easy to love and be loved by her own natural children, but when both she and the stepchild failed to respond to each other in stereotyped "familial" ways, she rejected *him* rather than the stereotype. Margaret and her husband created a nuclear family with their own babies born later in their marriage, but they apparently couldn't cope with the other reality of a stepchild who had loyalties to a mother who lived elsewhere, whom they wished to disavow, and whose very existence obliged them to acknowledge a network of other relationships. In other words, they tried to force the stepchild relationship into the mould of the nuclear family, and when it didn't fit they thought of it as a failure and gave up.

Margaret was a good example of how trying life can become when people bring set ideas of sex roles and "family" to second marriages. Carla and Anthony Renzetti were drowning in a similar pond, of course. Once again, when men and women think of themselves as "mothers" and "fathers" and attempt to impose those roles on each other's children, the kids will probably fight them tooth and nail. Children know that mothers and fathers cannot be replaced and that doing a sex-related job, like cooking or even throwing around a football, does not a "parent" make. In happy stepfamilies, shared activities can lead to friendships, sometimes deep and rewarding friendships, but there is usually still a parent in the wings, occupying a large corner of the child's heart. The parent in the wings may be dead, or the emotional quality of the relationship may be painful and unpleasant. But it exists all the same. Women get wounded on this particular battlefield more often than men because they are expected to become "mother" by virtue of their gender more often than men are expected to become "father."

Is biology destiny? The unwilling stepparent

If remarriage does become the most common form of the family and if a large number of people contracting second marriages have children from a former union, what choices will exist for women who prefer not to include motherhood in their life plans? The range of possibilities may become increasingly narrow. It may be extremely hard to find a partner who does *not* have a child in tow, at least on a weekend basis.

Men are less likely to face this particular problem because the range of available female partners is traditionally much wider. A middle-aged man can marry a woman of twenty-five or a woman of fifty, while women are conventionally limited to partners around their own age or older.

Anyone who thinks he or she is about to embark on a life-long idyll of love while ignoring the loved one's unwelcome little offspring is asking for a lot of trouble. People with children come as package deals, whether the kids live in the household full-time, part-time or only visit a few times a year. A stepfather who decides to leave all the parenting to his wife will never move beyond the status of guest in his own home, and certainly will never develop anything remotely resembling a real relationship with growing children. Women who withdraw from stepparenting their partner's children will face the same obstacles to family integration. They, however, may also be thought of as "unnatural." By virtue of their sex alone, it may be assumed they will instinctively adore the little darlings.

Sandra was a woman who thought she could compartmentalize her marriage so that *she* had a relationship with her husband and *he* had a relationship with his children (who visited every other weekend). Before they married, Sandra and Harvey never discussed what part the children would play in their lives, though it became clear that Harvey expected her to look after them and care about them as if they were her own. But Sandra had had different thoughts. She didn't want children at all. She vaguely expected Harvey's ex-wife to remarry and the children to disappear altogether.

Sandra wasn't interested in Harvey's children. She didn't know how to look after them and she didn't *want* to look after them. As far as she was concerned, they were his kids and *he* should look after them. She didn't see what they had to do with her or what she had to do with them.

"There was a general expectation that because I was female I ought to love the children. His mother and my mother both would sigh with relief when we had his kids for the weekend. They'd say, 'Thank God he's got the children.' I was made to feel guilty, as though there was something wrong with me and I ought to see a psychiatrist. Finally, I did. I saw one for six years, and it was through that therapy that I came to realize that I wasn't 'strange' while everyone else was normal. I realized that there were expectations being imposed on me and that I was being asked to be someone I wasn't. I wasn't their mother and I didn't want to be their stepmother, whatever that was supposed to mean."

Part of Sandra's problem came from the web of ambiguity surrounding her relationship to Harvey's children. She was expected to look after them, even to be filled with joy when the time for their visit approached. (The reality was that her stomach went into a knot on Thursday and didn't relax until Monday.) Although her own attitude was negative, she was also getting double messages from everyone else. She was expected to perform the duties of a parent, but she wasn't accorded the authority of a parent. In this everyone concurred: her husband, his ex-wife, *and* the children. The children took to taunting her. "My mommy says Daddy only married you to spite her," the oldest boy spat out whenever he saw an opportunity.

Sandra had a point—women are often expected to be the instant linchpin of a new family, and if they refuse the role it may be assumed, even by those closest to them, that there's something vital missing in their makeup. On the other hand, she and her husband were utterly unrealistic about their marriage. They never discussed the children or their attitudes toward them. And Sandra had an amazing fantasy that she could avoid the children altogether and leave the parenting to her husband.

The visiting stepchild

When children live with their other parent and only visit on weekends or holidays, roles may be quite difficult to sort out. The children, themselves, may resist the authority of Mommy's or Daddy's new partner, whom they may see as an intruder. A stepmother or stepfather may feel unsure about how to approach the relationship. To present oneself as a parent/disciplinarian feels wrong and inappropriate, yet at the same time no one wants to be ignored, treated rudely, or walked over with impunity.

The once-in-a-while stepparent needs to be as relaxed as possible and perfectly clear about his or her levels of tolerance. After five years of refraining from comment when her visiting stepdaughter made horrible slurping noises at the table, one woman finally blurted out her annoyance. "Smarten up," she said angrily. To her surprise, the child responded quickly and seemed more relaxed in her company. "I think she was as unsure as I was about whether she belonged in our family, and my correcting her manners made her feel she really did belong," the stepmother recounted, looking somewhat bemused. No doubt. After five years, a child might well begin to think that a stepparent who never, ever made any comment of a "parental" nature simply lacked interest.

Children should be made aware of whatever behaviour is expected of them, simply because people who live together, full-time or part-time, have to know what the terms are. There may be initial resistance of the "you're not my mother/father so you can't tell me what to do" variety, but if the ground rules are clear and the adults consistent, everyone will likely feel more secure.

It is true that visiting stepchildren must adapt to families with different rules and regulations and possibly different value systems, and they often do feel strained by divided loyalties. They need to feel wanted in both families; they need to know that an absent parent will not be belittled in their presence; and they need to know that there is not only one way to do anything. Families do do things differently, and provided that no one is malevolent or inflicts damage on anyone else, there is no harm involved. On the contrary, children who learn about differences at an early age probably have a distinct advantage over their "monofamilied" contemporaries.

Instant love, instant obedience

Women are most vulnerable to the myth that in a successful family everyone loves everyone else. And since women are expected to be the glue that holds the family together, they run into a lot of trouble in second marriages where many members of the family cannot and do not love each other, especially at the beginning. The successful stepfamily has come to terms with the reality that there is no such thing as instant love. Love, if it develops at all, takes root and deepens over time. It doesn't just happen because we believe it ought to.

Men, on the other hand, are most vulnerable to the myth of instant obedience. In sex-role conventions, women are expected to be the keepers of the flame, but men are expected to be the "head of the family." This notion, conjuring up as it does the image of a stern Victorian father seated at the head of a table flanked by rows of well-behaved youngsters and a docile wife, has subsisted mainly in our collective imagination. One would be hard pressed to find such a family today, but the archetype remains and sometimes gets activated in the remarriage family when men feel insecure. One doesn't need a dozen kids or a wing collar to hook into the notion that "Father knows best," but when "Father" is a stepfather and is seen to be assuming a role (and an unpopular one, at that), the consequences are readily predictable.

A well-meaning man entering a family where there are children from a former marriage may feel that he has to assert himself in order to make his presence felt. He may feel acutely uncomfortable if he lets things he disapproves of go by. He may think, for example, that the children won't respect him. But just as no one can command love to appear, respect, also, must grow. Once again, a certain distance is needed between people entering relationships they may not have willed for themselves.

A stepfather who can let a few things go by in the beginning until he gets a good sense of the way his new spouse is raising her children will be laying a basis for a real relationship. Especially if he concentrates on developing a friendship with his stepchildren.

Ironically, the stepfather who demands instant obedience from his stepchildren is often the most anxious to succeed in his new role, but, like his female counterpart, he pushes too hard. In the case of both men and women, stepparents seem to perform better in the long run if they can relax, laugh a bit, and ignore some of the predictable negative behaviour.

Here is the story of Alan Boychuk. Alan's marriage failed for the very reasons I've been discussing. Very common reasons. And very avoidable reasons.

The problems of a first-time parent

Alan Boychuk was what Gail Sheehy has called a "latency boy." He was a bachelor until he was thirty-eight, living with his mother until Wendy, his fiancée, cajoled him into moving into his own apartment while they were deciding whether or not to marry. Like many men who manage to avoid the upheavals of adolescence, he remained bound to his mother in a childlike way. She continued to criticize the way he dressed (he deliberately wore old clothes with stains in order to provoke her) and he retaliated by sniping at her.

Alan Boychuk may not represent the majority of single men who marry women with children from previous marriages and then have problems in their relationships, but he isn't a particularly rare type, either. Never-married men or women who have reached middle age might be expected to have a hard time adjusting to the demands of communal life under the best of circumstances, but when there are children involved the task is likely to be all that much harder. For example, people who have not had children may have unrealistic notions of what children are actually like. They may also have rigid ideas of what they *ought* to be like; and therein lies potential trouble.

Alan had come close to marriage several times. At thirty-seven he was still very attractive, with a mop of salt-and-pepper hair and a slim, lithe body. Professionally, he was a successful chiropractor in Calgary, Alberta, with a large following of people who swore he was a shaman with magic in his fingers. He was intelligent, articulate, and witty. He was playful—he liked to throw a ball around in the park—and, according to Wendy, he was an ardent and imaginative lover. Needless to say, women had always found him interesting, but from Alan's point of view there had been something wrong with every one of them.

One aspect of family life that he did long for increasingly as the years passed was fatherhood. Alan's own dad had worked at several jobs to support the family and was away from home for long periods of time, and Alan felt he had missed the whole experience of being fathered. He wanted a child of his own to nurture. Not just a child, but a son. Through this boy he planned to relive his youth and improve upon it. Alan had a detailed blueprint in his mind for the way he wanted the child to develop, but there was the constant problem of finding the "right" woman. "I made jokes about wanting to be a single father twenty years ago when it wasn't fashionable to do that," he said. "Being a parent was important to me all along."

When he was in his late thirties, Alan started to realize that he was being left behind. Not only had most of his friends married years ago (some of them were divorced and already remarried) but their *kids* were almost grown-up. His old buddies seemed to be exiting from a stage in their lives that he had never even entered. *He* was still wondering about whether or not to leave home.

Alan met Wendy in June, 1972, and fell for her like a sixteen-year-old schoolboy. She was fun, she was smart, and she was sexy; and after a few weeks of dating, Alan felt tempted to take the plunge. He suddenly saw himself at one step removed, with humour and not a little irony. He knew he was too old to believe his own rationalizations about what was wrong with this one or that one and why he wasn't ready to settle down.

Wendy was a widow in her early forties with one child—a teen-age son. Her first marriage had been unhappy and probably would have ended in divorce had her husband lived. Alan was the first man she had enjoyed sex with. He was experienced—far more than she was—and patient and encouraging. She, too, fell in love like a girl—with his delightful sense of whimsy, with his playfulness, with his lithe body and with his ardent passion for hers.

One thing that did worry her was his combined attachment to and dislike of his mother. It was fun to have a boyish man around, but sometimes he seemed a little *too* boyish. His games with her son were too intense, as though he didn't distance himself the way adults usually do. But he was very hard to resist, and Wendy didn't really want to. "There seemed enough that was positive in the relationship to take a chance,'' she recalled.

"I became quite conscious that one of the reasons I wanted the marriage was because I wanted to parent her son,'' Alan said as we sat over coffee in his apartment.

This did not diminish his wish to have kids of his own, but Wendy had already raised a child and she didn't want to start over again. After several months Alan decided he wanted to marry her anyway. Parenting her son, Joseph, would be satisfying enough, he told himself.

The unseen writing was already scratched into the wall. "I came into this family thinking of myself as a father, as *the* father,'' recalled Alan sadly. "His natural father was dead and I was going to be *it*. It is true that I had a romantic illusion about what it was to be a father, but I wasn't acting in complete isolation from reality. Joseph had talked about wanting an adult man in the house, and Wendy definitely wanted a role model for her son. I really wanted to be *very* involved with the boy. I wanted him to confide in me and do all those wonderful things that I now know take years of relationship to develop. I wanted to love him and I wanted him to love me.''

Before the marriage, Alan had tried hard to establish a friendly relationship with Joseph and had been quite successful. They swam together and the three of them went on picnics. He organized softball games for the whole neighbourhood. He pored over the movie page and treated everyone to hamburgers. He barbecued hot dogs on the grill, and when he found out that both Wendy and Joseph liked sesame-seed buns he crossed town to buy them. "At the age of thirty-seven or thirty-eight I could remember very well what it was like to be a boy, and there were lots of things I liked doing,'' Alan said. "I also liked playing with mechanical devices and taking things apart and putting them back together again. I thought I could relate to Joseph as a male.''

So far, so good. Their troubles only began when Alan moved into Wendy's house, because with the act of marriage he breathed life into his vision of what a "father" was. He expected Joseph to respond according to his blueprint. To Alan, being a father meant staying in control at all times. Children had to be moulded and shaped; and it was the job of a father to make sure they did not stray from the straight and narrow.

Plenty of authoritarian parents run into difficulty with their adolescent children, but a stranger playing the role of a strict parent, matched with a rebellious thirteen-year-old boy who is still mourning the death of his father, are set on a collision course. Furthermore, Joseph had been the only male in the house and he didn't like sharing the honour. Wendy remembered that when he was younger she would hear him chirping happily from the bathroom, "I'm the man in the house, I'm the man in the house." But Alan thought Joseph was "out of control" and needed disciplining. He objected to the boy's using the lawn-cutting tractor as a toy, and he insisted that all jobs be done with push-button alacrity. He patrolled the house like a cop on the beat; and nothing Joseph did was good enough.

Wendy didn't want to interfere. She firmly believed that a new spouse should be allowed to have a real role within the family; otherwise he or she remains a spectator and the natural parent continues to raise the child alone as a single parent. Wendy also conceded, though a bit reluctantly, that Joseph needed the tougher discipline Alan brought to bear. Maybe he *had* learned to get away with too much. So she stood aside. When Joseph complained that he was being disciplined too severely by Alan, she told him to take his grievances directly to the source. That seemed like good, sound thinking at the time.

Joseph's hostility to Alan was unmistakable. He refused to cooperate with Alan's carefully worked-out schemes for running a smooth household. He didn't do his assigned jobs; he began to rebel in school and he allowed his marks to drop. But the more entrenched he became in his opposition to his stepfather, the more Alan dug his heels in. Personality traits that Alan had previously submerged now exploded into life. He found himself locked in a full-scale power struggle with a thirteen-year-old opponent.

Alan knew, intellectually, that he was making serious tactical mistakes, but somehow he felt afraid to allow the boy to "win" at any level. "I saw him as someone who was opposing me and I thought, 'I'm such a nice guy, why would he do that?' Sometimes I was able to stand back and think, this is a thirteen-year-old kid and he's having trouble because he's been the rooster here and now I've come along. I was trying to understand that, but at the same time I thought it was part of my job to get this kid to deal with the realities of life, like responsibilities and doing what you're supposed to do. I only tried to follow through on the things I was expecting from him."

Eight months into the marriage, no one had to tell Alan that things weren't working out. Instead of confiding in him and wanting to play a game of ball, Joseph seemed to hate and fear him. And, Alan had to admit, the feelings were mutual. "I was angry a good deal of the time. In retrospect, I should have been able to say I disagreed and leave it at that, at least some of the time, but I had to prove I was right no matter what," he admitted with characteristic honesty.

The stepparent who strides into his new family like an army general is inviting trouble. Like any human relationship, perhaps even more than most, the ambiguous connection between stepparent and stepchild needs nurturing. It is a seed fallen lightly on sandy soil and it is unlikely to root without special care.

In Alan's case, everything suffered. Soon he was blaming Wendy for her son's behaviour. Joseph wouldn't be so difficult if she had brought him up properly in the first place. "I wasn't too tactful," he allowed later. But in permitting Alan to humiliate her son, Wendy was filling her own cup of guilt and resentment. She felt torn between a natural desire to protect her child from what seemed to be excessive disciplining and concern that perhaps Alan was right and Joseph did need shaping up. Perhaps she had lost her authority over him during the years of single parenting? And there was the marriage itself to consider. Knowing the stake Alan had in being a father to her son, Wendy felt sure he would react badly if she criticized his manner, or, more drastically, took back the whole responsibility for parenting. She suspected such a move might effectively destroy the marriage.

The things Wendy and Alan shared in common did not disappear just because Alan was having problems with her son. He was still fun and witty and awfully good in bed. "Our relationship suffered but it wasn't suffocated," Wendy said. "Somehow there was affection, and in bed I could forget my disappointment and anger. So could Alan. I think people who live together can somehow sustain themselves through difficulties with physical warmth and caring. Also, I was glad to have a family constellation, even if it was a lousy one. My own father died when I was very young, so I think I idealized family life rather unrealistically."

But Alan's demands on Joseph and Joseph's adolescent defences soon reached the breaking point. It became a point of honour for Joseph not to obey, for to do so would be to acknowledge defeat at the hands of this enemy-stranger who had entered his life under the guise of being his father. Alan, however, had spent his life waiting to be a parent and he had to "succeed" at any cost. That meant bringing Joseph into line with his own values and expectations. The marriage itself was Alan's first real commitment to a woman. There was a lot at stake.

Alan had to be in control and to be seen to be in control. One day, in front of several friends, he picked Joseph up and marched him over to the garbage cans. "Take them into the garage," he ordered, as everyone looked away in embarrassment. Inevitably, a series of events brought the struggle to a head.

It started when Joseph wanted to drop Latin. Alan, because he was concerned about Joseph's schoolwork, offered an opinion. He thought that any job requiring the correct use of English depended on a good, solid knowledge of Latin. But Joseph was failing the subject and his mother supported his choice. Finally they all agreed to consult the school counsellor, who concurred that it was useless to force a student to take a course he didn't want. It wouldn't work, she said. Alan knew she was right, but he was hooked on exerting authority. That night at the dinner table he insisted. Eventually the boy caved in. He would continue with Latin the following year.

Curiously, Alan was not pleased with Joseph's capitulation. "Although I had won, I knew I had lost," he admitted. "He would just horse around and not work. I knew that all along, but I felt I couldn't give in to him. And the more I realized there was no way to win, the angrier I got."

About an hour after his "victory" at the dinner table, Alan, seething with rage, noticed that Joseph had neglected to finish one of his chores. "Come down here and put these dishes away," he ordered. But Joseph had already gone to bed. Joseph often did that. He procrastinated, then waited to see how far he could push his stepfather. But this time Alan felt out of control. He felt dizzy with anger. He climbed the stairs three at a time, hauled Joseph from his bed, put him under his arm, carried him down the stairs and pushed him into the kitchen. "Do it," he roared.

Instead, Joseph took off his pyjama bottoms and fled into the cold March night. Sometime later, he returned with a policeman. He showed the officer the red mark on his side where Alan had carried him down the stairs. The policeman looked questioningly at Alan. "Yes," Alan offered. "That is what happened. I'd say this was a domestic dispute, wouldn't you?" The officer agreed and said good night. Joseph shuffled off to bed. "Wait a minute," called Alan. "You'd better do the job." Joseph looked at his mother for help. "You'd better do it," Wendy said quietly.

Alan thought he had tried his best to make Joseph into a responsible person and failed. He decided that from then on he would cease to "parent" him, as he put it; and he informed the family that he considered Joseph a tenant in the house.

They lived in this state for about six months, and, not surprisingly, Alan and Wendy's sex life cooled into a deep freeze. Alan was angry at Wendy for continuing to love and parent this boy who was the living proof of his failure. She, in turn, was inexpressibly angry at him. For six months they slept back to back without touching; then in March, 1977, she asked him to leave.

"I never anticipated how hard it would be," sighed Alan. "I thought I was a superman, capable of undertaking any challenge. I married Wendy because I loved her and we had a good relationship. I was under no illusions about how difficult it would be to parent Joseph, but I thought, 'Okay, this will be a greater challenge. I can do it.' I know now that part of my problem with Joseph was that he wasn't becoming the individual I wanted him to be and I couldn't accept him as he was, as a person with a lot of strengths. I wanted to change him. I do feel some regret, and I think if I had to do it all over again I'd do it differently—if I could.''

"However strong the stepparent's determination to be a parent and however skilled his efforts, he cannot succeed totally,'' wrote psychologists Irene Fast and Albert Cain. Alan Boychuk's first mistake as a stepparent was that he did not understand this basic reality.

Joseph was already a teen-ager when Alan and Wendy married, and certainly less than ready to have a new "father" descend on him and shape him according to his own lights. But, like many stepfathers, Alan sincerely thought that was the right thing to do.

All new stepfathers are faced with the task of finding a place for themselves in an established family group. They must be involved in setting up conditions so that the new family can function. If they are not involved they'll remain guests, but if they come on too strong, they'll be heartily resented. It's a fine line to tread, and the most successful stepparents walk carefully until they have won the confidence of the children. This is likely to take several years (the experts suggest between four and six, as an average), but when it happens and there is a cushion of trust and positive experience to relax into, the vicissitudes of daily life with its altercations and annoyances can be comfortably taken in one's stride.

Joseph had lost his father when he was eight, before he was old enough to cull loving memories that might have sustained him later on. His dad was a blank page which he had filled with his own mythologized and idealized characteristics. Since his father's death he had also been the "man of the house.'' He had grown close to his mother, and together they formed a tight little cocoon of comfort. So when Alan arrived on the scene, Joseph was less than joyous. It was fun having him around to play ball with, but marriage? A new father? *That* was different.

The further Alan pushed him, the more unhappy Joseph became; and the way he fought back was classic. First he failed at the job—i.e., school. He turned to his mother for help, but she seemed withdrawn and less available. So he went to the highest "authority"—the police. Domestic disputes, however, are not necessarily taken very seriously by the police. Faced with an articulate, reasonable adult man and a boy who had appeared in their station minus the bottom half of his pyjamas, they sided with the adult. It was a struggle of wills.

Through it all, Wendy felt torn—a common enough reaction for the natural mother who is caught in the middle. She wanted to help her husband carve out a place for himself in the family, but she was also a relatively passive woman who may have been secretly glad to have someone take over the parenting. She, too, had mythologized the "family," and she thought that any two-parent constellation was better than none. But when she finally felt the awesome power of Alan's need to control her son, regardless of circumstance, she began to reconsider. Then she made a choice and asked him to leave.

Dr. Paul Druckman is a family therapist in Toronto who has seen many remarried couples struggling with such problems. Druckman suggested in an interview that there are three categories involved in the adaptation of remarriage families. The first he describes as the "instrumental" stage. That is the level of basic functioning, where jobs get done. Beds get made, food gets bought and cooked, and the grass in the yard gets cut. But Alan Boychuk and Wendy never reached that first stage, because Alan came into the family with a specific scenario in mind for his stepson. He was less interested in getting the household operating than in moralistically shaping the boy into his vision of a properly responsible youth. He made no allowances for adjustment difficulties or predictable resentments.

Druckman's second category concerns the opportunities

available in a family for people to develop both emotionally and intellectually, and in this area as well, Alan's attitude also precluded success. Alan became an inhibitor of development. There were no lines of communication where people could actually hear what others were saying and negotiate compromises if necessary. His need for instant obedience prohibited communication of the sort that might have fostered emotional growth.

Dr. Druckman's third classification concerns the family's ability to prepare its members to cope with the world *as it actually is* outside the family. In this category Alan's attitudes were also counterproductive. By demanding uncompromising obedience and imposing rigid punishments when he was rejected, he was unable to do what a good "parent" must —i.e., teach children how to negotiate their way through difficulties.

Although he was intelligent and not indelicate as a person, Alan's own personal needs and inexperience with the vicissitudes of parenting made it difficult for him to respond sensitively to Joseph. Like stepparents who demand instant love because that is part of the mythology of the family, his own mythology, premised on instant obedience, instant responsibility, and "shaping up," also invited disappointment.

In the stepfamily, "reality" is a key word. And one reality is that the old mythologies need creative updating. The successful stepfathers who appear later on in this book have let their spouse's children come to them when they were ready, without initial demands for either love or obedience or anything other than polite consideration.

The ex-spouse and the "binuclear family"

In 1973, a seminal book appeared on the scene. Called *Beyond the Best Interests of the Child* and authored by several influential people (Joseph Goldstein, professor of law at Yale; Albert J. Solnit, child psychiatrist and director of the Child Study Centre at Yale; and the late, redoubtable Anna Freud), it had a profound influence on the thinking of social workers, psychiatrists and other professionals who work with families, and probably still represents mainstream thinking on questions of custody. The theory was that children of divorce are better off in one place they can call home while visiting the other parent at regular intervals: sole custody, in other words. The relationship to the other parent was thought best if limited to agreed-upon times. As far as the rapport between spouses was concerned, the same professionals considered it unhealthy if people continued to care about each other after their divorce. Too great an interest was thought to be pathological.

Recently, however, some quite revolutionary ideas have emerged that challenge these basic assumptions. New research suggests that children of divorce function best when there is genuine, ongoing parenting from *both* parents and when the children have open access to both. That sounds more like joint custody than sole custody, and although there is no conclusive evidence yet available on the success or failure of joint-custody experiments, some researchers are beginning to think it may prove to be the best postdivorce system we've come up with.

According to Constance R. Ahrons and Morton S. Perlmutter, both from the University of Wisconsin, the new thinking can best be summed up by the phrase "binuclear family." In an interesting paper called "The Relationship between Former Spouses: A Fundamental Sub-System in the Remarriage Family," they advanced the idea that it is the divorce process itself that changes a nuclear family into a binuclear family. That means two households instead of one. When the former spouses remarry, the households alter again to become "maternal and paternal stepfamily subsystems," an academic way of saying "Mom's and Dad's new families that include the children from both sides." The authors go on to suggest that the two interrelated households actually form one family system, a binuclear family system.

This may come as an unpleasant bit of news to those divorced and remarried people who want nothing more than to leave their former spouses behind, somewhere—anywhere—

preferably in Siberia. In reality, however, a large majority of divorced couples do maintain contact of one sort or another, primarily to discuss the children, but their interaction is often coloured by ongoing anger and unresolved bitterness.

According to research done in California by Judith Wallerstein and Joan Berlin Kelly and published in their 1980 book, *Surviving the Breakup: How Parents and Children Cope with Divorce*, it is precisely this sort of negative interaction between ex-spouses that interferes with the adjustment of children to divorce and remarriage. They found that in cases of sole custody, the relationship of the noncustodial parent (usually the father) to the child is essential to the child's psychological adaptation, including the child's ability to accept a stepparent after a remarriage, and that the quality of the relationship between the absent parent and the child depends greatly on the ability of ex-spouses to relate to each other as parents and on their ability to separate this role from the bitter remains of their married life. The opposite—shutting the door on one member of the family after a divorce—resulted in increased disturbance in the family. In other, related research, Judith Brown Greif of the Albert Einstein College of Medicine reported in an article entitled, "The Father-Child Relationship Subsequent to Divorce" that fathers who had only limited access to their children often became depressed and cut off contact altogether in order to lessen their own pain. Because they were so alienated from the daily lives of their children, many stopped seeing themselves as parents. The effect of this withdrawal on their children was predictable. They became depressed and angry and their relationships with the absent parent became strained and superficial. Even the sole-custody mothers, those whose former husbands had been amputated from the family, were more depressed. They were overwhelmed by the burden of single responsibility for their children.

Seeds of anger may be sown long before a remarriage takes place. People who have not adequately mourned the end of one relationship before they leap into another may remain emotionally bound to their former partner—with ties of love *or* of hatred. Or if one partner has remarried and the other hasn't, the unmarried person may continue to feel hurt and badly rejected. A new spouse may be jealous of a former spouse and use her stepchildren to denigrate the ex-wife in her husband's eyes. A father who has been "cast out" of the family may be frightened that his wife's new husband will alienate him from his children. (A mother may feel the same way.) Children, too, often learn that it is profitable to manipulate their parents by playing one against the other.

The binuclear family, where there is cooperation instead of antagonism, may be a lot harder to put into practice than to theorize about, given the anger divorce and remarriage can generate; but it is not impossible. The alternative can be bleak. If ex-spouses can come to terms with their divorce and evolve a new way of relating to each other, their present or subsequent remarriages will be that much easier.

In one family, both husband and wife were so obsessed by his ex-wife (although she lived in another city) that their own marriage never developed on an independent basis. Wife number one worked in a rather high-profile job, and it was she who had initiated the marriage breakup. She was also awarded custody of their three children. Her former husband had always felt somewhat envious of her success. They had married young, and when she began to develop professionally, he thought he couldn't keep up. When he married for a second time he deliberately chose a different sort of wife, someone who hadn't completed high school and was committed to staying in the home.

It was a rebound marriage, contracted before he had got over his feelings of rejection (which already placed it in jeopardy), but what he hadn't counted on was his new wife's insecurity with regard to her predecessor. The first wife continued to carry her husband's name, and the new wife felt like an afterthought.

She fought back. First she became pregnant, so that she could compete at least on that basis. Then she built up her strengths. She thought of herself as a fine mother and housekeeper (she also had a child from a former marriage) and compared herself favourably with the ex-wife. Her husband's job was to let his first wife know that she was inadequate—a poor housekeeper and consequently a poor mother. Because he hadn't overcome his own hostility or finished mourning the death of his first marriage, the husband was more than happy to participate. But the most destructive tactic the new wife adopted was to run down her "rival" in the presence of the woman's daughter, a sensitive girl in her early teens who was experiencing the usual early adolescent mother-daughter antipathies. The child had been quietly angry since her parents' separation, and her suffering had intensified because of the hostility between her natural parents. She missed her father badly and blamed her mother for driving him away. On the other hand, her new stepmother seemed appealing. She was considerably younger than her mother, and they even shared interests in common. But the main attraction was that the stepmother offered the girl a route back to her father's love.

For five years the stepmother and the father denigrated the girl's mother. They insinuated that she was stealing child-support payments and using them for herself; they announced that the girl's mother was a poor parent because she worked outside her home; they made fun of the way she dressed.

The girl was deeply disturbed by the conflict this engendered in her. She was being asked to choose, she knew that, but she couldn't do it. She became wan and tight-lipped in her mother's presence, and eventually she left home.

The new marriage also ended in divorce. The father and his new wife were never able to overcome their preoccupation with the ex-wife and adequately address the separate issue of their own relationship.

Fear and insecurity are common emotional responses when two families unwillingly find themselves joined by the reality of shared children. In the above case, real harm was being done to an adolescent girl by engaging her in a vendetta against her own mother, but in most instances both families are doing their best to protect the children. Things may get done differently from one household to another, but seeing the reality of differences may be to the child's advantage if he or she is not made to believe otherwise. When children are moving from one home to another they are usually quite able to adapt, as long as the rules of the household are spelled out clearly. And when children are encouraged to relate positively to all the adults in their lives (regardless of how the adults may feel about each other personally) they will not feel compelled to choose between their parents, nor will they suffer the psychological consequences of such an act.

One couple garnered their courage and invited both ex-spouses (who had acquired mythological proportions) over for a chat. The new wife, Judy, was fortunate enough to have a sense of humour.

"For the first two years we griped about my first marriage and what a bastard he was and for the next two years we griped about his first marriage and what a bitch she was and how she was poisoning his kids against him, then one day we realized that that was where all our energy was going. Our own relationship and our new family was taking second place to all the bitterness and anger we had stored up. My kids were living with us and they were quite wild. I guess they just felt lost. We were fighting a lot, too, and we started to wonder what we still had going for us besides our mutual hatred for our ex-spouses. One day we decided to invite them over. I really wanted to get a look at this monster who was ruining my life. It was the most difficult thing I ever did, but they came and we did talk about the kids and some other things that were sticking points, like the fact that my ex-husband spoiled my kids rotten on the weekends and made them dissatisfied with their life at home with us. It really helped—a lot. When I saw his wife, she definitely looked quite human to me. I don't know what I expected. I also understood how frightened she was that I was stealing her child's love from her. I felt for her, as one woman to another. I almost liked her."

It was easy to create a mythology about the "bitch-monster" who lived on the other side of the family. Judy discovered she was a woman like herself, fraught with fear at the imagined prospect of losing her child to another.

How can ordinary, well-intentioned people with ordinary human frailties avoid falling victim to a disruptive ex-spouse or actually becoming disruptive themselves? How, for the sake of the children, can they improve relations with the one person who may have hurt them the most? One suggestion comes from Dr. Robert Garfield in a fascinating article entitled "Mourning and Its Resolution for Spouses in Marital Separation." Dr. Garfield argues that the successful transformation of the relationship between former spouses is a vital part of the healing process after divorce. "The parenting relationship is one of the most powerful channels for developing renewed trust," he wrote. "The spouses' continued commitment to their children affirms what was valuable in their past relationship. At the same time, spouses can partially rectify the painful situation they have created for their children.

"Cooperative parenting affirms a new model for relating to each other replacing the negative emotions. . . . Paradoxically, it can help spouses accept the loss of the marriage."

Dr. Garfield acknowledges that not everyone is capable of transforming the way they relate in one fell swoop, and he offers guidelines for proceeding. At first, he suggests, couples should keep their conversations to the business at hand, probably the children. They should avoid emotionally provocative issues and the desire to attack or blame the other. Gradually, as they feel more comfortable, they may be able to talk more generally, but by limiting themselves to the subject at hand, at least in the beginning, their interaction is more likely to be unemotional and neutral in tone. Dr. Garfield's second recommendation—and it is an important one—is that parents not grill their children about the details of an ex-mate's life—and that includes dating. Don't "use" the children at all, he advises. "Using children as emissaries of anger and blame or as targets for unresolved anger damages everyone."

Divorced people who have worked through their feelings of loss seem to be better prepared for remarriage. Otherwise, as we've seen, the new marriage may inherit endless complaints about, and comparisons with, the old marriage, and there just aren't too many relationships that can tolerate a frontal assault of that nature.

Money conflicts

Unless they are so wealthy that such questions don't even enter the picture, conflicts over money often emerge in any marriage—first, second, or third. But in remarriages where one or both partners have financial obligations to another family, things can get tight indeed. In fact, in a study of remarried couples conducted by sociologist Lucile Duberman in 1975, an overwhelming majority of people ranked money as their second most thorny problem. Children were the worst problem, as the reader must certainly be realizing.

Money has so many emotional uses. It can be used to display love or to dispel guilt. It can seduce and it can be used to punish. It can be withheld here and lavished there—to indicate preferences. It can determine who holds the balance of power in a family. In any number of ways, conflicts over money may substitute for other, less socially acceptable expressions of resentment.

Remarriage is a fertile battleground for money wars, and any number of possible situations may create stress:

1. He is paying alimony and/or child support to his former wife, and his new wife resents the drain on their finances.

2. He loses his job or can't meet payments, so wife number two becomes responsible for the payments to his former wife. *That* may evoke a number of negative feelings in wife number two.

3. Wife number two is receiving child support from *her* first husband, but it is inadequate. She'd like husband number two to help, but he's already stretched thin with support payments to *his* ex-wife.

4. Wife number one is in financial difficulty. (In the Wallerstein-Kelly study, twice as many women as men were in financially unstable situations five years after the divorce.) If her ex is slow with his support payments she may cut off visiting until he catches up, causing stress to everyone involved, including the children.

5. Wife number one may tell her children that their father

doesn't care, since he isn't supporting them to their former level. The children will transmit this message and probably feel deprived and resentful, especially if there are children in their father's remarriage family who seem to have more than they do.

6. Father and his new wife may try to win the children by becoming weekend fairy godparents. One teen-age girl whose mother was struggling in a low-paying job would come home with expensive imported clothing and complain bitterly about her mother's "values."

7. Father and wife number two may insinuate that the custodial mother is misusing child-support money, thus disparaging her in her children's eyes.

8. A stepparent may hesitate to include stepchildren in estate planning and wills. The action may be unconscious but represents real ambivalence about the relationship all the same. A husband may likewise "forget" to change his life insurance and will to his second wife's name.

These are but a few of the subtexts that may underly apparently straightforward money problems. In the nuclear family, there is one pot of money and it gets divided according to the priorities of the family. After a divorce, the same salary may have to support two households, and if there is a remarriage, both families may have financial problems. The question of where the available pot of money gets directed is of direct practical and emotional concern to everyone.

Potential money complications underline once again just how important it is for people planning a second marriage to talk about all the gritty details *before* they move in together. Both men and women have a right to know just what the family income is going to be and how much is already allocated elsewhere. And when children are being used to transmit hate messages that appear in the guise of money issues there is a lot to be said for the direct approach. One mother who was being accused of squandering child-support money by her ex-husband (via her son) drew up a budget and showed the boy what came into the house and what went out and what part the child-support payments played in the total scheme. Her son stopped transmitting messages and started to understand how he was aggravating the problems between his families.

Ideally, all the members of the family—including former spouses and their mates—will communicate about issues of mutual concern. These people exist in the life of a remarriage family, so they may as well be acknowledged. If sitting down with an ex-spouse and his or her new mate is just too much to contemplate, it might be easier to do with a trained professional in the room whose job it is to assure everyone that things will be kept under control.

SUGGESTIONS

1. Be aware of fantasy expectations. To blame a stepchild because he "disproves" preconceived notions one has held about oneself, as Margaret did, is grossly unfair. Nowhere is the ability to remain open-minded and flexible more crucial than in the stepfamily, where just about everything is a new experience.

2. Recognize from the start that a lover who has children does not travel alone in this world. He or she comes as a package deal, and a prospective mate will ignore this reality at his or her peril. Discuss the role children will play in your remarried life before and not after the event, trying to avoid stereotyped assumptions about biological instincts. If, after discussion, you discover that you do not want to be a participating stepparent, bow out early.

3. A willing stepparent must be allowed the necessary authority in order to have a true position in the family. This is often very hard to concede for even the most enlightened natural parent, but it is crucial for the integration of the remarriage family. Men like Harvey, who side with their ex-wives against their new wives on grounds that they alone are the "real" parents of the children, are preventing the stepfamily from taking root.

4. Set up ground rules for children who live in your house on a part-time basis, just as you would for full-time children. Just because they are allowed to eat cookies in bed at the other house doesn't mean you have to allow it. The clearer you

are about your own standards (provided they're not unreasonable) the better the children will know you, understand you, and, with luck, respect and like you. You'll like yourself better too.

5. Both men and women should enter their remarriage families gently. Just as a new member on an executive team usually tries to get a feel of things before running for the presidency, so a new spouse-stepparent ought to take a while to observe the way the single-parent family has been functioning and then not be too critical. During the sensitive transition period almost everyone will be feeling a little nervous, or worse. Hold on to a sense of perspective and your sense of humour.

6. Be prepared to be flexible. People who have never raised children before must be particularly careful not to bring rigid, untried notions about children into their marriages. Anthony Renzetti proved that a preconceived script about the roles men and women play in the family won't work in the same way in a remarriage. Alan Boychuk learned that a preconceived script for the behaviour and development of a child also was destined to fail.

7. Never try to replace a real parent in a child's mind or heart. Alan Boychuk suffered from reincarnation fantasies. He thought he could march in and "become" Joseph's father.

8. With the "binuclear family" as an ideal, work toward whatever level of cooperation is possible between the remarried family and the ex-spouse. Everyone will benefit. If interaction is difficult, start by avoiding emotional issues and remaining as neutral as possible.

9. Talk about finances before you remarry, not after.

10. Be aware of a possible subtext when money matters become a problem. If there is one, try to deal with the underlying issue.

CHAPTER THREE
Voices of the Children

PART ONE: WHAT CHILDREN WORRY ABOUT

The problems facing children in remarriage families are often the mirror image of their parents' problems. The perspective is different, of course, and because they are children, they are less able to conceptualize their feelings and take steps to improve their lives. Sometimes their conflicts are quite unique. Losing one's place in the sibling hierarchy of a family is something no remarried adult ever has to confront.

Parents, however, should take heart. During the 1970s, several studies of people who grew up in stepfamilies indicated they had developed into adults with the same positive characteristics as children from nuclear families. In other words, the growing-up process may be considerably harder, but there is no evidence that the majority of children from divorced and remarried homes are permanently scarred by their experiences. Without diminishing the problems, it is worthwhile remembering that as humans we're a remarkably adaptable lot.

On the other hand, the anger, confusion, and suffering children may experience during the transition periods is palpably real. Indeed, most children who are brought into a remarriage family will have to deal with at least some of the following concerns.

Abandonment

The principal worry of just about every child whose parents separate is that he or she will lose the presence and the love of the departing parent. Children may believe the breakup is their fault—if only they had done what they were told, Daddy wouldn't have gone away—and they may perceive the separation as a rejection of themselves. It is important for parents to state clearly that this is not the case—and the message may have to be repeated many times over.

Sometimes children fear their remaining parent will also leave them; after all, if one parent vanished, what is there to prevent the other from doing the same? This is a terrifying prospect. One boy of five whose parents had recently separated called out from his bedroom one night, ''Is it against the law for mommies to leave their children?'' The child was appealing to the highest authority he could think of: if love couldn't hold a parent, perhaps the force of the state would. His mother understood the question. She went back into his room, hugged him in the dark, and promised she would never leave him.

Like adults, children may become depressed and angry. They may have tantrums and regress to a more babyish stage. Six-year-olds may start to soil again, remembering at some level of consciousness how secure it felt to be a baby and have their needs looked after.

Worries about being abandoned are often reawakened at the time of a remarriage. Now it is the single-parent family that is being threatened, and children may worry about losing the one parent who has remained. Far from being welcomed, a stepparent may be seen as a threat to the only security the child has.

A child who has responded positively to Mom's or Dad's new friend when the relationship seemed casual may suddenly turn on the stepparent. Stepparents who understand the basis of such fear will move slowly, and natural parents will make sure they continue to set aside time to spend alone with their children.

Children are often unable to understand why their parent

would even *want* to remarry. Isn't the parent satisfied with having just them? In one family, the father had remarried some years earlier and the teen-age daughter (who lived with her mother) seemed quite accepting, but when her mother wanted to remarry, the girl flew into a rage and threatened to leave home. "Why was it all right for your father to make a new life for himself and not for me?" her mother asked. "Because you had your children," replied the daughter, speaking a child's essential truth.

Misconceptions and myths

Many children harbour the hope that their natural parents will reunite long after that prospect ceases to be a possibility. Rationality is beside the point: Some continue to hope even after a parent's remarriage. Such children are unlikely to accept a stepparent and may actively try to break up the new relationship, but for the majority a remarriage signals the end of their cherished wish, and they must mourn their loss anew.

The parents of one sixteen-year-old girl had been separated for a decade. Her father had been living with a new woman for at least four years, and her mother had a comfortable ongoing relationship with a man who visited the house frequently. When the father decided to marry the woman he had been living with, the girl was visibly upset. "I guess you guys aren't going to get back together," she said to her astonished mother.

A child moving into a remarriage family may also feel uncertain about what will happen from a material point of view. Children need to know what to expect. Will they be sharing a bedroom or will they have separate rooms? Will they be moving to a new house, and will they have to attend a new school? If a couple can afford to move, it's probably wise to start fresh in a new house, where neither partner feels like an intruder in someone else's family home. Children should also be involved in decisions as much as possible. They can come along on house-hunting expeditions and choose the furniture for their own rooms. They ought to be involved in any redecorating of their rooms. Most important, they must be assured that their possessions will be respected. No one is going to leave their favourite toy behind. The old life will be integrated into the new life as much as possible.

Spying games and loyalty conflicts

"When you attack a child's loyalties, you are attacking the child's basic structure. Depending upon the degree that you are successful in making a child more loyal to you than to his other natural parent . . . you have undermined the child's ability to cope . . . Trust becomes dangerous to him because he feels that if he trusts anyone and loves anyone he may have to end up being disloyal. That is a very painful thing to handle, and it brings lots and lots of guilt."

The quote is from child psychologist Jean Chastain, and it puts the problem succinctly. There is nothing sadder than the child who has had to face a separation in the family and must now cope with the additional pain of hearing one parent belittle the other. Children have a right to go on loving the two people who brought them into the world, regardless of how those people may feel about one another, and they have the right not to be used as spies and messengers of hate. Rarely, a wise child simply refuses to become involved, but more often children are entangled, to their personal detriment.

What if there are unpleasant things about a parent that a child must eventually be told? First, parents must be clear about their own motives. How self-serving is the need to tell and how much is based on an honest desire to inform and help?

Children will observe for themselves and come to their own conclusions. A parent who proclaims his or her love from the mountaintops, but rarely comes to visit and appears to show little real interest in the child's activities, doesn't need "interpreting" by the other parent. Here, as elsewhere, actions speak louder than words. These may be painful realizations for children, but when they represent reality it is better for the child to discover the truth for himself, over time.

When there is information about an absent parent that must be imparted, parents and stepparents need to tread cautiously. They must realize that criminals, scoundrels, and social pariahs of every stripe are often loved profoundly by their children.

Sexuality and the ambiguous incest taboo

Can one really speak of "incest" in the context of stepfamilies? Do an adolescent boy and girl become "brother" and "sister" just because their respective parents have married each other?

The answer is almost certainly no, on both counts. Yet the incest taboo must operate in the stepfamily just as in the nuclear family, in order to protect its members. Sometimes the taboo takes effect quite unconsciously. One man who is now in his early forties said he automatically transformed his stepsister into a confidante and friend although he had dated her in the past. From the moment their parents married and they lived in the same house, he stopped seeing her the same way. He never actually thought about it, he said, it just happened.

But the incest taboo *is* on precarious footing in stepfamilies, and the easy familiarity of bathrooms and bedrooms can quickly become erotically charged. Sexual interest can come from any quarter: from a stepson towards his stepmother; from a stepdaughter towards a stepfather; or from either stepparent towards a stepchild; but the most common combination is between stepsiblings, and the most delicate time for children to start living together is early adolescence.

Parents sometimes deny evidence of sexuality between teen-age stepsiblings, and understandably so. The denial is part of the fantasy that the reconstituted family is the same as the original nuclear family—or ought to be. In their book *How to Live with Other People's Children*, authors June and William Noble told of a family in which the husband's twelve-year-old son and the wife's fourteen-year-old daughter had taken to spending the night in each other's rooms. The mother saw this as evidence that the young people had "very similar interests." No doubt she was right.

The stress on the children may be considerable. A boy who feels attracted to his stepmother may mask his feelings by being unpleasant and gruff, and adolescents in the family may fight incessantly to camouflage their unacceptable feelings.

If children are overtly seductive with a stepparent, it may be wise to deal with the subject directly, without being too serious. One fourteen-year-old girl began sitting on her stepfather's lap and whispering little secrets into his ear. Fortunately he understood her and was amused rather than threatened. With his wife's consent, he told her that she had the wrong guy. He could be a friend and even a "parent" if she could accept that; but he was in love with her mother. He also reassured her that she would meet someone closer to her own age who would be special in her life.

Adults may find themselves attracted to their adolescent stepchildren just as natural parents occasionally find themselves attracted to their own children. In both cases, one can only rely upon the insight, self-control, and maturity of the adults concerned.

Some couples who are bringing adolescent children into a remarriage have considered solutions in advance. One family placed their teen-agers in bedrooms on separate floors and made rules about who could visit whom and at what times. And from the start they were a lot stricter about parading around in the nude than they had been in their first families.

Where do I belong?

Remarriage disrupts a child's life. Besides worrying about material questions such as where the family will live or fears about possibly losing the love of a parent, children also feel unsure about what their place in the new family will be. If a child was the oldest in the family, there were certain attitudes and privileges that went along with the station. The child who was "number one" may find herself displaced, like Cathy

STEPFAMILIES: MAKING THEM WORK   67

Renzetti, for example. The same is true for other family positions. The baby of the family may suddenly find himself a middle child. Overnight one may have to compete for attention with a host of people who weren't even there a matter of hours ago. In addition, a child with a quiet temperament may find herself frightened and lost in a remarriage family of noisy, demanding stepsiblings.

Adults need to recognize the fears that result from a family reorganization and pay attention to the children's specific needs. In the transitional stepfamily, roles need to be delineated more clearly, perhaps, than in the nuclear family. The fact that people belong to and have a place in the new family needs to be underlined and reinforced.

Visiting the other family

When children live full-time with one parent and visit the other, they often feel like outsiders in the second family. Men who are remarried to women who have children from a former union may find that their own offspring are quite overtly jealous. One little boy who lived alone with his mother suddenly refused to continue visiting his father, who was remarried and living in another city. After some prodding he acknowledged that he found it painful to be so removed from his father while his stepsiblings actually lived with him. "They get to be with Dad all the time and they're not even his real children," he whispered tearfully to his mother.

In addition, visiting children often have no friends in the new neighbourhood and are dependent on parent and stepparent to occupy them. Sometimes they don't have a permanent place to sleep, or keep their belongings in the other family home.

Chris Spankler is a woman of thirty, but her memories of growing up in a stepfamily are as vivid today as the events were all those years ago. Her parents had been unhappily married for many years. Both had ongoing love affairs, and when they decided to separate, they also decided to marry their respective lovers. One summer, when Chris was twelve and at camp, she received a letter from her mother saying that she and Chris's father had separated and that they would both be remarried before she returned from her vacation. There were no further niceties.

Chris was shocked by the brutality of the announcement, but at another level scarcely surprised, since she knew her parents were unhappy. She didn't like her stepfather, of course. She wasn't given a chance to get to know him, and furthermore she blamed him for the breakup of her family. He tried to "butt in" all the time, she said. He didn't like the way she talked back to her mother, but she had always talked that way and resented his interference. Finally her stepfather gave up. He still mumbled remarks about Chris's conduct, but her mother began to make all the family decisions alone. Once this happened he became irrelevant to Chris's life and easy to ignore.

The most painful part was going to visit her father and *his* new family. "Somehow I was expected to fit in with all these people including my stepmother's children and their friends but I didn't know anyone at all and I didn't even want to know those kids," recalled Chris. "I was supposed to amuse myself doing things, but I was never sure exactly what. The stepsisters and brothers were told to take me places, but they didn't want to, and that was very awkward. I was expected to fend for myself.

"When I was unhappy everyone would tell me to pull up my socks and grow up. It was even harder because I went there to be with my father, but he was usually just around the house doing whatever he happened to be doing. I didn't have a place there, but it was assumed that I did. I didn't feel like a member of the family, but I kept going back because I wanted to be close to my dad.

"My real father withdrew from me and I never let my step-father get close, although now, as an adult, I like him better and respect him. It was the strangest thing, really. Although I had two fathers, I grew up feeling that I didn't have a father at all."

Chris's story is instructive. Chris thought she was visiting so she could be with her father, but he assumed she would melt into the tapestry of his new family and become "one of the kids" while she was there. She didn't. Furthermore, no one seemed aware of the special problems she faced as a visitor who had no permanent place in the family. When she complained, there was little sympathy or understanding.

Had her father taken the trouble to introduce her to the children in the neighbourhood, she might have been able to establish friendships outside the family even though she was there only on an intermittent basis. Had he made a point of spending time alone with her, she might have felt more welcome, and her visiting, over the years, might have had more emotional content.

After she left home in her early twenties, Chris lived for five years with a man who provided her with the security she craved. When she felt stronger, she left him. She said they were not suited, even though he was the kindest person she had known. At the time of our meeting she had a high-profile job in industry—one that required a clear intelligence and good administrative abilities. She lived alone.

Although there was no suggestion that the breakup and reorganization of her parents' lives had damaged Chris in any permanent way, there was clearly a sadness, an ongoing sadness, that two fathers had not added up to one.

HOW TO HELP YOUR CHILD ADJUST TO A REMARRIAGE

1. Be sensitive to the child's fear of abandonment at the time of a remarriage. You may be gaining a companion, lover, and friend, but your child is likely worried about losing the only full-time parent he or she has.

2. Be aware of symptoms of regression, especially in younger children.

3. Make sure children are informed in advance about any material changes that will occur in their lives. Make an effort to include them in house-hunting and decorating choices. Try to maintain continuity wherever possible.

4. Do not use children to spy on or transmit messages to your ex-spouse. Nothing will frighten a child away from a re-

marriage family faster than the suspicion that it will be used as a vehicle to alienate him further from his other parent.

5. If at all possible, let children discover the truth about their other parent by themselves. If negative information must be imparted, do it gently. Stepparents should always avoid running down their predecessor.

6. Be aware of sexual undertones in the stepfamily and address the issue directly (but gently) if it seems necessary to do so.

7. Recognize that family reorganization will probably upset the position a child has held in the age hierarchy of the family. This may represent a major loss of status in addition to other worries, and he or she may need special help in adjusting.

8. Remarriage families who have visiting children should try to allow time for natural parent and child to be alone together if the visit is to be meaningful. And do not assume that your visiting son or daughter will automatically fit in with the other children without assistance.

PART TWO: FOUR ADOLESCENTS ON LOVE, LOSS, AND REMARRIAGE: NORMA, ANNE, LIONEL, AND RANDY

Norma Jason

Norma Jason was twenty years old, big-boned, and tall. She had shoulder-length brown hair and blue eyes, and her perfect teeth had apparently been the object of much orthodontic attention. The library of her mother's home was plush, comfortable, and, she said, soundproof. Norma peered into the outside hall to make sure her younger sister wasn't listening, then shut the solid wood doors firmly behind her.

Norma's mother, Gail, had just remarried for the third time, and for as long as Norma could remember she had been preoccupied, if not obsessed, with her mother's love life. The worst thing that had ever happened to her, however, was the loss of her father; and although that event had occurred when she was only eight years old, more than half a lifetime ago, the memory remained as jagged and as sharp and as raw as it had ever been. The loss of her father had coloured and shaped her entire life, and her mother's subsequent involvements had only added to the problem. For Norma, none of these emotional roadblocks had ever been resolved.

Her anger had been directed at both her parents, for not loving each other enough and for destroying her family; and her bitter mood over the years had left a lasting imprint on her face. Her blue eyes were appraising and cool, a defiant tightness had pulled her mouth into a permanent pout, and a rough, impatient note sounded in her voice. Norma had long ago surrounded herself with protective armour. Now that she was older and definitely more in control of her life, she was a lot safer; she could afford to let go a little, and she was trying. But the old habits of anger were well ingrained, and they would be with her for a long while to come.

She poured coffee, and the familiar social ritual seemed to put her at ease. She relaxed visibly onto the brown sofa and began to speak. And what she chose to talk about was The Event: that traumatic moment so many years ago when her life stood still, then veered sharply in another direction.

"I was eight years old and we were visiting with my grandparents in California. I was listening in on one of my mother's telephone calls, and I heard her say she was going to take the children and leave. I felt so upset I could hardly breathe. I barged into her room and I started to shout and scream and cry. All I knew was that we were going to be separated from my father.

"I had always been very close to my father. When I was little my mom used to say that he paid the most attention to me. He used to treat me like I was his little princess—the whole bit. Maybe some kids are closer to one parent than the other, and in a way I leaned toward my father in those days. When I heard my mother on the phone I knew she was going to take us away and we wouldn't see him. That's what I thought that day, and that's how it turned out."

Gail Jason returned home to Buffalo, New York, and did precisely what she said she would do. She took her two children, aged eight and two, and moved into her brother's house. But Norma was devastated. She felt as though she had been torn into two halves, one belonging to her father and one belonging to her mother; and in her childlike way, she wanted to make things up to her dad.

"I remember telling my mom that I didn't want to live just with her. I wanted to live with both of them, because I didn't think it was fair for me to be with her all the time and leave him all alone. So Mom said, 'Sure, if you want to try it out and live with him for a while, that's okay with me.' So I stayed with him for a couple of days, but I felt so strange. Maybe because he was male and I was female. I don't know. I really missed my sister, and my mom, too. I just wanted things to be the way they had always been.

"But after that, my dad sort of stopped seeing us very often. He travelled a lot and he was busy with his own life, getting things back together and all that, and then he moved to another city. Now he says he really wanted to see us more, but he didn't want to interfere. He said he would say bad things about Mom and she would say bad things about him and it would confuse us, so he thought it would be better if just one parent brought us up. He thought we'd turn out better and that we wouldn't be torn between both parents.

"But I didn't agree at all. I was so resentful because he didn't see us. When I used to speak to him on the phone I was very hostile toward him, and I used to cry and yell because I wanted him to care about me. I wanted him to come to visit us and be a part of our lives. But he didn't. He just totally stayed out of our lives."

For Norma the separation was like an amputation. This beloved father had favoured her, had chosen her to be his special princess. Then, without warning, he was gone, and it seemed he no longer loved her. What else was she to think? What could his well-considered reasons for staying away possibly have meant to her as she waited beside the telephone, weekend after weekend, hoping he would call? She thought there was, perhaps, a reason he wasn't telling her about. Maybe she had been bad and he was punishing her.

Perhaps loss through death is easier for a child of Norma's

age to accept. An eight-year-old will eventually understand the finality of death. She may derive comfort from knowing that her lost parent loved her. And she can obtain solace from her surviving parent, who is likely to speak lovingly of the other. But Norma's father's disappearance seemed inexplicable, and there was little comfort available from her mother. Gail had nothing good to say about her ex-husband.

"I have never heard her say anything nice about him," said Norma bitterly, "but *he* doesn't put *her* down. It's been as though she had tried to brainwash us into believing that it was one hundred percent his fault and that she's done everything right. I resent that. I mean, a marriage is fifty-fifty, and both have to make it work, the man and the woman."

As Gail Jason struggled with her personal despair and the reality of being a single parent to two children under the age of ten, Norma began to feel newly responsible. She also began to see her mother as a person who needed help and protection. "I tried to support her. I don't know if I succeeded, but I was more protective of my little sister and I started to do a few things around the house," she told me.

But Norma was feeling more than ambivalent, and she expressed her sense of loss in anger. She was angry at her mother, angry at her father, and she closed in tight on herself. "As I got older I decided I wasn't going to depend on anyone," she said thoughtfully. "I figured I had to depend on myself, because I had depended on other people and it hadn't worked for me. I had depended on my father, and my father let me down. He went away. I had depended on my mother, and she went and got divorced from my father. I was just sick of depending on other people."

She was a fighter and she refused to accept her father's rejection. What could she have done to deserve his indifference? she continually asked herself as the years passed. At age twenty she was still thinking about him—but less often, she was quick to add. The Event, however, was still in her conscious life.

"Lots of times I remember the past when Dad and I used to play together, and then I have recurrences of hearing my mother say we were leaving and of running into her room, screaming. The whole scene just keeps coming into my mind, and it's very hard to deal with. Sometimes I wonder whether I rebel in certain ways because I didn't really have a father. Like I'm missing something in my life. Or maybe I'm rebelling because I'm resentful and I wish things were different or had been different.'' Norma had lots of theories to explain her difficult adolescence. She wished she understood better.

"You know, I speak to him on the phone more often now that I'm older, and lots of times I tell him that I don't love him. I tell him that over and over again. But it's not really true, because deep down I love him very much,'' she admitted softly, her eyes fixed on the coffee cup she held in her hands.

Just one year after her separation and divorce from Norma's father, Gail Jason remarried. The news came as a fresh blow to Norma. Her father had left her and now she felt sure her mother would leave her too. That's what the remarriage meant to her. Why, she wondered, did mother even want another man?

"I figured all she needed was us," she said, her eyes still blazing with the injustice of it all. "When we were young she always told us that the only thing that was important to her was her children. Her children were the sunrise and the sunset. So I was totally puzzled. Why would she marry someone else when she had us? I mean, why would she *need* anyone else?''

At twenty Norma didn't have to be told the answer to a question she asked herself at age nine, but something remained in her voice that suggested she didn't *really* understand, even yet. Her reaction to the news of her mother's remarriage was a child's gut reaction. Mommy, after all, is forever. Mommy belongs to her children. And Norma didn't want to share her mother, especially when she already felt her father had abandoned her.

Norma fought the marriage with everything in the arsenal of a nine-year-old. She was nasty to her stepfather, Simon, and to her mother, whom she pined for but also thought of as a traitor. She turned over her food at the dinner table and talked so rudely that Gail gasped with dismay and surprise. When she was sent to her room as punishment she let herself out the window and waited until her mother was distraught with worry before she returned. She did poorly in school and got into trouble with her teachers.

The wedding ceremony itself had been especially hard. Norma felt she was being "pushed aside," a phrase that continually popped up in her conversation, and she took out her anger on the lady her mother had hired to organize things. "She had me standing facing the wall," recalled Norma with fresh indignation. "Finally I turned to her and I said, 'I'm not like that. I don't like being put in a corner. How would you like it if I stuck *you* in a corner?' The lady was surprised, I guess. I just remember standing there. I did not want to be there. I could not *believe* my mother was marrying this man. He was just awful. He just tried to buy us and pretend that he liked us. And he let both of us get away with murder. I mean, he had no discipline and everybody knows you have to bring kids up with discipline. He was just too nice to be real."

This marriage broke up when Norma was eleven, but nine years later she was still too angry to be aware of having said she had hated a man for being too nice. In fact, Norma would not have accepted any man as a stepfather. She had not accepted the loss of her father, nor had she overcome the anger she felt toward both her natural parents. She had never understood why her father had not wanted to visit her when they had been so close. She was torn between loving him and hating him. She was torn between loving and hating her mother. And she was deeply afraid that whatever bad thoughts she had had—the ones that made her father leave— might also make her mother reject her. The painful "proof" was that the worst was about to happen. Simon would steal the affection Gail gave to her. She would be pushed aside, made to "stand in the corner." Gail needed more than she and her sister could provide, and that was frightening.

Simon's title of "stepfather" also felt like a threat. Norma already had a father whom she was trying to recover. She didn't want Simon to be a "father" of any description.

"I was really scared that my little sister, who didn't know my father that well, would think of Simon as a real father. She did start calling him Daddy, and that was awful. I always called him Simon, but he was the first father figure that my sister ever had, and she really took to him. When she called him Daddy I would get really angry, and I told her so. I said, 'He's not your father, so don't call him Daddy. Your *real* father is Daddy.' Then I had to explain. I said, 'Daddy is the one we see sometimes at Grandma's.'

"That's why I really resented Simon. I thought he was trying to make Anne think he was her father when he wasn't. I got so upset about that that I got into a fight with him and I started punching. I mean, that really, really got to me. I just couldn't take that."

Norma was flushed and breathing quickly. The intervening years seemed to have made so little difference. In her mind, her mother's remarriage had effectively orphaned her. The downy cocoon of childhood, where the world looks safe because Mommy and Daddy make it so, had been torn away and she fought to restore it.

"Was Simon friendly to you?"

"Yes, but to no avail," she replied, her eyes flashing. "No bloody way."

An additional complication was the fact that Simon had custody of his daughter, who was just a little older than Norma. Just like Cathy Renzetti, who refused to accept her new place in the family hierarchy, Norma also rebelled against being displaced.

"I was the oldest girl and I always have been," she said angrily. "Then this new girl came into the house and all of a sudden she was supposed to be my equal. Well, I didn't *have* an equal!"

Her stepsister, Lilly, was ten years old. She was fat and she had pimples on her face, and Norma never let her forget it. Once again, Norma felt the intrusion in terms of being "pushed aside," and she fought back tooth and nail.

"If I had to do it over again I wouldn't hurt Lilly so much, but that was the only way I knew how to deal with it. I mean, *she didn't belong there*. She didn't fit in."

Norma's anguished and heartfelt cry, "She didn't belong there," was a direct personal rejection of Lilly, but it hit the nerve centre of a problem affecting stepfamilies in general. In remarriage, the old, closed boundaries of the family are disturbed as new people enter the sacred circle and claim to be family members. The question is: Are they or are they not?

So far there is no generally accepted definition of what these new family "boundaries" might be in remarriage situations. It's all a little ad hoc, and there's an element of choice involved, which, of course, never exists in the nuclear family. People who like their steprelatives are simply more likely to accept them as family members than people who don't.

This was the choice Norma made. She bluntly refused to recognize the legitimacy of the new family ties.

Norma became a problem for everyone. She became a magnet for all the family tension. All the adjustment difficulties in the Gail-Simon merger focused on her. She felt she had been "put in the corner," as she told the wedding consultant, and she began to play the role to the hilt. She did things—"bad girl" things—that would confirm her perception of herself as a rejected outsider.

"Whatever anyone said to me, I snapped back at them. I didn't have time for anyone. I couldn't be bothered with these people, even my mom and my sister. I was sick and tired and I knew deep down, I just *knew* Mom had made a mistake. I wanted to tell her. I didn't want to see her get hurt again. I guess I was trying to tell her in my childish way, but I didn't know how. I just rebelled totally.

"One day we were at the dinner table—Mom always made such a big deal about having dinner together—and my mom said something and Simon said something and my sister said something. It was so-o-o civilized. His daughter, Lilly, just sat there. She was scared to death of me. I just sat there, too. I was sick and tired of listening to them, because I also wanted to say something and no one was asking me my opinion. Finally my mom asked me something very politely and I just exploded. She looked at me. She was astounded that I would get upset over something so little, but she didn't realize that I was reacting to the whole horrible scene because I hated it so much. So she sent me to my room. That's what she always did. I slammed the door. Then I decided I would run away, so I cut the screen out of my window and I jumped down, about six or seven feet. I had a bicycle underneath my window just waiting. Running away was another way of rebelling, because I thought if I stayed in my room I'd be *taking it*. I'd be consenting. I'd be agreeing with her. I'd be saying, 'Oh, yes, Norma is a bad girl and she belongs in her room.'

"So I ran away. Of course I came back when I was hungry and when I knew she'd be beside herself with worry. She was, and of course she sent me to my room again. It was so dumb. I figured she should have come out in the open and said, 'Why are you running away?' even though I thought it ought to be pretty obvious. But I guess it wasn't obvious. She just thought that was the way I was. Difficult."

Norma probably would have hated Simon regardless of the circumstances. She was quite clear in her mind about that. But she did acknowledge that he might have seemed less threatening if she had had a chance to get to know him a little before he married her mother. As it happened, Gail and Simon decided to marry fairly quickly. They had known each other for several months, but Simon had never been what Gail called "a special beau." He was only one of several men she was dating. Gail sprang the news quite suddenly without preparing her daughters. Like so many single mothers, she thought it best to protect her children from seeing a lot of men pass through her life, and especially from any hint that her relationships might involve sex. So, as far as the kids were concerned, the men she dated were cardboard figures who said hello and goodbye and occasionally chucked them under the chin. It was easy to mock them, too. They weren't quite human, the way teachers aren't quite human to their young students. Norma and her sister enjoyed sizing up their mother's dates and passing judgement. This one had thin hair, that one was too fat. And that one waddled when he walked.

"The only time we spent with Simon after they got serious was when we were with my mom," recalled Norma. "So we only knew him through her. It wasn't on an individual basis. I think they should have let Simon be with us without Mom so maybe we could have formed a relationship with him. If he had taken us to the zoo or something, we might have liked him. As it was, the relationship was forced on us. He was just my mother's husband.''

After two years, Gail and Simon separated. Norma was part of the reason. She had made life in the beautiful house hell for everyone. She had made young Lilly's life miserable.

Norma had won, and when news of the separation came through she was ecstatic. ''I was so happy,'' she said, a contented smile spreading across her face and her blue eyes shining. ''I even felt a little badly about the way I had treated his daughter. I was a little older by then, and I thought it really wasn't her fault. I actually felt quite sorry for her, and after they got their divorce we even became friends. I told her if she ever needed someone to talk to she could talk to me. I said I knew I was contradicting myself because two years earlier she couldn't have come to me with a gift. I wouldn't have accepted anything she gave me or anything she wanted to tell me. But after the divorce it just felt different.

''Oh, God, it was such a relief when they left. I felt like the negative parts were swept out of the house and now we could start fresh. I felt we had our family again. We didn't need this intruder and his daughter.''

The old boundaries of the traditional family had closed in again. Norma had helped kick ''the intruders'' out and resurrect the ''real'' family. And she didn't feel guilty about either. ''Their separation had nothing to do with me,'' she claimed defensively.

But she did feel upset for her mother; and now she tried, again, to protect Gail, as she had after the first-marriage breakdown. A role reversal took place. ''My mother had been hurt and I wanted to protect her so badly, but I couldn't. I had tried to warn her. I thought she had got married just for the sake of being married, or why would she have married *him*? She always let her heart tell her what to do instead of her head. It was just like she did things deliberately that would hurt her, and I really pitied her for the situation she was in.''

Norma had mixed feelings about playing caretaker to her mother. On one hand, she loved the role. Now she ''knew'' her place in her mother's heart had been restored. Now that the rival and his daughter had been cast out of the family she could relax and devote her energies once more to recapturing her father's love. But on the other hand, looking after her mother was frightening and added to her sense of being alone in the world without enough support.

For the next eight years, Norma lived with her mother and her sister, and as she matured she began to see Gail as an adult who was lonely and who had needs beyond her children. But Norma was wary. These new glimmerings of adult understanding did not yet extend to wishing her mother would remarry. The family boundaries were closed and that was the way Norma liked it. The only real worry she had was when Simon appeared back on the scene a couple of years after the divorce. Her younger sister, Anne, was happy to see him, and Gail seemed happy, too. So Norma took matters into her own hands. She reprimanded her mother. "Here you are, a young, single, beautiful woman, and you've got this louse chasing after you," she scolded. "Why don't you throw him out?" She also made it clear that she didn't want to see Simon in the house. "You're already divorced and you know how I feel about him," she chided. "Please see him elsewhere if you have to see him." Feeling guilty, as single mothers often do, Gail complied with Norma's wishes.

By the time Gail married her third husband, Howard, Norma had reached that stage in late adolescence where her main drive was to separate herself from her family. Thoughts of future schooling and career choices began to loom large in her mind, and she felt propelled to take a few, tentative steps away on her own, the way babies are propelled to pull themselves to their feet and then to walk. Was she strong enough to make the longed-for move into independence? she wondered. Was she ready?

In any case, life at home had begun to feel too constricting. She was still rebelling and Gail was still correcting her in a parental way. As long as Norma lived at home Gail would probably continue to "mother" her, but at age twenty Norma had had enough of being mothered—or so she felt. She thought of herself as standing at the edge of a moat separating home from the outside world. She wanted to leap across—but she hesitated.

Thus preoccupied, Norma was hardly upset at all when it looked as though Howard might become stepfather number two.

Several hours had gone by and the oak-panelled library had darkened. Norma's words seemed to have filled the room: her loss, her sadness, her fear, her love for her mother, her anger. Now she was emerging from childhood, and new possibilities beckoned from a world outside the family where she hoped she might live undisturbed by echoes from her own troubled past.

"It's strange now, Mom being with Howard," she said quietly. "It's like when I was younger, except then I had less knowledge and less experience. I feel as though I have been through stages of growth—an early stage, a middle stage, and a later stage. I feel, Well, here we go again. Only it's different. Now I feel very good for my mother and I think it's wonderful that she has found somebody who can make her happy again. I think Howard is a very good person and I have total trust and faith in him. I know he's a stable human being and I know he wouldn't do anything to hurt my mother. I actually feel the family has been expanded. I feel very warm towards Howard and his daughter. I haven't met his son, but I'm sure I'll feel just as warmly about him." She looked reflective. "You know," she added, "I do think a lot of my attitudes have to do with me and not him at all. I'm older and I think when you get older you can't be as easily provoked. When someone says something, you just leave it because you start to realize what things are important. And if my mother has found love in her life, then all that can happen is that the family will become closer and closer."

Norma was about to leave for college. The school, Sarah Lawrence, was far away, and that was perfect. Norma was becoming more detached—and she knew it.

"In a way, I'm saying all this as an outsider," she acknowledged. "If I knew I was going to be an insider here in the family and living in the house, I don't know if I would say the same things."

"Let's pretend that you were not going to be leaving

home,'' I suggested. ''Then how would you feel about the new marriage?''

A pained expression crossed her face. ''To tell you the truth, I'd feel cramped, like I was being pushed into a corner. I'm even starting to perspire.'' She laughed a little. ''You see, I really do have to leave home now. I just need my independence.''

Norma wouldn't have to live with Howard or think of him as a ''father'' of any description, she said. But she was not too old for a friend. Howard had wisely approached Gail's daughters in just that way—as a friend and not as a parent—and Norma respected him for this. ''He talks to me as a friend and I see him as someone who knows more than I do. He's a friend who gives advice if I ask, but he doesn't expect anything in return. And that's the best way for him to be right now.''

And with Howard on the scene, Norma could finally let go of the caretaker role she had created for herself. Now she could drop the heavy load she had insisted on carrying.

''I like to make sure everything is in order and running smoothly, and this has been difficult for me,'' she said, acknowledging the fact that the balance of power had long ago shifted in her direction. ''I feel I have been responsible for the family for so many years. I feel that as the older daughter I had to watch out for my sister. I'm very loyal, and I think that will never, ever end. But in a way, that's why I can't continue to live at home, because those feelings of responsibility overtake me and then I can't do anything else. I feel my mother has had a very hard time, a lot because of me, I guess. I've become obsessed with responsibility. Now Howard will look after things, and that's fine with me.

''Another thing that's new is that I can see Howard as an individual and not just as my mother's husband. I mean, he's a person. He's got things that have happened to him. He's got children. I can see my mother as a person, too, and I can see that they need each other.''

Her voice had quieted. ''I even hope that he will like me for what I am and not just because I'm my mother's daughter,'' she added softly. ''Maybe he'll like my values and the way I think and the way I question things. I don't know how to express it exactly, but I want him to recognize me for who I am, not just for the fact that I'm in the family.''

This was the twenty-year-old fledgling adult speaking, the girl who had just okayed her college program for next year and had begun to delve into translations of Honoré de Balzac because a respected friend had recommended them. This was the emerging adult who could analyze the troubled years of her childhood with intelligence, the young woman who was honest enough to talk straightforwardly about her anger and her love. But at age twenty (and for many years to come) there is a flip side to all of this, and on the flip side of Norma's maturity lived the child who struggled, still, to understand why her own, beloved father had turned his back on her. Sometimes she thought she understood him and the reasons he had given—but then she would doubt again.

''What I'm still confused about is why my father never took more of a role in our lives. I still cannot understand that. I mean, he tells me how he thought it would be better for us if he stayed away, but that's not perfectly logical, because he's a father and, well, he only had two kids. In his whole life he only had two kids, and they're healthy and there's nothing wrong with them . . .'' Her voice trailed off as she struggled to control the familiar surge of sadness. ''Why wouldn't he take a paternal interest in us?'' she asked, as though a stranger might provide an answer to the central question of her life.

''You know, I told him all this, quite recently. I said, 'I think there's something wrong with you, Dad,' and he said, 'Well, you'll understand when you're older.' But I said, 'Dad, we *are* older and you don't realize it. We're older and we're all going to be far away, and where are you going to be? You'll be all alone without your children. You ought to get to know Anne before it's too late!' And he just said, 'Well, if she doesn't want to know me when she's older, that's her loss, not mine,' and I said, 'Oh no, oh no, you're wrong, because it's *your* loss, not hers. I mean, you're the one who's going to be alone, because we have each other—Mom, Anne, and me—and what do you have? Think about it.' Well, he hasn't gotten back to me, so I guess he's still thinking about it.

"The thing is, he wouldn't know what to say to us anyhow. What can you say to a kid you don't know after you've said, 'Hi, wanna play baseball?' Lots of times I've said, 'Dad, you don't know me,' and he says, 'Yes, I do,' so I say, 'Okay, what's my favourite colour,' or 'What's my favourite food?' Well, of course he doesn't know, because he doesn't know me at all. I mean he sort of loves us in a way because we're his children, but not because of who we are as real people. Because he doesn't even know us."

Norma looked crumpled and dejected. She couldn't acknowledge the reality of a weak father who probably hadn't cared enough. At the same time she fought a deep-seated conviction that he had rejected her because *she* wasn't good enough. Norma knew that to give in to that thought would be disastrous. Instead she stubbornly went on hoping he would want to know her and that he would love her again.

The scrappy street fighter in Norma's personality had helped her through, and her search for common ground was unyielding. "I'm a lot like him," she said, reaching for her elusive father. "My father has had a lot of hard things to go through in his life, just like me. He's a fighter and a survivor and so am I."

Anne Jason

Anne was the little sister to whom Norma had spoken, in desperation, about who was and was not a daddy in this family. Unlike Norma, she was tiny in stature and looked even younger than her fourteen years. Long, dark hair fell softly around her face and neck, and her expression was gentle.

Where Norma had carefully constructed an aggressive exterior to ward off further hurt, Anne had not. She was immediately responsive and eager to talk about herself. She had been actively looking forward to this meeting, she said. She needed to talk to someone.

Fourteen is a funny age. Children may be in full rebellion

against their parents and the limits they impose, but at the same time most of them know they're not yet equipped to leave home and look after themselves. Anne Jason still thought of herself as needing parental care. That care had to come from her mother, Gail, for the mother-daughter relationship was the one unequivocal, no-strings-attached emotional bond Anne had been able to count on. Her short history was one of loss—Anne was well aware of that; nevertheless, she was better able to take emotional risks than her sister. A second stepfather had recently entered her life, and although she was wary, Anne was also hopeful that they might connect in a positive way. She hesitated to trust Howard, but she was willing to admit that she liked him and to hope he liked her.

That took guts, because Anne hadn't had much luck with those elusive creatures known as "fathers." Sometimes she thought she would like to write a book about her life, even though there weren't too many years in it so far.

"What would you write in your story?" I asked.

She paused, her expression serious. "Well, it would seem like a fantasy—no, not a fantasy, they're usually good. It would seem like a nightmare," she corrected herself, straining to attach the right emotional tone to her tale. "It would be a nightmare because no child would want this kind of story in their family. We have gone through so many marriages, and we'll probably go through a lot more in life. My mom is very happy now . . ." She hesitated, considering how to reconcile her mother's current happiness with her own ominous vision of the future. "It's just that we're so full of experience," she added with a meaningful glance.

So full of experience. Her sister Norma was also "full of experience," but of a somewhat different sort. Norma was still grieving over the loss of her father and fighting to recover his love, but Anne had never really known this man whom she referred to only as "my first father." She was just two years old when he and her mother separated, and of course he had almost never visited. On the very rare occasions when he did come to the house or telephone, he spoke briefly with Norma. Not once had he ever directly asked to speak with her. Anne said she "hated" her first father.

The man she missed and still longed for was her "second father," Simon. Anne was still a tiny child when Simon and Gail had married, and her earliest memories were of him and the time they spent together. "I remember my second father because he'd take me down to the lake or on a picnic. I remember him dipping me into the lake. I have lots of memories like that. It seems like just a few years ago that we did all those things, just like last year," she mused.

Anne was six when Gail and Simon separated, and she began to think that a relationship with a "father" was as likely to dissolve as a sand castle on a beach at high tide.

Anne thought her first father was a loser, or worse. She used to think she could ignore him, but in fact he had burrowed through to her heart like a tick carrying poison, and with every move a shiver of pain shot through her. Indeed, she was presently experiencing a flare-up. After many years of living in Texas, Paul was planning to return. Anne didn't know how she would react.

"I just hope he doesn't start coming here, because I don't want to see him," she said defiantly. "But I know I will, eventually, and when I do I think I'll just say, 'Hi, Father, how are you?' And that'll be it. That's what I always do whenever I see him. Then he pushes a five-dollar bill in my hand and the interview is over. Like he tries to give me money, and money is not what I want. It's the love and support a child needs, and if you can't get that from your parents, where do you go?" She sighed audibly. "Oh, I just know I should have my second father here to help me," she added plaintively.

Gail Jason knew her children had experienced serious loss, and she was anxious that they not lose touch with their paternal grandparents as well. She felt it would be tragic for the older couple, were that to happen—her daughters were their only grandchildren—and also that her children needed their love. Although relations with her ex-in-laws were strained, Gail made sure that the girls saw them at least once a week, just as though she and their father were still married.

Anne loved her grandparents profoundly, but something had upset her ever since she was a child. They always insisted on telling her over and over again how wonderful her father was. They showed her pictures of him and commented on how handsome he was and how well he dressed. Whenever an opportunity arose they pulled out a yellowing newspaper clipping of their son and Gail on their wedding day. There were her parents waving at some unseen audience, looking so naïve and young and happy.

Anne thought the picture was ridiculous. The wedding may have been nice, but the marriage sure wasn't, or why would they have divorced and made so much trouble for everyone? Anne wanted to tell her grandparents that she hated their son, and that he wasn't her "father" just because he had once engaged in a sexual act with her mother, and that he had never cared a hoot about her or come to visit her or even asked to speak to her on the telephone. But she couldn't bring herself to hurt them like that. However, she resented being caught in the middle, between her grandparents, who were constantly promoting their son, and her mother who despised him.

For example, certain arguments seemed to be ongoing. Once, years ago, Norma had almost drowned in a swimming pool. Gail claimed credit for having saved her, but so did her first father, Paul. Naturally his parents backed him up, and they always talked about it, years and years after the fact.

It seemed silly to be fighting over this particular detail for all these years, but since the underlying subject of the argument was which parent loved Norma most, the issue was deadly serious. Anne had opted for her mother's explanation. "I don't believe my father," she told me angrily. "I think every word he says is a lie."

Now that his daughters were older, Paul had initiated a campaign to justify himself. When he told Norma he had thought it would be better if he disappeared from his children's lives and allowed their mother to raise them, he was likely speaking the truth. He and Gail had separated years before fathers got custody with any regularity, or even tried for it, and long before joint custody was considered acceptable. And many noncustodial parents do drop out after a divorce.

Dropping out is always to the disadvantage of their children, but in the long run the parent is also the loser, as Paul

Jason was beginning to discover. On one occasion he told Anne he had been "driven out" of the family by Gail's father. But Anne adored her maternal grandfather, and to hear him criticized by this man whom she blamed for so much of the disappointment in her life literally made the hair on the back of her neck stand on end. "How can you criticize him?" she shouted. "Don't you dare say *anything* about my grandfather."

"But you don't understand," replied her father. "You don't know my side."

"I don't care," cried Anne. "I know the *truth.*"

Anne's face was flushed with the memory of this encounter, which had occurred about six months earlier. "He got mad at me and he yelled at me, but I still defended my grandfather," she said. "But I found it so terrible, because I really didn't know who was right and who was wrong, even though I said I did. The only thing that was obvious was that each part of the family defends itself, and I was defending the part of the family I was close to.

"It's so upsetting to be caught in the middle. For instance, my father's parents had a fiftieth anniversary party and I brought back the flowers and put them on the table in the dining room. But my mom said to take them away, because she didn't want a memory of the event. I was shocked, and I said, 'You don't care about them,' and she said that they didn't love her and that she had done so much for them even though she was divorced from their son. That was just like a stab in my heart. It was so painful because I love my grandparents very much and I love my mother very much and I wasn't going to pick sides between them, so I just said, 'Okay, I'll take the flowers up to my room and you won't have to look at them.' "

Something else had happened at that fiftieth anniversary party that had upset Anne and made her angry at her first father. It was a happy occasion. The champagne was flowing and so were the compliments. But when Anne's grandfather stood up to thank his friends and family for their wishes, he read a speech that everybody knew was not his own. Paul had written it. It was about divorce, and it was part of Paul's attempt to rationalize his ten-year absence to his parents and, more specifically, to his children.

Anne didn't really understand the speech too well. It was about people who aren't right for each other and how sometimes they split up and it was full of big words. In the midst of delivering it, Anne's grandfather began to cry.

"It was just killing me," said Anne, tears standing in her eyes. "My father had no right to write grandpa's speech. It was so philosophical, like he had copied it out of a book or something, and I know my grandfather doesn't use words like that. My father was using my grandfather to say his speech. Here was this happy occasion, this fiftieth-anniversary party. I just wanted to punch my father in the nose, because he had no right to do that."

Paul had tried to explain himself to his daughters, but this one wasn't listening. The inner conflict she experienced was threatening to overwhelm her.

As a small child of four, Anne glued herself to Simon, her "second father." Simon was easygoing and caring in the way he related to her, and now that he was gone Anne looked back on those days with more than a little idealization. In her mind he had been the ideal father, the perfect man. Simon did what her first father never did; he cared about her as a person. "He helped me with my problems in school and with my friends and all those things. Even though they were little problems, to a young girl they were big problems," she explained.

So when the hero revealed his clay feet, Anne was stunned. It seemed that Simon's weekend trips away from the family had less to do with business than pleasure, and when his girl friends began telephoning the house, there was no more pretending.

Norma was delighted, naturally. Simon's misdemeanours only confirmed her low opinion of him and precipitated his departure from the house—along with his hated daughter. But Anne was crushed. Her second father was leaving her. Just as Norma believed something was wrong with her because Paul had withdrawn his love, so Anne believed with all her heart that there was something terribly wrong with her. When two fathers leave, the "evidence" begins to build up.

Simon moved away, but he was sensitive to the attachment Anne felt for him and came to visit twice a year. At one point, several years after the divorce, Anne thought that he and her mother might try again, but nothing ever came of it.

Anne looked forward to Simon's visits, but she really didn't know what she ought to think of him. Norma kept saying what a terrible man he was for having deceived Gail and lied to all of them. Anne found it painful to hear her sister criticize Simon, but she could see her point. "I could understand her feelings because he wasn't really her father," she said, nodding sagely.

Anne meant that she and Norma had different fathers. "The first one was to be Norma's father and the second one would be mine because I was young and just starting to grow up when he came to us," she explained. But Norma's accusations confused her. Ought she to continue loving someone who had hurt her mother and abandoned her?

Eight years slid by, but questions about Simon remained. Anne missed him terribly as she grew from childhood into adolescence. She got along with her mother and with Norma, but there was a pervasive sadness about her that others noticed. She did succeed in making friends, though, even though it was embarrassing to explain the marriages and the divorces and especially the name changes. Her name had gone from Jason to Sandringham, which was Simon's name, and back to Jason. But increasingly, Anne was having trouble concentrating on school. Her mind seemed too full of thoughts.

When Howard entered her mother's life, Anne's first thoughts were fearful. Was the merry-go-round of love and disappointment cranking up again? This time, however, she was a teen-ager and a little cynical about her mother's love life. "We've been through a lot of marriages and we're going to go through a lot more," she had said. Howard seemed like a nice enough man, but Anne wasn't going to get too excited.

The really wonderful thing was that Gail was happy again, and the transformation in her mother melted much of Anne's apprehension. "It's taken her so many years to find this happiness, and after all she has done for Norma and me, she de-serves it. Just to see them cooking in the kitchen is so cute," she said, smiling with love.

But as far as her own commitments were concerned, Anne would hold herself aloof. She certainly did not want Howard to think of her as his daughter. "I'm not his daughter and I don't want anyone to pretend I am," she said. But that did not prevent her from hoping she might learn to care about him and be cared about in return. In a low voice she clarified her thoughts. "It would be nice to be close *as if* I were his daughter. I want to be close like a daughter, but not be a daughter."

The fly in the ointment was the whole issue of trust. Anne thought Howard might be a "fake," and she was afraid her mother would be betrayed again. That thought was dis-turbing because she saw that Gail trusted Howard com-pletely. Anne was slightly critical of this. She thought her mother ought to hold back a little, the way she was doing.

Anne also noticed that Howard had taken over certain par-enting decisions, and this made her nervous. "I think Mom's trying to give him some say, which is nice, and I agree with that," she said. "But I don't want her to give him too much." Anne was willing to allow Howard into the family, but she was worried that her mother might abdicate her authority as a parent.

There was another element that was a little harder to talk about. Anne was glad that her mom was happy but, ironi-cally, the happier Gail became, the lonelier Anne felt. Gail had belonged only to her and Norma for so many years, and Anne was dependent on that love. Unlike Norma, she was not emotionally ready to try independence. Anne recognized the problem with considerable maturity and didn't blame Howard, but ever since the couple had become serious about each other, she had been feeling progressively more fearful.

Before Anne could allow herself to become emotionally in-volved with Howard, she desperately needed to talk to her mother about Simon: about why he had left, about whether he loved her, and whether or not he was still her "father." She felt alone. Friends in whom she had confided had disappointed her by gossiping to others, and the guidance counsellor at school was not sympathetic to personal problems. But Gail seemed unapproachable on this subject.

"There are some things I can't discuss with my mother. Maybe when I'm older and I've got more out of life and my Mom sees that I've become more responsible, she'll listen to what I have to say and she'll tell me what is true or false. But right now I feel that every child has to tell someone about their feelings, and parents don't always know this. Maybe I'll be able to talk with Howard some day. I know he wants to be close to us, because Mom said one of the reasons for him wanting to live here was that he felt close to Norma and me. I liked that. I know it's hard for a man to move in with children who have had a close bond with their mother and who have had a lot of rough times with other fathers, but I think we just have to be ourselves and let him be himself and tell him if we're upset with his actions.

"I still need my mother, though. I know I still need her care. And I've never had a real relationship with anyone like I do with my mother. But I know that she needs a relationship, too."

Anne interrupted her narrative to choose a juicy apple from a glass bowl on the coffee table. Her eyes opened wide as she bit through the red skin, and for a moment all her attention was focused on the pleasurable experience. She was still a child, as she said she was. An intelligent and knowing child.

"Howard's presence in the family has confused me a little," she resumed quietly, "but then, I've always been confused. It makes me think about the times I spent with my other fathers and about some of the bad things that have happened." She paused and the room was quiet.

"Sometimes it's a bit scary. I see that there's a lot of trouble in the world and I look ahead and I see that I may have children, and my children will have children. I know history repeats itself, and I think there are births and deaths and marriages and divorces and it's all going to repeat itself in me and my children and my children's children. And they will all have to go through what I've gone through."

She looked away and took another bite out of her apple. I

watched her, so gentle and so unsure. And I hoped that father number three would stay in her life and disprove her sad predictions.

Norma and Anne Jason are sisters and their experience within the family naturally overlapped; but in an important sense their suffering came from different sources. They both had lost "fathers"—but different ones.

Norma had been consumed with rage since the age of eight, and the sources of her anger touched on several problems that are common to divorce and remarriage. She had never overcome the pain of having been abandoned by her father, but more than that, she had been traumatized by the way it had happened. The most important event of her lifetime, the moment she constantly returned to in speech and in memory, was overhearing her mother on the telephone saying she would take the children and leave the marriage.

Norma wasn't alone in remembering this decisive moment in her life. Other children have reported remembering everything about the exact moment when they heard the news, including what they were wearing, what the room looked like, what expressions people wore on their faces, and the exact words they used. The way in which children learn about the breakup of their families can affect them for years to come.

There was, however, another reason why Norma still carried her anger like a sheathed knife ready for use more than half a lifetime after her father had left the family. Her mother remarried just a year after the event. Norma had been unable to mourn her personal loss before she was called upon to cope with another unwanted and threatening event.

The idea that grief may be the first phase of a healing process is relatively new and not particularly easy to accept. We have a long tradition of admiring stiff upper lips that tends to get in the way. Dr. Paul Steinhauer defined mourning as "the gradual taking back of bonds of love and caring that bound the child to someone he or she loved who was once available." What happens in such a case is that gradually the child comes to understand the reality of the loss and, in the case of divorce, to accept the inevitable changes in the relationship with the noncustodial parent.

But a child can't really grieve without help. She needs adults who will allow her to feel sad and angry over an extended period of time, and unfortunately she needs this when the adults in her life are probably least able to cope. In Norma's case, her mother had difficulty accepting her daughter's sadness. In Gail's mind, her ex-husband had no redeeming virtues and was not worth grieving over. Especially, she thought, when he was so callous that he didn't bother visiting his own children.

The Wallerstein and Kelly research (referred to in Chapter Two) consisted of a five-year follow-up study they had conducted with fifty-eight families of divorcing adults and their children in California. They recorded the immediate responses of family members at the time of the breakup and then again at yearly intervals, and they found, not surprisingly, that for children as well as adolescents the separation was the most difficult period of their lives. "The family rupture evoked an acute sense of shock, intense fears and grieving which the children found overwhelming," they wrote. "Over half the group were distraught, with a sense that their lives had been completely disrupted . . ." Wallerstein and Kelly also reported that a child's early reaction to separation is not governed by an understanding of the issues that led up to the divorce, or even by the fact that he or she may have been exposed to physical violence during the marriage. For better or for worse, the family was the centre of the child's world and the only source of protection. The divorce signified a loss of that protection, leaving the child feeling alone and frightened.

Among children Norma's age—those who were six to eight when their parents separated—the most striking response was an overwhelming sadness. More than half the children directly expressed their sorrow to the interviewers the first time they met. They sobbed during the interview or seemed on the brink of tears.

But the children carrying the heaviest load of all were those who had been abandoned by a parent or who had tried continuously to reestablish a relationship and failed. These children "suffered intensely" according to the authors, and most began early to show signs of depression. They became sleepless or had psychosomatic troubles such as headaches or digestive upsets, or they were unable to control their anger, or they began to do poorly at school. The most stressed were those children whose relationship with the lost parent had been warm and loving. "Where the disruption occurred in what had previously been a good [parent]-child relationship, the blow seemed an almost impossible one for the child to absorb," wrote the authors.

All this was true for Norma. She was angry and upset, and there was no possible way she would have allowed a stepfather to enter her life. She already had a father and was fighting to get him back. Her mother's remarriage was nothing less than a betrayal. And, as if to underline the important symbolism the word "father" carried in her mind, she became utterly terrified when her younger sister began to call Simon "Daddy." No pretender to the role would be allowed to usurp the title.

Norma's fear that the remarriage would separate her from her mother was also fairly typical. This anxiety is often hard for parents to understand because they, of course, are absorbed in each other. But the child of a single parent who has grown close to that parent over the years may be struck with terror at the idea of a remarriage. If Mom's or Dad's attention is directed elsewhere, what will they become? What will their place be?

Norma spoke constantly of feeling that she had been "pushed aside." Her father had left her for no reason she could decipher, and now her mother had brought in a strange man to be her companion, sleep in her bed, and be Norma's stepfather. Norma thought she had lost everything.

According to Dr. Steinhauer, a child who has not resolved feelings of loss may be deeply disturbed by the appearance of a stepparent on the scene. "The presence of a stepparent may reactivate and at the same time block the discussion or working through of the feelings of helplessness, abandonment and rage that originated with the original loss," he wrote in a paper entitled "The Child with Four Parents: Some Common Dilemmas Faced by Children Whose Parents Have Remarried." These same unresolved feelings may result in a state of continuing depression, which, in the case of children, often means ongoing behaviour problems.

Had Gail and Simon realized that Norma's hostility came from fear and insecurity, they might have been able to handle it differently. (I say "might," because Norma's unresolved feelings about her dad almost precluded the possibility of success from the start.) Simon, for example, might have encouraged Gail to spend more time alone with Norma; and Norma might consequently have recognized that his presence in the family was not going to deprive her of her mother. Gail and Simon might also have done more with the children as a family. Maybe it's not terrific fun taking twelve-year-olds along for a night out on the town, but doing things together is one way of consolidating a group of people into a unit with a minimum of common experience to build on.

Projecting even further back, Gail might have been more open about dating and about the fact that although she loved her children, she also wanted to include men in her life. Norma had had the impression that she and her sister were "enough" for Gail—Gail had said there was nothing more important in her life—and Norma was truly perplexed and hurt to discover that her mother wanted more. Even as a young woman, she didn't want to understand her mother's needs.

"It is absolutely essential to have an open, honest family relationship where the children can accept that the parent is an adult and that there is a possibility of a remarriage," said Lillian Messinger, one of the foremost researchers in the area of reconstituted families. "Without that preparation, the shock can be quite profound."

Norma's sense that she had to look after her mother instead of being looked after herself was also not unusual. In the Wallerstein-Kelly study, the adults were often in a state of emotional disarray immediately following their separation, and many of them turned to their children for love and support. Quite young children became helpers and companions and even advisors, and traditional boundaries in the parent-child relationship sometimes got lost in the process. This finding was confirmed by John and Emily Visher in their book *Stepfamilies: A Guide to Working with Stepparents and Stepchildren.* One teen-age girl they interviewed was so distressed that she couldn't imagine her mother carrying on without her and her sister. "What are you going to do?" she asked her mother. "We'll soon be grown-up, and then you won't have us to talk to."

Norma had manipulated events constantly throughout her mother's marriage to Simon by making as much trouble as she could. If things got bad enough for everyone, then maybe the marriage would break up, she reasoned, correctly. When Gail and Simon did separate, Norma felt powerful indeed. She had succeeded in ousting Simon from their lives—or so she thought—and she convinced herself that her mother needed her protection, a reversal of the usual parent-child relationship.

But this sense of being in control was one of the reasons Norma eventually needed to leave home. "I feel I have been responsible for the family for so many years," she said. And it was beginning to overwhelm her.

The most confusing element of all was Norma's sense that society provided some tacit support for her rejection of her stepfather. It was the old "kin" controversy once again.

The question, "Who 'belongs' in the family?" remains a psychological stumbling block in remarriage situations. It is also poorly understood in society in general. Norma could say, "Simon and Lilly are not members of our family," because in terms of the old nuclear family they weren't. In those terms, the only "real" family members were Gail, Norma, and Anne.

Our traditional notion of marriage is based on the nuclear model of the family, which means that we owe our loyalty to one household containing our closest human ties—our parents, brothers, and sisters. Other relatives are secondarily attached to the nucleus: two sets of grandparents, uncles, aunts, and cousins.

One of the defining characteristics of the nuclear family is its exclusivity—a few people are "in" and everyone else is "out." Sometimes friends may enter the family through bonds of affection—most of us have had an "Uncle" Joe or an "Aunt" Sophie in our lives—but the "aunt" and the "uncle" are perceived to have quotation marks around them in order to identify their real status. In the same vein, a family may "adopt" friends of their children, but in either case, the distinction amounts to the same thing. The nuclear family is by nature exclusive.

Second marriages challenge these deeply held convictions and leave us questioning what used to be unquestionable. The boundaries of the family, which we have understood to be clearly defined and more or less immutable, are disturbed and reshuffled. New people enter our lives and claim to be family members and we, in turn, are now apparently "related" to their kin.

Kin is the all-important word. What one author has called the "divorce chain" means that a child may find herself with a "family" that would have challenged the wit of the late Groucho Marx. What, for example, is she to make of a family that may now consist of four parents, eight grandparents, and any number of stepbrothers, stepsisters, half brothers, half sisters, step-aunts, half uncles, and second stepcousins twice removed?

Some years ago, I personally received a revealing telephone call. An unfamiliar female voice introduced herself. "Hello," she said. "I'm your ex-husband's wife's ex-husband's wife. I'm calling to tell you that your ex-husband's wife phoned from the Caribbean to say your children will be home on Saturday."

This is the language of our era, I laughed to myself.

The problem is that nobody really knows who is a relative anymore. If we continue to think in traditional terms, most of the newcomers are not relatives, but second marriages have forced professionals as well as ordinary people to reconsider definitions. Sociologists and psychologists are earnestly examining the new relationships, and anthropologists are crowding in to study kinship structures the way they used to rush off to the Samoan Islands.

Norma, then, had "grounds" for rejecting her stepfather. She didn't like him, and in her rejection she insisted he was not a family member. Given the general confusion that still exists on the subject, who was to tell her she was wrong? Her strongest feelings after Simon and his daughter left the household were of relief. "I felt we had our family again," she said. "We didn't need this intruder and his daughter."

At age twenty, her problems seemed to be resolving themselves somewhat, but not just through insight or understanding. Rather, she was growing up and growing away from the family. Her main concerns were now directed elsewhere— towards schooling, towards her peers, towards her future. It was okay for her mother to remarry now, because Norma didn't need her in the same way. Norma could afford to be more generous.

But the one open sore that refused to heal was the abandonment of so long ago. That wound would likely fester until the day Norma allowed herself to mourn the loss of this beloved father and to accept the fact that he never would be the "Daddy" she longed for with such terrible passion.

If Norma was angry, her sister Anne was melancholy. Anne held a deep conviction that personal relationships would go badly for her and for everyone she loved; and she envisioned an endless cycle of betrayal and loss.

Anne was in such conflict that her schoolwork was suffering, but she had no one to talk to. She "hated" her first father, as she called him, so she couldn't talk about him with Norma, who wanted him desperately. Yet, at the time of our conversations she was very anxious about his imminent return to the city.

Norma, in turn, hated Simon, so Anne couldn't talk about him, either. Anne was very confused about Simon. She suspected that no one had told her the entire truth, including her mother, and she wanted to know the whole story. Was the breakup just a case of marital infidelity, or was there more involved? Most important, how did Simon feel about *her*? It seemed strange to be longing for a father who wasn't even her father. When she had tried to discuss her problems with her friends, they only gossiped about her; and when she went to the school counsellor, he made it clear he was overworked and hadn't time for anything other than school problems.

Her grandparents weren't possible confidants, either. She loved them dearly, but they added to her problems by doing public relations for their son. Anne thought it was pathetic the way they brought out that frayed newspaper clipping to show her how handsome he had been the day he married her mother. Anne's grandparents on the other side were equally inaccessible. The whole family had taken sides and evolved immovable "positions." They would have been unable to listen sympathetically without pushing their point of view.

It was particularly sad that Anne was unable to confide in her grandparents, because grandparents can play a pivotal role in helping children through divorce and remarriage. In the best of circumstances, they provide an island of trust and safety by refusing to line up against either parent. In remarriage families involving stepgrandchildren, intelligent grandparents are careful not to discriminate, no matter how strange things may feel at first.

Paul's parents, however, were playing an unwittingly destructive role in Anne's life. They had an axe to grind. Perhaps they thought of themselves as representing their son's interests in his absence. Perhaps they believed they should counteract the negative propaganda Gail unremittingly spread about. Perhaps they were afraid of being overlooked or eventually shut out because their son had so little contact with his children.

Had Gail been more neutral, she might have felt better able to confront her ex-in-laws with their behaviour because it was upsetting Anne. But she couldn't. This was a situation in which outside counselling might have been helpful.

Anne seemed to need help urgently: Her sadness bordered on depression. But there was one promising sign: She seemed genuinely hopeful about a potential relationship with Howard, stepfather number two.

Lionel Duffy

"I didn't like my stepfather. That's the first thing that happens when your mother gets together with a new father. It's just automatic. It's because you're so used to your own father and you think that now he's all alone and maybe your mother is torturing him or something. I got to see my dad, he always came to visit and all that, but I really missed him a lot."

Lionel Duffy was seventeen years old and a high-school dropout. He had answered my ad in the newspaper because he needed someone to talk to, preferably a stranger. His mother had married, divorced, remarried, separated, and now she was living with someone new in another apartment.

Norma and Anne Jason had also lived through their mother's divorces and remarriages, but Gail was always there as a constant in their lives. Lionel, on the other hand, had been cast aside like last season's coat. The stepfamily relationship had been quite happy, but one year ago, in her haste to start life afresh, his mother had asked both him and his stepfather to leave. They did. And since then, everything had seemed so confused. Lionel said his life "fell apart," and he still worried about being struck down by something he referred to vaguely as a "nervous breakdown." At the same time he felt some tentative optimism. He had a new job, in a factory where they made Styrofoam cups and lids, and he thought he would go back to school for night classes. But his self-esteem had been damaged, and his favourite expression throughout our conversation when he referred to other people was, "I don't want to be a burden on their backs."

Lionel lived with his stepfather, Jim, in a row house in a tough working-class suburb of Toronto. He seemed disorganized; in fact, he had forgotten our interview and just happened to be at home when I arrived. He also seemed a little apprehensive, since, as he explained, talking personally to adults was not something he did very often. Adults were a bit like teachers, and teachers were not quite like regular people, he explained.

That confession out of the way, he offered a cup of instant coffee and dug out some cookies; then, having satisfied the social requirements of host, he managed to relax.

The most striking feature about Lionel was his eyes. They were brown and gentle as a doe's and in marked contrast to the rest of him, which was burly and scruffy and generally indistinguishable from the other neighbourhood toughs. He also spoke with sensitivity. Just a year ago things had seemed so fine, he said, but now everything was mixed up. His mom and dad had married very young because his mom was pregnant, but the marriage hadn't worked, and on Lionel's seventh birthday his mom told him they were going to move into her boyfriend's place. "I didn't know what divorce was, so I didn't really care," Lionel told me. "But when I realized Dad was gone I was really surprised and hurt."

At first the new living arrangements seemed like a joke. "I was confused," he recalled. "I'd wake up in the morning and he'd be there and I'd think, 'Who's he?' Then I would sort of think it was fun. Like I didn't really care because I was little and didn't know what was going on. But after the first few days I decided I didn't like my stepfather at all. Like I said, that's just automatic with a new stepfather."

His mother seemed happy with her new man and Lionel came to care for him as well. For one thing, Jim never pushed himself too hard. He allowed Lionel to come to him when he was ready. Lionel knew how much his stepfather had given of himself over the years, and he appreciated what he had learned from him. "Oh, he taught me a lot," he said without hesitation. "He really gave me all my manners. I would have been a total slob today if it wasn't for him." Lionel also remembered that Jim had given him things to take to school for Show and Tell when he was little. He was grateful.

When his mother and Jim decided to marry, Lionel was genuinely happy. At age twelve, on the edge of puberty, he felt as though the wedding ceremony cemented his relationship with Jim and the three of them as a family. In his memory he, too, was "married" on that beautiful day.

"We were married right here in this house," he told me proudly.

"We were married?"

"I mean my parents were married," he said, correcting himself hurriedly.

"Did it feel as though you were getting married, too?" I asked him.

"Oh, yeah. I got to stand right up there with them and everything." He beamed. "I was glad to see them finally married. It's just the way life should be, I guess, when people care about each other."

But, happy as he was, Lionel was always very careful to keep the relationship with Jim straight in his mind, in his stepfather's mind, and in the minds of his friends. He made a point of stressing the *step* in stepfather when he introduced Jim. He respected him, even loved him, but his natural father also occupied a place in his heart. In this relationship as well, Lionel felt lucky. Throughout the period of separation and divorce his father stayed by him. Lionel was conscious of the efforts his father had made under trying emotional circumstances and also that his dad had continued to contribute to his support. That meant a great deal. "He always gave the cheques to me, personally," Lionel said, nodding vigorously. "He wrote them out in front of me and gave them right to me."

His father had also remarried, and he and his new wife had a baby. Lionel adored the child and wanted to be close. So much so that he refused to call him a "half brother." "I prefer the word 'brother,' because I've never had a brother," he explained. Still, he didn't need to be a full-time member of his father's new family, because he felt secure with his mother and Jim. He felt at ease with the idea of having two families: one he lived with and felt closest to, the other he visited.

All things changed when his mother asked him to leave. She was in her thirties, a time when women often make major breaks in their lives. She was feeling restless. And she thought she was still young enough to start again.

She told Lionel that Jim had "wasted" ten years of her life, and Lionel was distraught. "She used to be fat when she was in her teens and her twenties, and suddenly she was dieting and she got really thin," he said disdainfully. "She's in her mid-thirties but she thinks she looks twenty-five. She's on a real ego trip, sort of acting like a swinger. And she didn't care about her family anymore. She wasn't acting like a mother and I didn't think that was fair."

The child's vision of "mother"—always there and, above all else, devoted to her children. Certainly not sexual in any way. But Lionel's mother was feeling her sexuality. She wanted to be rid of the trappings that had tied her to domesticity since she was eighteen years old, and she tried to leave her son just as she had left the men in her life.

When she asked Jim to leave, Lionel felt betrayed. Jim was his father in the emotional sense of the word, the man he identified with, the man who had sent him to school with items for Show and Tell and taught him his "manners." He was fond of his natural father, but Jim was the man who had prepared him for adulthood and for the world outside the family.

The fights began. Lionel's mother was unhappy about having an almost-grown child underfoot. He made her feel guilty when all she wanted, she said, was a tiny taste of independence. Finally she told him to leave. Lionel asked Frank, his best friend across the street, if he could live with him. Frank asked his family and they said it was okay. "Mom," he said, "I've got a place to live and I'm moving out."

"Go," said his mother, and she wrote him a cheque for $120.00 in rent.

Lionel quit school in order to continue paying room and board to his friend's parents.

The disintegration of the remarriage family threw Lionel into a tailspin. He started to drink and smoke dope and to worry about having a "nervous breakdown." When he felt up to it he scurried about frantically looking for affection. His mom had had a falling-out with her own parents six years before and had cut off contact, but now Lionel went to visit his grandparents. That was a strange and unsatisfactory encounter. He hadn't seen them for so long that it was like visiting strangers. He also felt newly anxious about belonging to his father's new family. He asked his father and his wife if he could live with them and was devastated when he felt their hesitation. His stepmother was pregnant again and they had just moved to a new house. Lionel didn't pursue the issue and he knew they were glad he didn't. They had their lives to live and he was practically grown up. "I just didn't want to be a burden on their backs," he said ruefully.

Sometimes he was invited for dinner, and if his stepmother's family was also there, twelve people might be seated at the table. He yearned to be one of them and sometimes he actually thought he was—sort of. But the feeling didn't last. There was something bland and shallow about the way his father and stepmother related to him. He was a visitor. "When I go over there for Sunday dinner, Dad says, 'Hi, how's it going?' Then nothing. Because he doesn't really know what else to say. Then they both say, 'Call us if you have any problems,' but I don't. Because I don't want to be a burden on their backs."

After six months or so, Jim invited Lionel to live with him in the old house, and Lionel gratefully accepted. But it didn't feel the same. "We used to feel like a family when we used to sit down and eat dinner together," he complained. "But now Jim and I come in at different times and make our own dinner and eat at any time, then do what we want. There hardly ever seems a time when we're both here together."

All the same, he was with Jim, and Jim was his only "parent." But, good man that he was, Jim did sometimes feel overwhelmed and resentful at the oddity of his situation and then he lashed out unfairly. Twice he said, "You're not my kid. I'm just supporting you." That really hurt. Once he added, in anger, "Why don't you go to hell." A natural father might say that in a moment of rage. It would hurt, then perhaps be forgotten. But a stepparent treads a finer line, and when Lionel heard those words from Jim he felt as low as he had ever felt in his life. Then it seemed there was no one who truly loved him.

Lionel, however, wanted to believe he was loved, and he was willing to forgive. "I'm sure Jim loves me," he said. "He just doesn't show it. I love him and I respect him, but I'd never tell him that. We just can't talk that way."

One year after his mother's rejection of him, Lionel was

thinking about the future again. With Jim's support, he was planning to return to night school. And he thought he might be able to afford his own apartment. Like Norma Jason, he hoped a separation from the family might resolve the accumulated pain of marriage, divorce, and remarriage; of stepmother and half brother and parents who appeared, then disappeared, shifting like the desert sands.

"I'm sort of glad that almost everyone is happy now the way they are," he said, straining to sound fair. "I don't want to be a burden. I'm growing up and I'm almost out of the house, too, so I'm going to start worrying about myself now. Because I've got a job and I'm holding on to it. When you're a little kid and you go to school, you think, well, when I get out of school it's going to be Easy Street, but it just gets harder and harder. I'm at a point now where I have to clamp down and find out what I'm going to do.

"When I was a little kid I said I'd never smoke or drink or smoke pot, and I do all of that now. And, I don't know, I think I've got bad nerves, too. My dad had two breakdowns when I was little, and that worries me now. When I think back to the times I cried in bed wishing my dad was there, my real dad. I was already about nine or ten then. But I could never tell my dad. It's just that you sort of lose that closeness with your family when you don't live with them for years.

"I'm sure going to be super choosy when I get married, because I don't want my kids to go through their teens like I did. Like, love is going to have to hit me like a rock for the chick I marry."

He banged his hand on the table for emphasis.

"I guess I'm pretty happy now," he volunteered, not very convincingly. But when he added, "I'm just going to watch out for myself now," I believed.

In Lionel's case the graft of the remarriage family took. Like all the children I spoke with who were relatively happy in their stepfamilies, Lionel felt genuinely known and liked by his stepfather. He was not merely tolerated because he was the son of the woman Jim loved. He was cared about for himself.

This is a common enough human emotion, but so difficult to achieve in the stepfamily, where conflicting loyalties to natural children and to parents who live elsewhere often prevent real feeling from taking root.

Lionel felt utterly destroyed when his mother left him, and then he began to experience the feelings of loss and exclusion so many children report. His stepfather, too, had been kicked out, and his real father had made a life for himself where he, Lionel, was not really wanted on a full-time basis. Lionel was a half-grown colt and too old to be petted. At seventeen he was an encumbrance to his father and his young wife.

It was his stepfather, Jim, who took him in again and shored him up emotionally until he was ready to leave of his own accord. In spite of Jim's occasional resentment at being a single parent to his stepson, his willingness to protect Lionel when he was vulnerable was testimony to the dedication Jim brought to the task. It was also testimony to the potential for real caring between stepparent and stepchild, in spite of the difficulties inherent in the very nature of the relationship.

Randy Colberg

When Randy Colberg was just five years old, his parents separated; and then began a long, dark night. "I had a lot of bad dreams for many months," he said very seriously. "It was a period of disruption that affected the rest of my life."

Within a year, Randy's mother had met and married her second husband, a man who had a daughter Randy's age who lived with his former wife and whom he missed deeply. Randy's stepfather could never bring himself to pay attention to Randy. He felt too guilty about having deprived his own child of his presence.

Randy, however, did not remember that his stepfather didn't like him. He remembered, rather, that he didn't care very much about his stepfather—or, it seemed, anyone else in the family. For years and years, nothing that happened in his home seemed to affect him at all. He claimed to be "indifferent" and "independent." The truth of the matter, however, was that, like many children who cannot find enough emotional support in their families, he withdrew and turned to a peer group. "I spent most of my time with a tightly knit group of friends, and they really became my family," he said. Later on, the group (which was made up of "misfits," according to Randy) fastened onto a young adult man they named, not insignificantly, Papa George. Papa George gave them advice and listened to their confidences.

Randy was now twenty-one years old and emerging from his protective shell like a duckling from an egg; and with the same fresh, wide-eyed interest in the world, as though he had never seen it before. "I'm at a time in my life when I'm trying to understand things," he said earnestly. "I'm trying to get in touch with things from my childhood, and I'd really like to be able to talk to the people who've had an effect on me. Especially my real father. It's more his lack of presence that's been an influence than his presence."

For the past year Randy had been living on his own and working part-time in a milk store while he attended school. The physical distance from his family, their approval of what he was doing, plus the financial independence his job provided, all created an atmosphere in which he could, for the first time, ask the perennial adolescent question: Who am I? Until now Randy had been deadened by the rejections in his life, his heart squeezed in a vise.

The first of what he called his "weird" relationships was with his natural father. For a year or two after the separation, his dad would visit on weekends and take Randy and his younger brother, Jimmy, out for the day. They would eat all the junk foods they were never allowed to have at home, and when they slept at their father's apartment he let them watch television "until four o'clock in the morning." At least it seemed that late. The certain part was that this weekend dad didn't really do the things Randy thought a "dad" should do. Randy didn't think he should be eating all that glop, even though he loved it. He also felt uneasy about not having a bedtime. Dad just didn't seem like a "parent."

Randy's dad married a lady called Barbara, but that only lasted a few months. Randy said he was "indifferent." Then he got married again to a woman who didn't like to have Randy and Jimmy around. The couple moved to another city and one summer the children were invited to visit for a two week period. Randy was twelve years old and impressionable. "It was horrible," he recalled. "They were fighting each other and yelling at us. Their marriage was just falling apart. They were really both too busy to bother much with us, so most of the time we just wandered around and watched TV."

Randy wasn't exactly "indifferent" to that episode, but it did push him further into withdrawal. For several years he did not see his father at all. The father divorced again. He was unemployed and looking for work.

When Randy was nineteen his father wrote him a letter. "I'm going to be in town next week," the letter said. "Let's have a drink together." A drink? Randy was thrilled. A real man-to-man evening with his father—and over a drink!

They met and Randy noticed that his dad was shorter than he remembered. He also had a beard. That night Randy's father told Randy some of the things that had gone wrong in his last marriage, but he still didn't talk about Randy or what had happened in his marriage with Randy's mother. Still, it was a momentous occasion. "I thought, 'Wow, a real father-to-son chat after all these years.' " Then his dad disappeared again. "Once in a while he telephones, but that's about it," said Randy flatly. "But I would like to see him," he added, becoming agitated. "I'm trying to understand things."

The rejection in the stepfamily came early. His stepfather, it turned out, was able to relate closely to Jimmy, Randy's little brother. The age difference between Jimmy and his daughter at home apparently eased the guilt that prevented him from "fathering" Randy. So Randy withdrew further. He put it this way: "I always felt a certain distance between myself and the family—so if I had to leave for some reason it wouldn't bother me too much. I just didn't feel a part of things, not when I was there and not when I wasn't there. I'd stick to my room most of the time and just come out for meals. It's not that I felt uncomfortable. I just didn't feel emotionally involved."

Around his tenth or eleventh year, Randy began to feel

closer to his mother. She had always been there, a buffer between her husband and her son, who was being ignored. There was nothing she could do to change the emotional climate, she told him many years later, except to nag and complain. But deep inside, during those years he hid in his room, Randy knew that his mother was available. Fortunately for him, he was able to use her love to break out of the darkness.

During the process of asking himself who he is and what kind of person has emerged from the years of closed "indifference," Randy has decided, rather amazingly, that he actually had a happy childhood. He said this to his mother recently and she replied, "You had *what*?" But Randy now believes that the web he spun around himself buffered him from the pain. He adopted a persona and inside the mask he was free to be himself. "I knew that my stepfather and everyone else thought I was weird and a misfit, and that made me aware that really I could do almost anything," he explained. "If you were weird, people expected you to *act* weird. That gave me a lot of freedom. Now what I'm really trying to understand is how I could go through all the commotion in my life and have emerged quite normal."

Back to the duckling analogy: Randy was also seeing the members of his family with new eyes. People who had occupied roles were now beginning to assume full human dimensions. His father. His stepfather.

"What I'm really trying to do is to see the real people behind the titles," he noted. "Like mother, father, stepfather, grandmother. Maybe one day I'll make a real effort to know my stepfather. I might like to because obviously my mom loved him and still loves him, so he must be an okay guy. He's been around for fifteen years and I guess he has had some influence on my life. Maybe I'll find out what it was."

Randy was trying with an intensity typical of late adolescence and early adulthood to put the pieces of his past together. It was certainly the healthiest task he could have set himself and a challenge he would have to meet before he could proceed. He had had very little help in coping with the real trauma he had experienced before he was six years old—

the departure of his father followed by the arrival of a remote stepfather. But Randy was a fine example of the basic resilience that can often carry children through the most trying of childhoods and see them emerge with, as the studies indicate, positive characteristics similar to children from nuclear families. Norma, Anne, Lionel, and Randy were all struggling to overcome the disruption they had experienced and get themselves back on a normal developmental track. They had all felt rejection and tried to cope in individual ways. What they had in common was courage.

SUGGESTIONS

1. Children, like adults, must have time to mourn their losses, and in a supportive atmosphere. Gail's total rejection of her ex-husband, Paul, made Norma's and Anne's adjustment much, much harder.

2. Noncustodial parents have a real role to play in their children's lives and must insist on that right. Lionel, for example, profitted from his father's continued involvement. Norma and Anne suffered from their biological father's lack of involvement.

3. When a parent seems to be truly indifferent, children need help in accepting the fact that this is not a reflection on their personal worth.

4. Disruptive behaviour in children is often a sign of depression, not "badness."

5. Openness is important. Anne desperately needed to talk to her mother about Simon but was unable to.

6. Grandparents can play an important, supportive role in helping children adjust to the momentous changes in their lives, but they must refrain from any "parent-bashing" if they are to be effective and not merely an added disruption.

7. Norma's and Anne's positive response to Howard demonstrated the success of the "friend" rather than "instant parent" approach to a stepchild, especially in the beginning.

8. Mid-adolescents like Lionel are at risk because they are often thought to be too old to need protection. Lionel certainly did, but he was rejected by his mother and thought of as past

needing care by his father and stepmother. Fortunately his stepfather demonstrated loyalty.

9. The remote stepparent can compound a child's sense of rejection and be as problematic as his or her overbearing counterpart. People who feel guilty about attending to stepchildren because they are no longer parenting their own children on a full-time basis need counselling to help them overcome the psychological hurdle. This should be part of the open discussion and planning that precedes a remarriage.

CHAPTER FOUR

There's Light at the End of the Tunnel

HOW ONE FAMILY BEGAN TO RECTIFY
ITS MISTAKES

An outsider peering through the keyhole at the McIntyre-Logan family during the first two and a half years of their life together would probably have recoiled in horror. The two units, consisting of a parent and two daughters each, argued constantly. Once, someone's finger was broken during a squabble. Even their family pets hated each other. But in recent times their fortunes had taken a turn for the better. They were beginning to get along—the two individual families were beginning to unify.

Stella McIntyre and Syd Logan were both working-class people. By virtue of joining their respective incomes they had managed to buy a substantial house in a middle-income section of Toronto, and it was this move, above all else, that had bound them to each other during the rough years. Together they could offer a better neighbourhood to their children and more amenities. Apart, as single parents, they would have struggled merely to keep their heads above water.

Here is the story of their misconceptions, their early mistakes, and the steps they took to introduce a different reality into their lives.

Stella McIntyre

After eight years of marriage to an alcoholic husband who beat her up and didn't bother coming to the hospital when her babies were born, Stella McIntyre had thoroughly enjoyed being single again. She was raising two daughters, working hard, and attending night school in the evenings; but then she had always worked hard, ever since she left school at the age of fifteen and cajoled the owner of the local greasy-spoon restaurant into giving her a job as a waitress. During her seven years as a single parent she had occasionally felt lonely—she especially missed having a regular sex life—but God knows, she was busy enough. She even found time to help initiate a singles club in the community where she lived. For a while she dated a man who had four children whom he missed terribly because they lived with his former wife. He wanted to marry Stella, but every time he saw his children he would come over to her apartment and cry. He would get so upset he couldn't even talk about it, and it would take him a week to get over each visit. Stella felt sorry for him, but she just couldn't take it. "I wanted someone to cheer *me* up," she said.

One day she went to a fortune-teller who said she would meet a really nice guy who was a Virgo and had kids of his own. Of course he would be tall and dark and handsome. That went without saying. So when Stella just happened to get introduced the very next day to a tall, dark man who had two children, she was more than a little intrigued. His name was Syd Logan, and when she told him about the fortune-teller he laughed out loud. Even if nothing at all developed between them, it was an amusing way to start.

Syd's wife had skipped out on him and he was having trouble with his thirteen-year-old daughter. She was avoiding school and staying out half the night, and Syd wanted Stella to tell him what to do. Stella thought, "Oh, God, here we go again; what do I need *this* for?" But he seemed like such a nice person, and there *was* the prophecy to consider. . . .

They saw each other for about a year—enough time, they thought, to allow their four daughters to adjust. At first the kids seemed to like the idea of a blended family. One of Stella's daughters actually said she had always wanted an older sister. The idea of moving in together appeared to make practical sense as well, since alone, neither Stella nor Syd could afford to buy a house. Stella was still doing waitressing and Syd worked shifts in a factory. Together they would be a lot better off, they reasoned. So they scraped together the down payment for a substantial three-bedroom house in a middle-class district of town, informed their respective daughters that changes were about to take place, and took the plunge.

Like so many prospective stepparents, Stella was as innocent as a newborn. "I thought that because we cared about each other, things would be great." She sighed. "There would be a new mother, a new father, and the kids would adjust. Ha! Kids don't necessarily adjust at all. After we moved in together things got worse than we had imagined, and for a long time we didn't know what hit us or what to do."

Stella's and Syd's naïveté matched that of thousands of people entering second marriages. Carla Renzetti thought her remarriage was a second chance at the golden ring. This time she believed she had met and married the *real* Prince Charming (not a pretender to the throne like her first husband) and that fairy-tale happiness was a realizable goal. Stella McIntyre, on the other hand, pinpointed her own false expectations when she said there would be a new "mother" and a new "father" in the family, and therefore the kids would adapt. But one of the many realities of remarriage is that mothers and fathers are not replaceable in their children's lives. Stepparents must aspire to something else.

Stella was about forty, a large, strong-limbed woman with a determined look in her brown eyes that suggested she wasn't fazed by most events. This had been different. Uniting their families had evoked such strong hostility in both sets of children that she and Syd felt quite overwhelmed.

After three years of communal life, every spare penny was still going into the mortgage, the existence of which accounted, more than anything else, for the fact that they were still together. It was hardly a sentimental bond, but because they could not afford to separate, Stella and Syd were forced to look around for ways of making their family life more tolerable. They sought out counselling, it helped, and now there were several signs that they had, indeed, weathered the worst of it. The past six months had been decidedly more peaceful, and, although Stella wasn't prepared to say anything definite about the future (she was superstitious, she said), the quality of their life had definitely improved.

The front hall of the house was full of teen-agers' paraphernalia. Stylish winter boots were lined up along the wall and four pairs of white figure skates hung on hooks. Matching scarf-and-hat sets lay in disarray over an entrance table, burying schoolbooks and stray sheets of looseleaf paper. Stella introduced the girls, who hung around, peering through the living room door at intervals so they could hear what was being said. Stella didn't seem to mind. She charged ahead in full-throated voice.

"I liked being single," she said loudly, "and if it hadn't been for the kids I would have stayed single. But I started to think I wasn't giving them a proper life. I thought they didn't really have a father and they needed one. I used to call their father on occasions, like birthdays, and ask him to get in touch with them. He liked the older one, but he ignored the younger one, and it made me so sad and so tired. I just thought they deserved to have a mother and a father in the house."

This, of course, was one of the very worst reasons for moving in together. Stella thought she ould replace the children's father simply by bringing another man into the house—and that by the same token she could also become mother to Syd's daughters. But the children themselves quickly put her straight. Their first reaction was to lash out in rage, and for three years their anger did not subside. "We put the girls in two bedrooms, two sisters in each, but they just screamed at each other and carried on all the time. The sisters also began to fight between themselves, although mine had never done that. I guess they were really upset. Syd's kids would tell him that my girls were stealing their money or their nail polish or something like that, and my kids would come to me and do the same. Or my kids would ask why Syd's girls were allowed to take food into their rooms while they weren't. They complained that Syd was always criticizing them and never disciplining his own daughters.

"It was a mess, and the worst of it was that they almost succeeded in doing what they were trying to do, which was to split us up. Syd's kids were very open about it. His oldest daughter sneered at me one day and said, 'My dad will never marry you. He loves *me*.' How do you like that!" Stella's eyes widened at the very memory of the girl's audacity.

This was the nub of it. Stella wanted Syd more for what he symbolized than for what he was. He symbolized the role of "father," and Stella had decided that her girls needed one of those. But she, personally, would have preferred to remain single! The marriage was to be a convenience undertaken for the sake of other people. Syd, as will become apparent, had his own priorities, which had as little to do with Stella as an individual as her priorities had to do with him.

The children were quick to pick out their respective parent's lack of commitment, and they ran away with that knowledge like dogs with a juicy bone. After all, they reasoned, if the relationship between the adults was so tenuous, they might be pushed into a breakup, and then, of course, there was a *chance* that the old life-style would resume. Syd's daughter could present herself as the real love in her father's life because she knew she was speaking the truth. Syd and Stella didn't love each other and everyone knew it.

If they had seen that their parents were truly united, the children might still have been destructive and manipulative, but with far less success. As things stood, Syd began to blame Stella for her children's behaviour, and she him for his. Syd was particularly resentful because his former wife had handled all the discipline and he saw that as a woman's job. Like Anthony Renzetti, he expected his children to obey Stella simply because she was the "mother" of the household.

"Have you seen your kids' bedroom lately?" he challenged her one evening.

"What about *your* kids' room?" Stella countered.

"It's up to you," he replied angrily. "You're looking after this house."

"Now, *that* conversation was the beginning of some understanding around here," recalled Stella, "because I just said, 'Hey, we're both working full-time and I'm trying to go to night school as well, and this family is not just my responsibility.' I just couldn't do it. Four kids and a big house and a full-time job and school besides? It was a joke. I said, 'If you want to hire a cleaning lady, that's fine. I'll pay half.' His kids had the same attitude. Their mother had been a housewife and she did everything for them. She shopped and cooked and sewed on all the buttons and did the laundry. So they thought I was supposed to do all those things because I was the adult woman in the house."

That confrontation led to the first real communication they had shared. The attitudes Syd and his daughters had brought into the household regarding women and mothers and their role in the family weren't working in this new situation. For the first time Syd and Stella faced each other as people and not as puppets playing a part in each other's fantasy of the family.

"We made *them* responsible for the house." Stella laughed. "We drew up a schedule. My two did the cooking one week and his two did it the next week. They also divided the laundry until they complained about having to do our clothes. We agreed and now we do our own laundry and each set of girls does her own. They also keep their own rooms neat."

This was the beginning of family cooperation, because the children saw, for the first time, that their parent and their stepparent were a unit—a unit *in charge*. Eight months of chaos had passed before these most minute beginnings emerged.

Stella felt encouraged. They had been successful in setting up the most elementary conditions for living together, the actual functioning of the household. It wasn't much, but it was something. Still, there were so many other problems that she awoke each morning filled with apprehension.

Stella's daughters had lived alone with their mother for seven years (which in itself can cause difficulties in a remarriage situation), but Syd's daughters had only recently suffered a severe emotional trauma. Their mother had walked out on them to live with a neighbour with whom she had been having a supposedly secret affair. But her elder daughter knew and had suffered in silence. This girl was badly troubled. She began to stay out all night with a series of boyfriends and occasionally to bring them home. Syd was concerned, but he simply didn't know what to do, which was one of the reasons he was attracted to a strong, competent woman like Stella. His younger daughter had responded to the shock quite differently. She withdrew, and for months she barely spoke a word. Three years later, she still had difficulty articulating her thoughts.

Perhaps out of fear that Stella would refuse to live with him, Syd neglected to mention that his older daughter, Terry, had had an abortion when she was thirteen, or that the problems he had had with both girls were ongoing beyond the first months. "I can't even tell you how upset I was when I saw what was going on here," said Stella, her face reddened. "I went in blind. Syd had implied that things had improved. But I needed to know what was expected so I could handle it! Terry would skip school and I'd get called at work because Syd was on shift and they couldn't reach him. But what could I do? I didn't know where she was. She wouldn't listen to me anyway, and her father refused to do anything. Then she would bring her boyfriend home and he'd stay overnight. I said to Syd, 'I don't need this; there are three other young girls in this house,' and he said, 'What am I supposed to do?' He felt helpless. It was too much for him. He never spoke much anyway, and he just couldn't think of what to do. Finally she let me take her to a birth-control clinic and she stopped sleeping with her boyfriend in our house, but there was really nothing I could do about her behaviour. She'd been sleeping around since she was thirteen. But I didn't want the rest of them getting into that too early. With four teen-age girls all upset about what was happening in their lives, I can assure you that sex and running around was a terrible problem for us."

This was another basic problem that might have been

avoided. Stella came into the marriage prepared to be a "mother." Syd expected her to be a mother, the school expected her to be a mother, even *she* expected herself to be a mother. After all, she had already put in years on the job with her own kids, she reasoned, so it shouldn't be too hard to take on a couple more at the same time. But her husband did not tell her what every "mother" knows—the past history of her child. Stella's role was impossible from the start. She didn't have the information she needed, and, secondly, the object of all this intended mothering refused her attentions. Mothering Terry was a joke, an empty shell, a word, a meaningless job description. But Syd had married her for precisely that reason, because he himself did not feel up to doing it alone.

It was a no-win situation and, once again, spotlighted the false expectations that had carried them into this relationship.

The mortgage continued to hold them together. And their own sex life. Whatever problems they had during the day did not seem to affect their willingness to lose themselves in each other at night, and after an abusive marriage followed by seven years of single parenthood, Stella was reluctant to give up this small corner of happiness. It was a trade-off. But how much could she tolerate before nothing at all could compensate for their daily family life?

Eighteen months after they took up residence together, Stella thought she had reached rock bottom. Two things happened. The first one took place one evening after a particularly tense day. Syd's younger daughter was swearing at her and calling her names, and Syd was tacitly approving by saying nothing. Stella thought she didn't deserve the abuse. She felt light-headed, then suddenly the taut wire that held her rage in check snapped in two. "I hit her," she told me angrily. "It was on the stairs. She punched me back and I fell and broke my finger. Does this sound like a soap opera? It felt like one, but there was no commercial break. I just felt helpless.

"After that I didn't want to come home at night. You could feel the tension in here as soon as you walked in the door. It was as though a bomb was going to drop on you. Like, what are the little monsters going to do tonight?"

Around the same time, another situation made the split between the families so clear that it was impossible to avoid the implications. Syd's younger daughter graduated from elementary school. She invited her father, her real mother, and her sister, but not Stella and her daughters. Furthermore, the date of the event was to be kept secret. Syd was in on it, and when Stella asked him about the graduation, he pretended not to know. The hurt, she said, was indescribable.

But the graduation episode revealed more clearly than anything else just how divided they were and how successful the children had been in manipulating their parents into antagonistic postures. It wasn't a hard job. Both Stella and Syd felt guilty about having changed their children's lives, even though they thought they were doing the best thing for them. And their relationship was fragile to begin with.

The "family" was ready to break up.

"I told Syd, 'This is it,' " recalled Stella. " 'Either I pack my bags and leave or you and your kids come into counselling with us.' He thought about it, then he looked at me real strange—I'll never forget it, then he said, 'We'll try the counselling.' "

The girls had to be pushed and coaxed, but they went along. At first there was a lot of "crying and hair-pulling and carrying on," as Stella put it. Even the counsellor felt at a loss. "I've never handled a situation like this," she told them, "so I'll treat you as an ordinary family with problems." She was sensitive and patient, and eventually the complaints and the stored-up hurts and the accumulated anger were spoken aloud. Stella and Syd learned, for example, that all the children thought the whole affair had happened much too quickly and that they hadn't been given enough time to get used to the idea of living together. Syd's children thought Stella was horning in on their mother's rightful territory, even though their real mother appeared not to have the slightest interest in them.

It is safe to say that none of these crucial feelings would have been expressed within the family without outside help, and at the end of their sessions, which lasted about eight months, they all felt considerably better about each other. At the counsellor's suggestion, they instituted Sunday bull sessions where the week's grievances could be aired. They eyed each other warily and began to learn to get along.

"I guess Syd and I finally decided that we'd stand together," Stella said. "It had got to the point where he'd be with his kids and I'd be with mine and the two groups were at war with each other. So we decided it had to be the two of us against all of them. I know it sounds funny talking about kids that way, but that's the way it was. We had to tighten our relationship. We had to sit down and talk more about things and about how we felt and try to get the kids to talk, too. Syd and I also decided we would go out alone every Saturday night so we could talk privately and not have four kids sitting there with their ears flapping in the breeze. I mean, we had no privacy at all."

Therapy helped them correct the area that was at the root of their troubles: the very lack of commitment to their own relationship that had opened the door to being manipulated by unhappy children. And when they began to support each other, the whole spectrum of relationships within the family improved.

Therapy also helped them understand that their problems were not necessarily specific to them, but common to all remarriages, and had to be seen as such. It allowed them to understand that much of their mutual unhappiness came from sources outside themselves, from the ghosts they had refused to acknowledge and incorporate into their lives. The leading ghost in the family was Syd's former wife. Her relationship to her ex-husband and her daughters had not been resolved, and her "presence" was preventing Stella from taking root in the family.

Therapy helped Syd's girls articulate their fears: Stella is trying to take our mother's place, they were able to say, but even if mother left us and even if she does not love us, she is still our mother. We have not forgotten her nor have we finished mourning her absence.

Remarriages may be filled with just such shadowy webs of unspoken fear and longing. A skilled, neutral counsellor can help to unravel the threads.

A calm had descended on the McIntyre-Logan family, and a peace flag waved, but a residue of bitterness and exhaustion remained all the same. "I have to tell you something," Stella said, lowering her voice for the first time and glancing suspiciously toward the living-room door. "If I had known then what I know now, I'm not sure I would have done any of this. At least I would have learned a hell of a lot more before I got involved with someone else's kids."

Syd Logan

Syd was so remote and so shy he was almost inarticulate. He seemed unaccustomed to verbalizing his thoughts, but what he did say, eventually, was that he had actively sought out a woman to fill the role his wife had vacated. After she left, he had serious difficulties. When he worked the night shift in the factory, his daughter Terry, who was thirteen, slipped out of the apartment, leaving eleven-year-old Jennifer alone. Jennifer would telephone her dad at work, making him frantic with worry, but he wasn't in a position to leave his job. When he was at home, Jennifer clung to him, never letting him out of her sight. In desperation Syd took both his daughters to the Children's Aid Society. A counsellor talked to him, and that helped a little—but only temporarily.

Syd doubted that he could cope as a single parent. He didn't want a "wife" in general, and he hadn't really wanted Stella in particular. He specifically wanted a woman to look after his emotionally traumatized daughters. "I felt my girls needed a mother, and I was surprised by the amount of resentment they felt towards Stella," he told me. "I felt protective of them, and when they would say they hated her for this or for that, I guess I would take their side. I would tell Stella she wasn't trying hard enough. It was a kind of 'his and hers' situation and it was awful. Now I think it's a little better."

"What kept you here?" I asked.

"The mortgage," he replied. "And the area. It's good for the kids. There's a good school, and I thought it would upset them more if they had to move again."

Never once did Syd refer directly to his relationship with Stella. He described their decisions and their actions uniquely in terms of the children. From his point of view, this had been strictly a marriage of convenience, and this attitude had, of course, contributed to the split between the families.

Our meeting was apparently a strain, and he twisted and turned and fell silent for many minutes at a time. "What would you advise people who want to combine their families the way you and Stella did?" I asked, casting about for a general question to set him at ease.

"Don't get a house," he replied after a silence. "When you've put all your hard-earned money into something, you don't like to see it go down the drain. But then"—and he hesitated again—"being tied together like that probably helped us stay together through the worst of it."

He turned toward me for the first time and smiled faintly.

"Would you do it again?" I ventured, wondering whether the insights he had subsequently acquired had given him a different perspective.

The smile slid off his face. "Definitely not," he muttered, looking morosely down at his shoes. "Well, at least I'd spend a lot more time thinking about it."

We shook hands. Then he fairly ran through the living-room door.

Terry Logan

Terry was eighteen years old and strikingly beautiful, with a full, ripe figure and long blond hair that fell halfway down her back. She seemed eager to talk about herself, and as she spoke she tossed her head in the habitual gesture of a girl accustomed to attracting attention to her beauty.

Terry was shocked and confused when she discovered that her mother, whom she adored, was having an affair with a neighbour in the apartment building where they lived. "I thought my mom and dad were really in love with each other," she exclaimed in a voice still filled with surprise after five years. "They never said they weren't getting along."

Terry carried her secret knowledge for a full year. Every Monday and Friday her mother told Syd that she was going to play bingo, but Terry knew she was lying. She had seen her mom and the man together. That year Terry lost eight pounds, failed at school, and could not sleep at night. But her parents did not notice her distress. They were preoccupied with the disintegration of their marriage.

The night she left the family, Terry's mother had an argument with her husband. Terry overheard and walked in on them, in the bedroom.

"Your father hit me!" her mother cried, lying, justifying what she was about to do.

Terry trembled as she listened to her parents hurl accusations at each other; then she blurted out the secret. She cried and cried, mostly with relief. Then she led her father to the apartment where her mother's lover lived. An ugly scene took place between the two men. Then Terry's mother packed her bags and left.

Terry was too upset and embarrassed to tell anyone. When people phoned asking for her mother, she said she was busy or out. And when her friends did learn the truth, Terry thought they were not sympathetic. She fantasized that they came from closely knit families and that they looked down on her for her misfortune. At home, life became chaotic. "I didn't want to show Dad that I was upset, and I was trying to keep Jennifer happy too," she told me. "Dad and Jennifer were always crying, but I would only cry when I was alone."

Terry was unable to deal with her mother's affair and then her leaving the family. "Mother" is a linchpin of the family, and the family is a child's source of stability. Terry was so overwhelmed by the threat to her personal security that she suppressed what had happened and refused to think about it. She was trapped whichever way she turned: To acknowledge what had happened felt like death itself, since her entire identity was wrapped up in the family. To deny it, as she did, brought other problems.

Had she been able to share her secret, or even let on to her mother that she knew, Terry might have been less traumatized by her mother's eventual leaving; but she hid everything and suffered for it. She denied her mother was gone, pretending to callers that she was out. She felt she had lost her status in the world and that her friends looked down on her. Because she was still an extension of her family, she felt that her very life was being threatened.

Terry began to skip school and tried, unsuccessfully, to find a job. In the evenings she escaped from the tense, unhappy atmosphere of home. Like many troubled adolescents, her way of handling the earthquake at the centre of her life was to seek affection outside the family. She made friends with a group of older boys and slept with them in turn. "I just liked meeting boyfriends," she said, staring defiantly and tossing her mane of hair. But what she really needed was an affirmation that she was deserving of affection, that even though her mother had left her she was both lovable and capable of survival on her own. Unfortunately, she wasn't; and the frantic sexual activity was the evidence. So was the pregnancy, followed by an abortion.

In her interesting book on women and depression, *Unfinished Business: Pressure Points in the Lives of Women*, Maggie Scarf points out that sex and pregnancy are a common expression of deep depression among female adolescents. "Sex and pregnancy represent despairing efforts to fill up an inner emptiness and loneliness. . . . 'Mistakes' are in some strange way a means of counteracting the awful isolation that exists within—of getting company inside one's skin," she wrote. Like Cathy Renzetti, Terry was trading off sexual intercourse for the pleasure of being held and stroked and comforted in her distress. The centre of her world had washed away and swept out all her familiar supports in its wake.

After several months of silence, Terry's mother resumed contact with her daughter, and Terry visited her on the other side of town where she lived with her new husband. But Terry never felt comfortable. She resented the fact that she and her mother were never alone together. The man's son always seemed to be "hanging around like a spy," or so it seemed. She blamed the man for her loss and her pain. It was so much easier to attack him than her mother, about whom she had so many different, conflicting feelings.

"He tried to be friendly with me, and he still does, but I don't like him," she announced categorically. "But he's old and he'll probably die soon." Her stepfather was fifty-nine.

Terry was angry. Sometimes, she said, her rage would rise in her throat and stop her breath. She felt betrayed and disbelieving. She felt abandoned by the person who had meant most to her. But still she yearned. When they were together she would feel the old urge propelling her into her mother's arms. She remembered the fragrance of her mother's skin and how soft her lap was when she curled up close. But the hard edges of anger set them apart. Yes, it was easier to blame the man.

Sometimes Terry's mother actually said she thought she had made a mistake and that she still loved Terry's dad. "Dad says that, too," Terry cried. "So why did they get a divorce? I think they would like to get married to each other again, and I think my sister wishes that would happen, too. But it's really just a wish, and I don't think it will really happen, because she went and married that new man and Dad lives with Stella."

Her mother's remarriage loomed in her mind as an unforgivable and weighty act of betrayal. "As soon as she got the divorce she got married, like the very next day," she sputtered angrily. "I hated her for that. I was invited to the wedding, but I didn't want to go. I felt she should have stayed living with him and not married him right away. It didn't seem right. Dad didn't get married to Stella! That way, if he doesn't like things he can always move out; but if my mom doesn't like things she can't move out, because she's married. I mean, she can move out, of course, but it won't be as easy."

When Syd and Stella moved in together, about fifteen months after Syd's wife left, Terry was thrashing about in a full-blown emotional crisis. She had not begun to resolve her conflict with her own mother. She vacillated between love and hatred and the fantasy wish, dear to the heart of every child of divorce, that her natural parents would drop their new relationships and love each other again. She was in full flight from the horror of her life—her sister was practically mute and her father seemed unable to cope—and she was trading sex for whatever comfort she could find. She had recently had an abortion. School was a huge problem. In short, all the underpinnings seemed to have been pulled out from under her, and she floundered.

Against this background, Syd announced that they were moving to a new house and that Stella and her two daughters would be living with them. It was, to say the least, not a likely scenario for the happy blending of two families.

One of the saddest things about divorce is that parents are often unable to help their children cope with the crisis. Terry had to help her *father* get through the day—and she was by no means unique. In their follow-up study of divorced families, Wallerstein and Kelly found this often to be the case. Parent-child roles get reversed. So Syd sailed into a remarriage with Stella while his daughter reeled with shock. Neither Terry nor her sister had been able to accommodate themselves to the reality of a single-parent family, let alone contemplate a reconstituted union with another group of people.

But Syd and Stella were oblivious of these problems—Syd because he was trying, rather unsuccessfully, to deal with the shock of having been deserted; Stella because she was preoccupied with her relationship with Syd and the response of her own two children to him.

There were early, ominous signs that the transition was going to be difficult. "I can remember Stella coming to our place on weekends with her two kids and everybody fighting," recalled Terry. "Jennifer and I would say, 'You're not coming to our house. No way.' One night I went out with my friends and when I came home her brats were both sleeping in my bed. I got *sooooo* mad. . . ." Terry's voice trailed off in breathlessness. "Jennifer and I didn't want nobody. We were still wishing our mother would come back, and it felt as though Stella was trying to be our mother. We really didn't know her, but she was telling us what to do and all that. It was like she was trying to take our mother's place, but even if I wasn't seeing my mother then, she was still my mother. And she still is."

In Terry's thirteen-year-old mind, Stella's presence threatened the last vestige of her relationship with her mother. If the empty space her mother had left was filled by a pretender to the position, what chance was there that she might come back again? Not surprisingly, the threat increased once the two families moved into the same house. Their fights intensified: Jennifer fought with Stella; Stella's daughter, Debra, joined in and defended her mother; Jennifer fought with Debra; and Terry fought with Stella. Anything at all could provoke a major confrontation. "You'd say the wrong thing and you'd get punched," Terry sniffed. "Dad tried to keep everyone from fighting, but my feeling was I had to protect him and Jennifer from Stella and her kids. Whenever there was something bad going on, which was all the time, Dad and Stella would start to talk about it and then *they* would start to fight. It was no good. Our bedroom was really close to Dad's and Stella's, and we could hear everything. We could hear what Stella was saying about us, and it felt as though my dad wasn't sticking up for us. I felt as though everyone had left me. First my mom and then my dad."

One miserable month dragged into another, and the shared mortgage, on which their mutual security seemed to depend, held them captive in the house—until the downward spiral ground to a halt in a therapy group. "I didn't want the counselling at first because I didn't think we needed it," Terry said, "but I have to admit it helped. At home we couldn't say we didn't like certain people or what they did without getting punched in the face, but there we could say it. Then every Sunday we had to sit down and say how we felt about each other. It helped. It felt as though a tight fist inside my stomach started to get loose, and now, touch wood, everyone gets along. I'd say it's been several months since we had a real fight here. We still have little arguments, but that's different."

As a result of the therapy, there were real changes in the way Terry related to her stepmother. "I used to hate Stella, but now, it's sort of funny, I almost don't think I could leave her," Terry said, looking slightly puzzled by her own shift in attitude. "She has definitely helped us a lot. She's not a mother, but she does give advice like a mother would. I ask her about school and other things. Like, just a little while ago I had something wrong and I asked her if I should see a doctor. Once I talked to her about my boyfriends and all that, and she told me that she went through what I'm going through when she was my age. I really think she's starting to understand me."

Terry, who had been so deeply hurt and troubled, seemed to be improving as a result of being helped to understand that Stella was not trying to undermine her real mother or threaten her relationship with her father. Part of the change was also the natural process of growing up. At eighteen she simply had more understanding, and more real independence from the family as well. But she and Stella seemed to have turned an important corner in their relationship. Terry had begun to trust; and that trust might prove to be the foundation of an abiding and caring friendship.

"Every way we tried to get rid of her, she just wouldn't leave," was Terry's way of saying she had begun to accept her stepmother.

From unlikely beginnings, these were indeed bright glimmerings of success.

Jennifer Logan

Like her father, Jennifer had never been talkative. As a young child she clung to both her parents, and after her mother left, when she was eleven, she cried with fear when her father went to work. That was when she turned mute for several months. Just closed up like a clam.

Now she was sixteen and more or less recovered from the trauma of having lost her mother, but she still found it hard to express her thoughts. Her memories of childhood all seemed to involve fear. "I felt really scared when my mother said she was going to leave," she recalled. "I didn't really understand what was happening at all. My sister and I went with her to this man's house and she stayed there. She told us she was going to stay with a friend, but she stayed there instead."

When Stella and her daughters moved in, Jennifer responded with fear once again. "I was scared, really scared, that Stella was going to try to be like my mother, to take her place. Then I got mad. I told my dad that I just wanted to be with him and my sister. I really wanted my dad all to myself," she added, voicing the universal longing of such children, perhaps all children.

Jennifer was unwilling—or perhaps she was unable—to discuss her view of the problems the new family had had to cope with during the early years. "We used to fight, but now I'm starting to talk to Stella a bit," she allowed, confirming that relationships were indeed improving. But the emotional deprivation she had endured became even more apparent when she was asked what she might wish for were she suddenly and magically offered three guaranteed-to-come-true wishes. This question often reveals underlying concerns children hold, as well as the full range of fantasy available to a child's imagination. But Jennifer could think of nothing at all. If a fairy godmother had descended from the sky at that very moment and in one glorious, glittering instant offered her the chance to realize whatever dreams lay hidden in her secret heart, she would have sent her away with her bag of goodies unopened.

"I can't think of anything," she whispered. And, like her father, she stared intently at her shoes.

Like Terry, Jennifer was nowhere near ready for a new "family" when Syd made his announcement. She had been the younger child receiving all the attention usually reserved for the family "baby," and now she and her stepsister had to slug it out for the middle position. The trauma she suffered when her mother left had not healed, nor had it even been addressed. Her father was too absorbed with his own troubles to help her, and Stella had her own worries. Both Jennifer and Terry would have needed much more time to mourn for their lost parent before feeling ready, emotionally, to accept the reality of a blended stepfamily.

Debra McIntyre

The happiest person in the entire family was Debra McIntyre. Debra was fifteen, vivacious, sociable, and sure of herself in a way that Syd's daughters were not.

The couch where we sat and talked stretched across the window area of the family living room, and on the other side of the pane of glass Debra's friends careened around on their bicycles. From time to time they knocked impatiently on the window, urging her to hurry up and join them. Debra shot them a look of scorn. "They're so immature," she commented disdainfully.

She, on the other hand, considered herself quite adult for her age, and she thought it was the divorce and remarriage that had done that for her. "I'm really quite mature now," she said with the straight-faced innocence of a child, "and I think I know a lot of things about myself that most people of my age don't know. I know more things about people and how they feel because of the divorce and because I've read a lot of books about it."

She was right. Studies of divorced children have shown that many of them are more mature in a worldly sense and definitely more independent. But Debra was astute enough to know that the sword had two cutting edges.

"I think I've benefitted in a way, but I've also lost, because I lost a parent," she said thoughtfully. "In a way, though, it was a good lesson. The divorce wasn't fun, but after it was over and my mom had custody, she let me see my dad. I can go and see him whenever I like, and that's really good because I can see for myself what he's really like. If I wasn't allowed to see him I'd always be thinking of him the way I did when I was four, when he went away. I'd always be thinking that something really important was missing from my life."

This was probably the most important insight Debra provided into her adjustment in the remarriage family. The credit went to Stella, for as much as she may have resented or even hated her ex-husband, she apparently had not communicated these feelings to her daughter. Debra knew she could form a reasonably accurate picture of her father without being prejudiced by the twisted perspective of another. That was, as she said, of inestimable value in her life. It allowed her to have as normal a relationship with both parents as possible under the circumstances. Debra was secure enough to acknowledge that her father had remarried a "nice lady" and that they had a baby, now two years old, whom she, Debra, adored. When I commented on her openness she nodded vigorously. "I'm a *very* open person," she exclaimed. "*Everybody* knows that."

But all this understanding was of quite recent vintage. At first Debra had actively resented the fact that her mother had left her father. "I would do anything in the world to say Mom was wrong about everything," she admitted. "But when I was nine years old I went to a day-care centre, and that changed things for me. I used to think all the time about the fact that they had broken up. I had all kinds of weird dreams about it. I thought my dad used to drink because I was a kid and he didn't want to have a kid. But one day at day-care they sat us down and they said, 'How many people in this room come from single-parent families?' About fifteen people put up their hands. I couldn't believe it! I thought I was the only one. After that I started to realize that my parents didn't get along and there was nothing I could do to put them back together again. That kinda made me feel better. Also, I stopped pretending I had a father. I used to say he was at home and stuff like that, then if my friends came over I'd say he was at work. But after that meeting at day-care I just stopped."

Debra liked Syd from the beginning, but she "hated" his daughters. "They were the worst kids I ever knew," she pronounced unequivocally. Syd wasn't the sort of man who pushed himself on people—indeed, he was so retiring, temperamentally, that he habitually waited for others to approach him. This worked well in Debra's case. "We're not close in a hugging way or stuff like that, but I know if I was ever in a bind he'd be the first to help me," she said softly. "He understands me and I think he really tries a lot." Debra thought Syd was like the father she never had, a welcome stand-in for the real thing. "But I would never tell him that," she added. "I'd be too embarrassed."

Like other children who remember their natural parents, although they may not have lived with them for years, Debra made an important distinction between Syd and the man who had engendered her. Whoever he was and wherever he was, this man was still her father. "I call Syd 'Dad,' but he's more like a real close friend. He can't be a real father, because I had my father until I was four," she explained. "I even wanted my mother to marry Syd. I liked him that much. But now I don't really care if they do. It's their business, and I'm not a big one for marrying, anyhow."

Debra had done a lot of thinking about the relationship between her mom and Syd and about the way the two sets of sisters got along in the household; and in the final analysis, she was content with the way things had worked out. The first couple of years had been "rough." Neither set of kids wanted to accept the other or the stepparent, and Debra resented the way Syd's daughters treated her mother. But now that life in the house seemed so much smoother ("There hasn't been a major fight here in six months," she said), she felt happier. "Terry and Jennifer have opened up to Mom and said, 'Hey, she's living with us.' And I also think of them more as sisters. Everybody believes we're sisters, and I don't say we're not. I like it. I always wanted a family and a house, and my mom really strived for that. We have a car and everything. We used to be not that well off, and at least we're a happy medium now. We have a bit more money for clothes and stuff like that, and we were able to fix up the house and buy a new couch." Debra stopped talking to stroke the couch appreciatively as though it were a beloved family pet.

Debra's wide-angle view of the remarriage closely approximated that of her mother and Syd. The blended family had practical advantages; and Debra was not one to overlook an opportunity for personal advancement. In her mind they had moved from the working class into the middle class. They were finally a "normal" family, more like the middle-class reflections of family life that beamed out from the television screen. This allowed her a new social status. Even her school marks had improved.

Her main problem had been not with a stepparent, but with her stepsiblings. "The one hard thing was not being the oldest anymore. I just *hate* it when they say, 'Debra, you're too young,' when before I used to be too old. Terry and I got along okay, but it was as though Jennifer and I were fighting for the middle position. I was younger by a little, but I was really much more mature. The first year we hated each other. In the second year we decided we liked each other and that we'd be twins. So we wore the same clothes. But this year we've decided to have separate identities.

"Lately everything has gotten better. For a while we had to sit down and say what we didn't like, and after that us kids also decided that we'd be more open with each other. We said that if we didn't like something we'd talk about it. We're still doing that, and it *usually* works. I can go up to anyone and say, 'You're bugging me.' "

Debra was watching her friends out the window and wanting to be with them, riding her bicycle up and down the road. "This definitely feels like a family now," she summarized. "I like it here, maybe I even love it; but I wouldn't tell anyone because you still have to be careful—if you know what I mean."

She leaped up from the couch and raced outside.

Judy McIntyre

If Debra McIntyre was the happiest child in the household, her younger sister, Judy, was perhaps the saddest. Judy was small and round and looked even younger than her ten years. Brown hair framed her serious-looking face, and her voice was sometimes inaudibly soft. What Judy longed for, but knew was lost to her, was the close intimacy of the single-parent family—her mom, Debra, and herself. Her mother and father had separated when she was a three-month-old baby, so she had never known her dad as a live-in parent. Her father had a new wife and a new family, and Judy felt only the most casual connection to them.

Judy had slipped through the cracks of the new family. The other girls were old enough to make their presence felt, or they had personalities that allowed them to carve out new territories for themselves. But Judy had been only five years old when this merger took place, and she was quiet by temperament. Now her mother had four girls to worry about, and one of them, Terry, was a serious problem. Since Judy was always well behaved and cooperative, she seemed to get lost in the shuffle. It was a case of the squeaky wheels in the family getting the oil.

Judy knew how much Stella had staked on this relationship with Syd, and, because she loved her mother deeply, she wanted her to be happy. She had also picked up her mother's expectation that Syd would be her "real" father. So her first reaction to Syd had been one of pleasure and excitement. "I was happy," she said. "I thought he'd get married to my mom, and I still hope he does. But I don't want him to be my father. I just want him to make Mom happy." She paused a long time and played with the tassles on a cushion. "I don't want Syd to be my father because I don't like him," she admitted finally.

Syd had disappointed her. Judy had hoped to find a "father," someone who played the role as she imagined it. She had to imagine because she had had no direct experience of a real dad and her images came primarily from television. "I don't have a real daddy," she told me sadly. "A real daddy would be different than Syd. I think he would be nice and happy most of the time and when he came back from work he would hug me and everything."

She thought she perceived other indications of her second-class status in the family, and they had to do with money. Money often presents problems in remarriages, coming right after problems with children (and a long way before sex and in-laws, which are major problems in troubled first marriages). Money gets tied up with emotional considerations of love and loyalty and it can be complicated. A man who is paying child support and/or alimony to his ex-wife will, for example, have less for his new family; and his new wife may be resentful. Another person may hesitate to change a will in favour of a new spouse because he or she hasn't really cut emotional ties to the first marriage. Such a person may also resist including stepchildren in financial planning because of ambivalence toward them, and that's the way the feelings get expressed.

Little Judy McIntyre was aware of the psychological uses of money but confused because Stella and Syd had not been clear about how they were dividing their financial responsibilities. She had noticed, for instance, that Terry and Jennifer were quite good at squeezing money out of their father for whatever they wanted, so she had tried the same technique. But Syd had told her to ask her mother. Stella was forthcoming with the money, but Judy felt rejected anyway. She didn't understand what the lines of communication were when it came to money. Her mother, she said, often paid for Syd's daughters' clothes.

Confusion of this sort made an already retiring child withdraw even further. "Syd treats his kids like number one, and he doesn't like me as much," she said in a tiny voice that barely rose above a whisper. She was frankly jealous of the attention her stepsisters received. "Terry and Jennifer just suck up to their dad all the time," she confided, emphasizing her words with a nod. Even the all-important symbol of love—the birthday present—had been missed. "I never get a present from Terry and Jennifer," she whispered. "Mom buys a present and signs it from them, but I know they didn't get it. Mom even tells me."

Unlike her stepsister, however, Judy was still able to fantasize about a fairy-tale future where her wishes would come true. Her first wish was standard television-inspired consumerism: She wanted to live in a big house with a swimming pool. Her second wish was for her mother—and for herself. "I wish Mom could have a big wedding and have a different husband than Syd, one that has no kids," she said, nodding seriously. Her third wish was that her mother and this mythical husband would "live happily ever after."

"I'd live with them," she added. And for the first time that afternoon, a happy smile broke across her face.

"Given the enormity of the task at hand and the intense and dislocating feelings that necessarily accompany it, the mystery is not why some families falter, but why and how others succeed . . ." Virginia Goldner of the Albert Einstein College of Medicine in New York City wrote in her article "Remarriage Families." Her point is worth emphasizing, because all stepfamilies, even those who have lived together for years and consider themselves successful, have had to negotiate their way through the most trying times. How could it be otherwise? In traditional circumstances a young couple evolves as a family slowly and in stages. First they get used to each other, then, if they have children, they get used to being parents. At each stage there is something new: toddlers, school-age children, adolescents. Family rituals evolve: a turkey at Thanksgiving, birthday parties, get-togethers at Christmas or Hanukkah, hiding Easter eggs . . . the occasions may be as individual as each family.

The remarriage family, on the other hand, has none of the cohesiveness and identity that grows in this way over the years. Its members are likely to be at different stages of development, and they have grown up in different environments with their *own* traditions, rituals, and rules. For months and often for years they may remain separate family units who happen to occupy the same house. Their task—and it is an awesome one—is to become a family with a shared history and some sort of shared value system, but to succeed they'll have to approach things slowly and acquire the ability to live with a certain amount of ambiguity. As we've seen, the "instant family" approach doesn't work.

People marry for any number of reasons other than love, and they've been doing so since the beginning of civilization. The lucky ones learn to care about each other along the way, but in remarriages (where a lot of alliances are contracted for reasons other than love) there just isn't as much time available. The family doesn't evolve slowly; it's just there. And if there is a lack of commitment between the spouses, an already difficult situation may become quite intolerable.

The experts call it "bonding," and if it doesn't happen, the new family will probably be in trouble. The kids, for example—his and hers—will know it immediately. The McIntyre and the Logan children did—and they used that knowledge to split Stella and Syd further in the hope that their natural parents might reconcile (Logan children) and that they might recover the lost intimacy of the single-parent family (McIntyre children). Poor bonding also caused problems in the Renzetti family, but the difference was that Stella and Syd decided to concentrate on building their relationship with each other. When they did, a truly dramatic shift took place, and the "family" began to unite.

Stella and Syd didn't know each other very well before they moved in together. Oh, they thought they did—they'd been companions for a year—but their individual deep-seated needs had clouded their vision. Stella thought her children "needed" a father in the house. She felt guilty about not providing them with a two-parent family and she thought Syd looked like a good candidate for the job. For his part, Syd had been deeply traumatized by the departure of his wife and hadn't really recovered. He was frightened—his girls seemed out of control. He knew he needed help, and Stella looked like a strong, competent helpmate.

They both had well-defined ideas of what their union should accomplish, but their own relationship played only a small part in the equation. They had a good sexual rapport that sustained them for a long time; but with so much anger in circulation, that, too, might have dissolved. Syd (like Anthony Renzetti) also carried stereotyped ideas of what a "wife" should do. Basically, he expected her to free him of the responsibility of his kids and take over the management of the household. For her part of the bargain, Stella thought she'd get a complete family and greater financial security as well.

With such a preproduction script, it was no wonder they didn't get to know each other during their year of courtship. They didn't have to; the story was already written in their minds, and the reality of who the other person really was and what their actual feelings might be would have interfered with the plot. Each projected his needs on the other in the expectation that a role left vacant by divorce would be filled. They set each other up as straw men, as "mother" and "father," but a huff and a puff from their children threatened the entire structure.

According to Lillian Messinger, successful remarriage families are led by "an executive couple"—in other words, the parents. In the most promising circumstances, she says, a couple planning a second marriage has learned something about the difficulties they're sure to encounter *before* and not after they begin to live together. They've thought about the roles they will play in the household and with each other's children. But neither Stella nor Syd had prepared themselves, which meant that with the sharp eyes they bring to such affairs, the children saw there was room for sabotage. (Most children brought into second marriages are initially confused and unhappy enough to attempt sabotage if they can.)

"If the couple relationship is strong and if there is real bonding before they begin to live together, people will usually be able to create some sense of family for the children," said Messinger in her office in the Clarke Institute of Psychiatry in Toronto. "The bonding is step number one. After that the kids begin to define their relationships and their own roles around the firm concept that each parent cares for the other. If this is established, the kids won't feel powerful enough to break things up, or even to try."

Although they are committed to each other, a couple still needs to be prepared for the fact that remarriage is always tough and kids have a hard time accepting it, especially if there is a living parent outside the home. Terry, for example, came into the new family feeling confused and rejected, her thirteen-year-old life in a chaotic mess. And because Stella and Syd were overwhelmed by the enormity of their problems, they were unable to help.

An observer watching the developments in Terry's life might have predicted just how difficult her adjustment in the new family might be. From the beginning Terry's experience was a classic textbook preparation for unhappiness. She was, to start, unaware that her natural parents were unhappy together, and her shock when she discovered her mother was having an affair was extreme. She responded by keeping her secret to herself, but the weight of it crushed her; it disturbed her sleep, interfered with her schoolwork, and caused her to lose eight pounds. Perhaps Terry felt that to pretend all was well would make it so; that if no one knew the truth, the family glue would not become unstuck. Finally, when her mother did leave and Syd was unable to cope, Terry did what many children do. She parented her bereft father, holding back her tears in order to protect him and her younger sister.

Terry was at an age where, under normal circumstances, she would have begun to detach herself from home and family. Adolescents take one step forward and two steps back until they are ready to leave for good, but Terry's parents left *her* before she could leave them, before she was ready. The emotional supports that provide the foundation from which adolescents venture, one step at a time, were pulled from under her and she fell sprawling into an abyss of fear.

In their California study of postdivorce families, *Surviving the Breakup: How Parents and Children Cope with Divorce*, Judith Wallerstein and Joan Kelly discovered that adolescents who lacked "inner controls, the consolidated conscience and independent capacity to make judgments" were left extremely susceptible by the divorce of their parents. Because they were unable to carry on independently without the security they needed, "the divorce left them vulnerable to their newly strengthened sexual and aggressive impulses and surrounded by the temptations of the adolescent world without the supports that would hold them to a straight course."

Adolescents who were aware of their parents' sexual activity were intensely disturbed. They were subject to vivid sexual fantasies about their parents, and their responses included "sexual excitement, acute anxiety, anger, outrage, embarrassment, dismay and envy." A few of the girls became sexually active when they discovered a parent's extramarital affair. One boy harassed his father's mistress, let the air out of the tires of her car, and tried to break the windows of her house.

Wallerstein and Kelly found that the danger of early sexual activity for adolescents is that they have not yet acquired the conscience and capacity for love and intimacy that are preconditions for loving relationships. When the sexual activity occurred as a reaction to the behaviour of the parents, they spoke of "pseudoadolescence." The child was not living out an emancipating adolescent experience, but responding to a frightening rupture in the family support structure.

Terry Logan was a classic example. At thirteen, she was still totally identified with her family. Her mother was her model of womanhood and a source of love and security; and when she left the family, Terry collapsed. The constraints she needed to contain her emerging sexuality were gone and she was easily vulnerable to the older boys she began to associate with. They provided her with the affection (or semblance of affection) she could no longer find in the shambles of home. She needed to be held. Terry's suffering was magnified when her mother refused to see her for months after she left, and when they did meet, the tension between them made communication almost impossible.

But still, Terry longed for her mother and nourished the impossible hope that her parents would reconcile, even though her mother was remarried and her father was living with Stella. With such thoughts, it was impossible for her to accept either remarriage family. Her mother's new husband remained a shadowy figure whom she blamed for her woes. And for years, Stella was a witch to be fought every inch of the way.

Because she hadn't sufficiently mourned the loss of her mother and the loss of her childhood family, Terry wasn't prepared emotionally for Stella, for Stella's children, or for the remarriage family.

Her sister, Jennifer, had different problems. Her muteness suggested a trauma equal to that experienced by Terry, but, being quieter and more inhibited to begin with, her response was to withdraw completely. Several years later she could talk a little—but only a little. The fear she had experienced when she clung to her father's leg and when she found herself alone in the apartment at night had never left her.

Emotionally, Jennifer was flat and distanced from the world around her, so frightened and so inhibited that she was unable to project her imagination into a fantasy wish for the future. But she too had begun to change with the therapy the family had undergone. "I'm starting to talk to Stella now," she had said.

It was a small but hopeful sign that the family was succeeding in changing direction and beginning to communicate.

Stella's children, on the other hand, were more articulate; in fact, Debra McIntyre was one of the most interesting children I met, because she was able to pinpoint with some precision which events and circumstances had made her feel good about herself again after the breakup of her family. It was this positive sense of herself that allowed her to accept the remarriage family and feel comfortable there, in spite of the difficulties the family had endured.

The first significant event for Debra happened in the day-care centre when she discovered, to her amazement, that she was not the only child in the world who had lost a parent to divorce. Until then Debra had lied to her friends, saying her dad was out or at work; but after the day-care experience she accepted the separation more realistically and could talk about it.

The key word is "reality," and when Debra was able to accommodate it, she had taken a giant step forward.

The second and probably most important circumstance was her open access to her father. Debra was quite clear about it; she could see him whenever she wanted and *learn for herself what he was like*. She didn't feel there was something missing in her life, as she was sure she would were she prevented from having a relationship with her dad. Her natural father and her stepmother had welcomed Debra into their family to the extent that she thought her stepmother a "nice lady" (no mean compliment for a stepmother) and felt quite committed to their child, her half-sister.

The research of Judith Wallerstein and Joan Berlin Kelly referred to earlier confirms Debra's experience. Their finding was that the relationship of the noncustodial parent to the child was directly related to the child's ability to adjust to divorce and later to a remarriage; and that that relationship was almost always dependent on the attitudes of the former spouses to each other. When there was open access, the child did not feel deprived of that crucial contact, and the noncustodial parent also felt an ongoing involvement with his child—to everyone's benefit. In her related study, Judith Greif found that at the time of a remarriage a child's mourning for a lost parent may become more acute. He or she may feel that an already tenuous relationship will be threatened even further by the presence of a stepparent. However, if a strong relationship with easy access between parent and child is already in place, the threat will seem less, and the child's ability to accept the reality of the remarriage will be greater.

These findings probably run counter to the feelings of many custodial parents who fear that if their child has a strong relationship with his natural parent he may be less willing to accept a same-sex stepparent. Some people become competitive and run down the natural parent to the child (almost always with disastrous consequences). In reality the opposite is true. A child who feels free to love and be loved by an absent parent will be better able to accept and learn to care about a stepparent.

Debra had a good relationship with her dad, and because no one tried to interfere with that, she could allow herself to like Syd. It helped, of course, that Syd did not push himself on her—he let her come to him when she was ready. But Debra was able to care about both her father and her stepfather without feeling guilty or unnatural. "We're not close in a hugging way or stuff like that," she said about Syd, "but I know if I was ever in a bind he'd be the first to help me." What greater accolade could a stepparent wish for?

Judy, however, had no such relationship with her father. She was only three months old when he and her mother separated, and her father had apparently lacked interest in developing the contact. So when Stella announced that Syd was to become her stepfather, Judy thought she would have a father at last. She fantasized about what that would be. A father would be "nice and happy most of the time," and when he came home from work he would hug her. She was so touching with her serious little face and dark eyes, this child who wanted a father. But a fantasy is a fantasy, and Judy wasn't prepared for a man who happened to have two daughters of his own whom he preferred. Furthermore, she yearned for the single-parent family she had known for most of her life. They had been a tight, close unit, Stella, Debra, and Judy; but now that special intimacy was gone, and Judy mourned its loss. She had had to give up the family she knew, in which she was most comfortable, and she had never found a place for herself in this one.

Even though Syd had apparently disappointed her in her search for a father, Judy held onto the dream that somewhere out there was a man who would be "it." This was Prince Charming in his paternal incarnation. Her wish was that her mom would marry this prince (someone other than Syd) who would, of course, have no children of his own. She and her sister, Debra, would be alone again and no one would ever forget her birthday present, nor would they hesitate to give her money when she asked. For Judy, this was the measure of love.

The McIntyres and the Logans had been together for three years and two and a half of them had been ghastly, but in the long run, the prognosis for the family didn't look bad. Estimates of how long it takes for the remarriage family to unify start at about two years, but Dr. Paul Druckman, a family therapist who sees a lot of troubled remarriage families, thinks it takes five. So, pain and suffering aside, the McIntyre-Logans were about average. Perhaps the important and positive new ways in which they had begun to relate to each other would have come about sooner or later (if they didn't separate before that happened), but there is no doubt that their decision to enter therapy helped the process along. Their therapist admitted she had never dealt with such a family (unfortunately this is too often the case), but she was sensitive enough to allow them to express the strange complexities of a remarriage situation without trying to impose expectations and attitudes that belong to the traditional nuclear family. Had that happened, they would certainly have continued to see themselves as failures. The therapist allowed them to talk in a controlled environment where they would not be assaulted for speaking their minds. And she encouraged them to set up a formal time, at Sunday brunch, when they could air their complaints. The tension these sessions released made a palpable difference in everyone's life. Terry and Jennifer relaxed enough to see Stella as a real person and not a witch who had come to deprive them of their mother. Terry's sexual acting-out seemed under control; Jennifer was starting to speak; Debra was happier in the family than she was willing to say aloud for fear of being embarrassed. Only Judy remained deeply sad.

Stella and Syd had begun to put their relationship first and the children were aware of this, but it remained to be seen whether that relationship had enough depth to keep the family going. They both said they would not do it again if they could roll back the clock: It had been just too difficult.

Now that they had come so far along the road, time was their ally. But in the long run, the family, like all remarriage families, would stand or fall on the strength of their commitment to each other and their tolerance of their differences.

There is a lot to learn from the McIntyre-Logans—a lot to avoid and a lot to admire. In the latter category is their willingness to risk real communication in therapy and to begin the process of making lemonade from a lemon, so to speak. It would be impossible, of course, to reduce all the nuances of their communal life into directives, but a few helpful guidelines do emerge from their experience.

SUGGESTIONS

1. Be aware that children's pain caused by a divorce or death in the family may be quite different from that of their parents. Syd's children were quite unready for a remarriage. They needed help in dealing with the family breakup first.

2. Tune in to divisive, manipulative behaviour on the part

of children. Never let them invite one side of the family to an event and not the other. Children who succeed in splitting spouses along former family lines will be on their way to splitting the family altogether.

3. Plan a strategy for developing family unity. A sense of a growing family "history" and "tradition" will help everyone's integration into the new unit, but it must happen gradually. Turkeys at Thanksgiving, trees at Christmas, seder at Passover, family trips to the zoo or to the theatre—plan it your own way, and take pictures.

4. Be aware that "promiscuity" among young teen-agers is more likely to be an expression of depression than of anything else.

5. Information can help children realize they are not alone. The day-care experience helped Debra accept the reality of the family breakup. She also read a lot, and said it helped. There are books written especially for children who have had a divorce and/or a remarriage in their families. The best are: *The Boys and Girls Book about Divorce* and *The Boys and Girls Book about Stepfamilies*, both by Dr. Richard Gardner.

6. Open visiting with the noncustodial parent is also helpful. Debra said it best. She was allowed to get to know her father as a real person and form her own opinion. (More on this in chapter five.)

7. Don't hesitate to get help. The main success of the McIntyre-Logan therapy was to strengthen the couple bond. This, in turn, helped the children and set the family on a more positive course.

A family doctor or school counsellor will be able to direct you to a service providing family therapy, but make sure the person you choose is knowledgeable about the special problems of stepfamilies (some continue to deny there is a difference between the nuclear and the remarriage family). And don't hesitate to shop around before settling on an individual you respect and feel comfortable with. You're doing the hiring in this situation.

CHAPTER FIVE

Remarriage and the Joint Custody of Children

"We have a good divorce. We got to keep Mommy and Daddy."
—Timmy

"AS IT IS now practiced, adversarial divorce with all its stress on fault, retaliation, win and loss, has no positive benefits for the contestants. Such legal battles over interpersonal relationships do not provide a healthy or just atmosphere for divorcing couples and their children. Lawyers are expected to act beyond their capabilities and judges must make decisions on matters outside their training . . . The single winner . . . often has an enormous burden of guilt to bear, while the loser . . . carries a soul-breaking weight of resentment and anger. Between the spouses, there is at least one legally sanctioned victor, but for the children there are only legally sanctioned losers."

The author of these angry words is Howard H. Irving, a professor of social work at the University of Toronto and a "divorce mediator." Irving works with couples who are prepared to resolve their custody disputes without going to court, and in his view the courtroom custody suit, in which one parent must call the other "unfit" and otherwise "prove" that he or she is inadequate, is always damaging. Indeed, how is one to explain to children that the "unfit" one will henceforth be paying regular visits?

In his book *Divorce Mediation*, Irving writes of the violence nherent in contested custody battles. We have laws to protect children from abuse, he says, but somehow the abuse intrinsic to the very nature of the court battle which treats children as property to be disposed of while parents degrade each other, presumably for the children's sake, is not recognized as abuse. Irving is appalled at what some parents do to their children in the name of love. His office has become a drop-off centre for children whose parents do not want their estranged spouse to know their address. He has talked to these children and heard them weep. Irving's advice to divorcing parents is to avoid court altogether if possible. Custody decisions are better arrived at by mutual agreement.

There's no final word on the sole custody versus joint custody debate. The more traditional defenders of sole custody believe that the best solution for children of divorce is to live with one parent, usually the mother, and visit with the other at preestablished, agreed-upon times. They believe that all the physical moving around involved in co-parenting arrangements is not good for children.

On the other side of the debate are those who swear that shared parenting represents a quantum leap in our attitudes to the divorced family and the most important new thinking to emerge in a decade or two or three. They point to the reality of the changes in current social structures, to the blurring of traditional sex roles, and to the fact that thousands more women are now in the work force.[1] The postdivorce family, they say, must reflect these new conditions: Women are no longer home full-time, and many men want to share equally in the raising of their children.

Eighty-five percent of custody awards are still made in fa-

---

[1] Statistics here are interesting. In the U.S. in 1970, 37 percent of women worked outside their homes, compared to 42.2 percent in 1980. In Britain during the same period, figures rose from 36 percent to 44.3 percent. The largest percentage increase occurred in Canada: from 34 percent in 1972 to 51.6 percent in 1983. *Sources:* Statistical Abstract of the U.S., 1981, U.S. Bureau of the Census; Social Trends, 1982, Government Statistical Service (Britain); Women's Bureau, Department of Labour, Government of Canada.

vour of women, based on the "Tender Years Doctrine," a policy which was formulated in the early 1900s in response to a growing body of literature that detailed the psychological development of children. Although historically wives and children had been legal chattels of the husband, the new doctrine broke with tradition by stressing the importance of the mother in early childhood; it held, quite radically, that "all other things being equal," she was best suited to the role of guardian.

The Tender Years Doctrine corrected a grave historical injustice by recognizing the important psychological component of the mother-child relationship (the chattel theory was political and economic in nature and preceded Freud), but, as often happens, it succeeded in creating another imbalance. A new punitive standard emerged, now directed towards men. Sex-role stereotypes grew: Mothers were perceived to have a "natural" semi-mystical bond with their children; fathers did not. So a mother's "natural" place was in the home and a father's "natural" place was in the outside world. In custody cases, this was translated into a belief that the mother was the more "natural" parent.

Theories of an exclusive maternal "instinct" and the lack of an equivalent potential for parenting in men have been stereotyped assumptions and are not supported by research. On the contrary, as fathers begin to fight for and win the right to remain involved parents after divorce, all indications point to their equal competence. In a 1977 study of ninety-two children living in varied custodial arrangements, psychologist Rhona Rosen concluded there was no significant measurable difference between those children who were living with mother or father. When the sex of the child and the age at the time of divorce were analyzed, no significant relationship emerged. "It would appear from Rosen's study that any automatic choice of custodial parent based on gender has no supporting evidence," said Dr. Irving. "This is an important consideration because many custody battles arise from the Tender Years Doctrine and the assumption that the mother has preference."

Opponents of joint custody often base their case on the

widely quoted book, *Beyond the Best Interests of the Child.* The authors' recommendation that children live in one permanent home and visit with the other parent was based on their belief that legal and physical single-parent custody was "the least detrimental available alternative."

However, in *Surviving the Breakup: How Parents and Children Cope with Divorce,* which was published about a decade later, Judith Wallerstein and Joan Berlin Kelly called attention to the enormous pressures on single parents, the resultant depression, and the appalling lack of social supports available for the single-parent family. They pointed out that opposition to joint custody derives in large part from the weight of precedent laced with plain, old-fashioned suspicion about new ideas. It becomes convenient and comfortable to recommend what has gone before, they wrote. Eventually, "the precedent of twice-monthly visits became not just customary, but somehow developmentally correct, morally right. Fathers pressing for [further] contacts or for joint custody were viewed with suspicion by legal and mental health professionals alike. 'It just wasn't done.' " Wallerstein and Kelly added that until very recently society thought it slightly odd for a father to want to spend a lot of time with his children. Mothers were warned not to give up too much, and some were made to feel guilty for wanting to share parenting with an interested father.

"The custom of alternating weekends . . . has continued despite a vastly changed society that by 1979 saw more than 60 percent of single mothers joining the work force," wrote the authors. "A rethinking of visiting issues must include the concept that both parents remain centrally responsible for and involved in the care and psychological development of their children."

Joint custody is only for committed, mentally healthy parents who are able to deal effectively with each other in spite of their divorce. It becomes more complicated, of course, when one of the parents remarries: The ex-spouses must absorb a new person into the parenting process. It is a difficult but potentially rewarding option.

Traditional arguments against joint-custody agreements in

remarriage are being seriously challenged from several quar-ters. *For example:* In nuclear families, boundaries are clear to everyone—some people are in the family and everyone else is out—and conventional wisdom holds that it is this sense of ex-clusive identity that makes people feel secure. But advocates of joint custody claim that although it is difficult to accept the notion of membership in two open-ended families, people who can do it will likely adapt to remarriage situations more easily. The remarriage family already has open boundaries, and having sole custody of children will not alter that reality. *For example:* It is often assumed that a diminished relationship with one natural parent will make it easier for a child to accept a stepparent of the same sex, but new evidence suggests that the opposite may be true. Children who continue to be par-ented by both their natural parents seemingly adapt better to the stepfamily, because they are, quite simply, more emotion-ally secure to start with. Judith Greif's study indicated that fathers who were denied an active parenting role became de-pressed and withdrew from their children. This, in turn, complicated the children's reactions. They had lost their fa-ther's physical presence in their lives and with that the ongo-ing proof of his commitment to them. The single mothers Greif studied were also more depressed, since they were forced to shoulder the entire burden of parenting alone.

The children in these circumstances were less prepared for the demands of life in a stepfamily than children who contin-ued to be parented by both mother and father, even though the latter were divorced.

Greif also found that in sole-custody arrangements, visit-ing between fathers and children was often unsatisfying for everyone. Parent and child both felt they had to ''court'' each other to ensure that the visits would continue. Fathers be-came sugar daddies. Children were afraid to address unpleas-ant issues or express anger for fear that the father would not return. It was much easier to direct anger against the parent who would be there the next morning. This made the role of the custodial parent even harder and the parents more de-pressed.

Furthermore, as a result of tiptoeing around each other

during their visits, both parents and children complained of a sense of superficiality in their relationships. Fathers who were visitors in their children's lives were saddened by the knowledge that at the end of each visit awaited another painful goodbye. They protected themselves from this recurrent hurt by distancing themselves emotionally, but this only accentuated the problems they had in meeting the children's emotional needs, or even knowing what they were. The effect was to reduce the father's sense of himself as an adequate parent even further.

On the other hand, co-parent fathers in the Greif study described a very different experience. They spoke of relationships that involved ''an open expression of the usual range of emotions. They did not feel as shut out from their children's inner lives and they sensed that their continuous availability to the child allowed for the child's spontaneous sharing of feelings.''

The issue boils down to a disagreement over how to deal with the experience of traumatic loss. Everyone concurs that people who have had a major loss in their lives must take time to mourn before they are emotionally ready to move on again; but until recently, moving on has been equated with giving up the past. In a book called *Attachment and Loss*, British psychoanalyst John Bowlby has suggested that there may be much more involved. In a study he undertook, healthy widows and widowers reported that they maintained an inner dialogue with their former spouses for years after death had separated them. They spoke to them and consulted them in fantasy and found this a consoling experience. In a very real sense they were able to use the lost relationship to help them cope with their present lives.

Robert Garfield of the Hahneman Medical College and Hospital in Philadelphia has added that it may be quite unreasonable to expect that former relationships can be excised from our lives without a trace, and even inconsistent with a successful divorce. ''Clinicians can help the mourner accept the reality of the old relationship, acknowledge its current role in his or her emotional life and integrate these in attempts at loving and living in a new family," he wrote, concurring with Bowlby's observations.

This new thinking is of particular importance to divorced and remarried people considering joint custody. The accepted wisdom is that there is something unhealthy, even pathological, about separated spouses who continue to relate positively to each other, the belief being that such people have not successfully cut their emotional ties. Although some people may try to maintain contact with an ex-spouse in the hope that the relationship will resume, continued positive interaction with a former partner doesn't necessarily mean that is the case.

In the binuclear family research project, former spouses reported that they related in a wide variety of ways. A full 85 percent described an ongoing relationship after a separation of two years. A few described themselves as "best friends" and a few as "bitter enemies," but the vast majority were in the middle. In every case, former spouses with joint custody got along more easily than the others.

The ability to continue a more or less comfortable relationship with an ex-spouse may indicate a *successful* resolution of a divorce and not the contrary. Again in the binuclear family project, 30 percent of those in joint custody arrangements reported their relations to be "generally caring, respectful and friendly," compared to only 20 percent of those with sole-custody agreements.

When parents can make joint custody work, everyone appears to win. Children profit from their parents' ability to minimize the trauma of a divorce and from having an ongoing relationship with both of them. The formidable pressures and the isolation of single parenting are lifted, usually from the mother; and the crucial contribution of fathering is recognized. As one divorced father with joint custody of his three children said with happy irony, "I'm the best mother I know."

THE VIKAR FAMILY

The Vikars are an extended remarriage family with joint custody of the children: two families in two neighbouring homes with two children who live two weeks here and two weeks there. It has been eight years since the original family dissolved and six years since the father remarried. The children are fine, but the adults had a difficult time and several problems persist. Some members of the family find it harder than others to tolerate the open boundaries and the sometimes unwelcome intimacy this alternative demands. But over the months and then years, many of their insecurities have evaporated and jealous fears have subsided. The Vikars believe they've made remarriage with joint custody work, although it will become clear that they have gone only part of the way. They were chosen because the kinds of problems they have struggled with are so very typical of the poignant human dilemmas people embarking upon this road can expect to encounter, to a greater or lesser degree.

Neil Vikar

Neil Vikar worked out of a comfortable office inside a complex of government administrative buildings. In his professional life he was one small cog in the machinery of the public service. As a middle-level manager of "human resources," as the bureaucrats called it, his wasn't a particularly inspiring career, but it was secure.

Neil liked security. His parents had scraped their way through the Depression surviving by the tips of their fingernails, and security was the value they had communicated above all others. Even in their emotional lives they had not taken many risks. Both of them feared that anger, for example, would threaten the union they depended upon. For as long as Neil could remember, the calm of his parents' household had never been broken. Potential disruption was smoothed down, rounded at the edges, and reduced to manageable blandness.

This childhood produced anxiety in Neil. As a teen-ager

his own anger rose, crested, then subsided, in towering swells of emotion. He would tremble in fear; his parents had made it absolutely clear that such negative feelings were not to be tolerated.

Neil's first marriage lasted for ten years, and during the entire time he worried periodically that it might end. Following his parents' example, he ignored the hints and then the obvious signs of his wife's unhappiness. When she started an affair with one of his friends, possibly to force reality upon him, he tried to ignore that, too. "I wanted to stay in my marriage forever and I would have if I hadn't been forced out," he said in a quiet voice, sitting opposite on the muted grey couch. "Every few months I had a few moments of extreme anxiety that I would succeed in overcoming. During our last few years together, my wife was clearly trying to end the marriage, but I never even entertained the idea of cooperating until I realized there was nothing left in it for me at all."

Neil was thirty-eight years old and, fortunately for him, a man with a sense of humour and an optimistic nature. He needed this optimism to carry him through a long period of disillusionment that followed his marriage breakup and the painful self-reevaluation that followed. He needed it, as well, during the early years of his new union, when the relationship between himself and his former and present wives seemed insolubly complicated. Six years into the remarriage, he continued to need it—that much was clear.

Neil and his first wife, Carole, were only twenty-one years old when they married. While he did graduate work in anthropology she supported both of them by working as a secretary. When he finished and two children had been born, he supported her return to school. Throughout, the marriage was egalitarian in structure. Neil and Carole both believed in fairness (although they sometimes succumbed to irrational feelings that influenced the way they actually behaved). But, by and large, mutual respect was one of the elements that carried them through the divorce without unduly damaging their children.

"I first became aware of how unhappy Carole was on our honeymoon," Neil said glumly. "She told me that deep down she felt empty, she felt nothing. I'll never forget. It was as though a chilly hand had gripped my heart.

"Later on I felt that I didn't give her enough support, but then I really wasn't that interested in climbing into her head or her heart. I wouldn't have known how. It was too scary, too much like the sort of activity my parents had steered away from in order to preserve their own marriage. When she sent me a very clear message by having an affair with my friend, even then I could do nothing about it. I couldn't *talk* to her about what was wrong. I became depressed instead—for many months."

In the eighth year of their marriage, Carole began to have dizzy spells and blackouts. In the ninth year she asked him to leave.

Neil left—but not before he had made it clear that he had no intention of giving up his children. Ingrid was seven at the time, and Joseph, the baby, was two. From the minute of their births Neil had adored them, and no private pressure or social convention was going to cut him out of their lives. He told Carole he was willing to go to court to fight her for custody if she wanted it that way, but that he would rather not, for all their sakes. Would she agree to joint custody? "I trusted what she did with the kids and I knew she trusted what I did. We had always thought of each other as good parents; that was consistent and unbroken regardless of what other things may have been happening between us," he said.

Carole was wary about joint custody. She had a friend, a social worker, who told her that joint custody was convenient for parents but hell for the kids. "We both saw that as possibly true, but there seemed to be another side that was worth the gamble," Neil said. "In a joint-custody situation neither of us would have to lose our children, okay, but even more important, they wouldn't have to lose us either. Neither of us would be forced to become a weekend parent. Nothing scared me more than the possibility of turning into a member of that sad-looking father brigade you can see every Saturday and Sunday in McDonalds, at the zoo, and in the playgrounds. I thought I'd die if that ever happened to me. I was a parent and I thought I had a right to go on being a parent, and if my ex-wife didn't want to share the job with me, I'd take her to court. Period. I realized a bit late that it hadn't helped to follow my parents' example. Blandness in my marriage hadn't guaranteed anything at all.''

Carole agreed, and for the first two years the co-parenting arrangement worked reasonably well. For one thing, it gave both the adults an opportunity to begin the slow transformation of their own relationship into a more mutual partnership focussed mainly on the children. They accomplished this by limiting their conversations to the children until they became comfortable talking about other things. Neil stopped making snide remarks about Carole's lover, who had been his best friend. Carole stopped prodding him to take note of her, to listen to what she wanted to tell him about herself. It was understood that all these things were now behind them, and that if they wanted to succeed as divorced co-parents they would have to tread carefully.

Early on they agreed to basic ground rules. The first was that under no circumstances would they run each other down in front of their children. For Neil that was one of the most difficult things he ever had to do. He was still deeply angry at Carole—he blamed her for ending this marriage he had wanted to last forever; but they had both agreed that everything they did would have to be in the children's best interests and that badmouthing each other would be harmful no matter how good it made the adults feel. ''For at least two years I practically had to punch myself in the mouth when I was about to say something mean,'' Neil acknowledged. He added with pride that he had never slipped and that he was quite sure that Carole had also upheld her end of the bargain.

They also agreed early on never to let the children play one parent against the other in the old Momma-Poppa game children of divorce often become so adept at—to their detriment. So if one child said, ''Mom [Dad] lets us go to bed at eight-thirty and you make us go to bed at eight,'' each parent would reply by saying he or she would discuss it with the other, but until that day the bedtime in each household remained fixed. They agreed as well not to turn their kids into messengers. ''It was so seductive for me to say, 'Could you please ask your mother to call me,' " recalled Neil. "But my feeling was that a kid has the right to be a kid and not have the responsibility of being a messenger too. Of course I'd rather not make the call, but each time I'd force myself to do it."

Neil and Carole talked on a regular basis at least once a week. They both thought it was nonsensical to disagree on small things like bedtimes, and from the beginning they tried to make mutual decisions that would provide the children with greater continuity in their lives.

"Joint custody was a decision we made without going to court, and it has worked quite well for us," said Neil. "We tried to make sure our decisions were not influenced by any bitterness we carried with us from the breakup. I admit that was hard, but being aware that it could happen helped. Now it's not an issue.

"We tried also to be as practical about things as we could. With money, we both knew very well how it can get used to punish and reward, and we tried to avoid that and stick strictly to the issue of need. As long as Carole didn't make any money, I supported her entirely for the children's costs. This payment was increased from time to time until she started earning a salary. I supported her when she was in need just as she had supported me when I was in graduate school. As far as I was concerned, the fact that we were no longer married was not a reason to renege on that debt. I was very grateful for her help and I wanted to show my appreciation.

"I think we have proven even more after our divorce than before that we are both effective parents. The bottom line is that we get along in terms of parenting. That took time, but after the first six to eight months I started seeing her less as my ex-wife and more as a sort of professional partner with whom I am in regular contact. Our current relationship is now entirely child-centred.

"Maybe the proof that all this makes sense is that the kids seem like well-reared, happy people. Of course the situation is essentially insane, living in two houses; but as sane as you can be in such circumstances, that's how sane they are."

Neil and Carole live in the same neighbourhood so the children will be in the same school district. It's been expensive because both of them have needed a house large enough to accommodate the children when they are there. The children must be at home in both places, with their own rooms and toys that belong there. The toothbrush doesn't move, the favourite books stay on the shelf. Sometimes there are duplicates of important items in both houses, like, for example, a favourite picture story.

In the beginning, the children moved every few days and then once every week, but now everyone has settled on a two-week period. Two weeks seem to allow enough time for both adults and children to relax into the rhythm of on-again, off-again family life. It takes everyone a couple of days to wind down from one cycle and rev up for the other. Neil has noticed that the children often seem withdrawn when they come to him from their mother's house. He does not interpret this to mean they are unhappy with their mother. He knows that they are trying to accommodate the change. Sometimes they are critical of him at this time, making sly comparisons to see what they can get away with. Neil himself is slightly tense during the transition. He and his new wife, Madeleine, must also emerge through a metamorphosis of sorts, from childless couple to instant stepfamily, with all the human interaction that entails.

Joint parenting became unexpectedly complicated when Neil met Madeleine, the woman he would eventually marry. Carole wasn't unduly disturbed as long as Neil and Madeleine weren't living together—she and Neil were still the only parents, and they continued to develop their new relationship in that role—but when Madeleine moved into Neil's house and began to "parent" her children, Carole became frightened. She couldn't tolerate the thought of another woman "replacing" her during the weeks she was separated from her children.

Neil described Madeleine as a "'meaningful adult in his children's lives" and said she had a "moderately close" relationship with them, but the jargon phrase "meaningful adult" and the qualifier "moderately" suggested his ambivalence. From the beginning, the lines of responsibility in the new-marriage household were fuzzy and difficult. Madeleine felt anxious about disciplining the children because she didn't want to turn herself into a proverbial wicked stepmother while Neil got away with being the loving father; but Neil did make a point of telling the children they had to ask Madeleine for permission as well as himself, and eventually she was able to assume more authority in the household.

Carole, however, seemed unable and unwilling to accept Madeleine's presence in her children's lives. She resented all signs of Madeleine's involvement in their parenting. When it came to the children's schooling, she refused to allow Madeleine to accompany Neil when they spoke to the teachers. At a psychological level, Carole refused to acknowledge that a remarriage had taken place. She tried desperately to keep Madeleine in the role of a girl friend so she and Neil could remain the sole parents of their children.

It couldn't work, and yet the alternative—accepting a truly binuclear family with new spouses attached—seemed too strange and too painful. Carole's despair was profoundly human; it summoned forth an atavistic fear of losing her children to a beguiling other woman who shared their lives half the time. The "other woman," however, angrily rejected the designation. Madeleine believed Carole was shunting her aside to maintain her primary connection to Neil, while she, the second wife, was left out in the cold.

In the middle was Neil—fortunately of optimistic temperament. "At the beginning I would feel upset when I talked to my ex-wife—I guess because this was the person who had hurt me so much—but that became less and less. But then I would have to talk to Madeleine about what Carole and I had discussed, and she would become angry. Madeleine wanted me to be more assertive and accusing when I had no need to be. I didn't know how to handle all the emotion coming at me. I refused to admit to Madeleine that Carole was a poor mother and an ugly person, because she wasn't and she isn't. The proof that she is a good mother is visible in her children! By the same token I will not downgrade Madeleine to my ex-wife. I have my loyalties. So I finally just stopped caring. Madeleine and Carole have sort of come to terms, but they cannot be in the same room together, and that's just the way it is. They don't deal with it and I've stopped trying. All I know is that even without the three of us being able to sit down and talk about these children we are all parenting, things have worked out quite well."

The stress on the children must have been enormous, especially in the beginning before a truce of sorts was arrived at. When she reached puberty, Ingrid, the older child, began to respond to the overt jealousy between her mother and her stepmother. Since the early teens are often a time when children "fall in love" with the parent of the opposite sex, Ingrid, too, found herself in competition for her father. Madeleine was aware of the girl's feelings. She could hardly avoid knowing, since Ingrid had begun to pass derogatory comments about her appearance and to suggest that Neil certainly found *her* more attractive. But it wasn't until Ingrid acted out her desires in a classically Freudian scenario that Neil was prepared to recognize that he had yet another problem on his plate.

Shortly after Neil and Madeleine got married, Ingrid decided that she, too, was going to have a wedding. She asked Madeleine if she could wear her wedding dress and invited all her friends, whom she dressed in old sheer curtains that had been discarded and stuffed into a bottom drawer. Then she got married—to her koala bear.

A picture of the occasion, taken by Neil, shows Ingrid with one arm flung back, her dress pulled down to reveal her shoulders and a bare leg displaying a blue garter. Her courtiers stood around her in their lovely sheers. Ingrid's happy expression was pure vamp.

These twelve-year-olds were engaging in a ritual of rehearsed sexuality, something little girls have been doing for as long as marriage has been held out as a pinnacle of female social and sexual success, and an amusing "marriage ceremony" of this sort might take place in any family. But the stepfamily (in its early stages) is often a highly sexualized environment. The adults are in a new, happy relationship and probably living through a period of heightened sexuality in their own lives. For adolescents, who are often obsessed with sex anyway, the atmosphere may be extremely stimulating. Furthermore, since children like to think of their parents as more or less asexual, evidence to the contrary may be disturbing.

This is not to suggest that adults should hide their sexual relationships from children. As Dr. Steinhauer pointed out in our interview, it is important to present children with the reality of a committed relationship, and sex is certainly a part of that reality. Obviously, though, the time adults spend alone together should be tempered by the needs of the children, especially their need not to feel diminished affection from a parent.

When Ingrid perceived that her father was the object of attention and jealousy on the part of both her mother and her stepmother, she felt she had to compete. Competition with a mother for a father might have occurred at this age in any family, but in a stepfamily it was just that much more likely to happen.

Neil and Madeleine were tuned in enough to understand what Ingrid was experiencing, and they handled the situation by clarifying the various relationships. "I had to make it very clear to her that I loved her and I would always love her, but that I loved Madeleine differently," said Neil. "I know that's the sort of conversation you often have with much younger children, but I think she wasn't as sure about that as another child might be, because she saw the conflicts in the other relationships.

"Both the children have had to deal with some difficult things. In a way, they don't have the freedom to be single, unitary human beings. They have to be a little bit different in the two houses; that's inevitable. On the other hand, they have the ongoing involvement and the love of both their parents, and of Madeleine too. The younger one was just a baby, really, when Madeleine came into his life, and he hasn't had any difficulty accepting her as a parent figure. As for me, I changed the direction of my career so I didn't have to travel as much and be away for such long periods of time. That was the only way I could see to be a successful parent—I mean a satisfied parent."

Things are still far from ideal, but lines of communication among the adults are now more open than they used to be.

Carole and Madeleine still cannot speak to each other directly, but Neil does discuss everything with Madeleine before he confers with his ex-wife. Madeleine's input is still somewhat secondary, but she does have an input.

"I can honestly say that as far as I am concerned I would choose joint parenting all over again," Neil said without hesitating. "There are many hurtful things that have happened to the children, but I feel that they were forgivable because we have both continued to care about our children so deeply and they know that, or they will when they are older. Maybe it sounds naïve, but I have always considered them absolute marvels. I am an absolutely adoring father, and I have let them know that."

Madeleine Vikar

"I think it's really important that you're asking someone like me before more and more people get into this sort of thing without really knowing what they're doing. Things have worked out okay in this family, but I wouldn't say it's really terrific. There have been rewards, but it has been very difficult—especially for me, I think."

At one time, the "difficulties" Madeleine Vikar spoke of were so overwhelming that they threatened to destroy her marriage, and after six years they had not been resolved. Her personal problems reflected complexities that are almost entirely new to the marriage experience. Madeleine and Neil and Carole—a rather unholy triangle—had no models to observe and little to guide them.

No matter how rational they think they are about their divorce, a man or woman can expect to feel a little uncomfortable with a former spouse's new mate, especially at first. It takes time to overcome old feelings of exclusivity and to accept that another person is occupying the familiar space, even if one gave it up gladly and is delighted not to be there any longer. The question of children may evoke even stronger emotions. Joint parenting has advantages in that neither parent loses the children entirely, but, in effect, both lose a little.

Women may suffer especially because society still "expects" them to be there on a full-time basis. Consciously or unconsciously, women may carry the same expectation and the prospect of someone else "usurping" their role part of the time may touch off deeply rooted atavistic fears.

Every new spouse must fashion a place in the family constellation, but where the natural parents are co-parenting their children, the stepparent may have a much harder time "fitting in."

Madeleine Vikar faced these stresses. She had difficulty acquiring status in her new family because the children's mother feared and resented her presence in the children's lives. She had transitional problems with the older stepdaughter, the adolescent who "got married" in Madeleine's wedding dress, and she felt confused about her place in the hierarchy of her husband's affections. "For a long time I continued to feel like a girl friend," she said. "His ex-wife had a lot more status than I did."

After six years of marriage, Madeleine was still jockeying for position. She had succeeded in finding a comfortable place for herself in the children's lives and in the marriage itself, but she had still not learned to accommodate Carole, the ex-wife and co-parent.

Madeleine was a vivid-looking woman of twenty-nine. Thick auburn hair curled below her shoulders, her skin was clear, and her eyes were green. She was a clothes designer, and her home reflected her artistic tastes. Lithographs and prints hung on walls that had been stripped in the latest fashion to reveal the underlying red brick. The small living room was full of textured materials: velvet corduroy on a two-seater couch and a shag rug on the floor.

The first thing she had noticed about Neil was how unselfconscious he seemed about being a single parent. Madeleine had met men who were less forthcoming about having children when they thought it would decrease their "marketability," but Neil made it clear from the first phone call that going out together would depend on being able to arrange baby-sitting.

Three months after they met, they moved in together.

Madeleine didn't anticipate any problems. She had always loved children, and Neil's little boy, Joseph, was a joy. The first time she met him he sat gazing at her for a long time, then got up and climbed into her lap. This relationship had remained good. The girl, Ingrid, wasn't unfriendly, either. The problems came a little later.

"I thought I would be a *kind* of parent," Madeleine recalled. "Neil was a little tense around the time we moved in together, and I actually saw myself as the children's ally. I certainly didn't think of myself as a 'mother.' I wasn't *old* enough to be Ingrid's mother."

The relationship to Carole would soon emerge as the major difficulty in all of their lives. "Neil presented Carole to me as a really wonderful mother and a very intelligent woman," said Madeleine, becoming visibly agitated at the mention of Carole's name. "He used all these superlatives when he talked about her. Now I realize that he was trying hard to be conscientious and fair and not be one of those divorced people who badmouth their ex, but I really think he went overboard. I felt a little bit competitive with her. I guess I was afraid I wouldn't measure up."

The day she met Carole, Madeleine had the distinct impression she was being "presented" to the person who still occupied centre stage in her husband's life. "It was like walking into a deep freeze. He said, 'Carole, I'd like you to meet Madeleine,' and she sort of crinkled up her eyes and examined me and said nothing. I thought maybe she had a headache or something, but they were still getting invited to the same parties, and soon after that we saw her again. This time Neil actually marched up to her and introduced me again, because she hadn't really acknowledged me the first time, but it was clumsy because she was in the middle of a conversation with someone else and she just sort of nodded and turned away.

"She loomed so large to me. She was older and more educated, and I had heard about how beautiful she was and how intelligent and what a wonderful mother. I didn't know where to put myself or who I was supposed to be. Was I central to Neil's life or not? I felt that she played too large a role in our life and yet I understood that that was the child-care arrangement.''

Madeleine had pinpointed some of the difficult problems remarried couples with co-parenting relationships must resolve. Where does the new spouse fit in? What role does the ex-spouse play in the new family? To what extent can the families be seen as separate?

"It soon got to be unbearable." Madeleine's white skin was flushed with remembered anger. "He would interrupt anything to speak to her, including making love to me. If I answered the telephone, she would simply ask for him. He was afraid of her, afraid of losing his kids.

"I saw no future for myself with him, and one day I moved out."

During this separation Neil and Madeleine spent hours talking about whether it was possible to improve relations. Madeleine wanted Neil to "denounce" his ex-wife, but he refused. He knew his future as a co-parent depended on maintaining good terms. At the same time, they both thought Carole was being unfair in refusing to acknowledge Madeleine's right to be a factor in the children's lives. They decided to ask if she would consent to see a counsellor with them. To their surprise, she agreed, and Madeleine moved back into Neil's home.

The counselling was not a success. Remarriage with joint parenting is so new that professionals are not always in tune with what makes these families different from the troubled nuclear families they meet. And, of course, joint parenting is not universally accepted by the counselling community. The Vikars hit upon someone who was unable to channel their confusion, anger, and fear, or help them in any way. The one session they all attended was "a disaster" according to Madeleine.

Madeleine stayed in the marriage, having decided to try a new strategy. She desperately needed to prove to her husband that she, too, was a good mother. She convinced herself that Carole was cold and intellectual in her dealings with the children and that they were starved for physical mothering. Her feeling for the children was real enough—fortunately, that *had* developed in this steprelationship—but when she held little Joseph in her lap and hugged Ingrid, thoughts of how Carole might react to hearing how wonderfully affectionate she was did occasionally dance gleefully in her head.

Carole, of course, remained unmoved and disdainful, but curiously, Neil's and Madeleine's wedding did bring about a change. Madeleine was reassured of Neil's commitment to her and became secure enough to allow that she might have exaggerated Carole's "power." Carole was forced by the marriage to take Madeleine more seriously. It seemed more obvious that Madeleine might be around for a very long time—for the rest of the children's lives, in fact. Carole began to accept that Neil needed to discuss the children with his new wife and that Madeleine's input did have some value.

Madeleine, however, continued to feel like "a second-class person." Carole now said "hello" on the phone, but she still fumed when Madeleine attended Meet the Teacher nights at the children's school. Their lives had improved, no doubt; but Madeleine, Carole, and Neil had not yet overcome the thorny human problems of joint parenting and remarriage. Of all five members in this binuclear family, Madeleine remained the least integrated.

Carole Vikar

The surprising thing about Carole Vikar was her appearance. Madeleine had portrayed her as a magnificently beautiful woman, but Carole, though attractive, was not at all beautiful by conventional standards. At thirty-eight, her figure was broadening noticeably.

Carole was a woman of strong loyalties and firm commitments, and in another age her marriage to Neil might have survived. Divorce as a solution to their problems was something that was simply "in the air," she said, and was perhaps the easiest way out. Carole thought it was Neil who had first suggested a separation, while Neil was sure it had been her. At some level of consciousness, neither was willing to take responsibility for having initiated the rupture.

Carole came from a family that stressed unity, a family of strong, believing Christians who promoted all the traditions and values that accompanied that way of life. They were angry when Carole announced that her marriage was over; from the beginning they had been wary about the prospects of a marriage contracted so young, and now there were unmistakable intimations of "I told you so."

Carole laughed to remember her initial fantasies of what joint custody might amount to. She had imagined a smooth continuation of parenthood with shared activities and warm feelings. "I had an image of spending a lot of time with Neil, planning for the kids, and maybe even doing things together with the kids. I thought we could both be at birthday parties and events like that, and I was truly surprised when this turned out to be so uncomfortable we only did it once. I thought we would have two houses that functioned pretty well the same way, since we knew each other so well, and that we'd both be free to drop in on each other."

It took a while to accept the reality of the unexpected discomfort and to set up more formal arrangements, but once they did, both Carole and Neil thought things were working well. They decided that birthday parties would alternate between the parental houses. They set up a regular time to talk together—every Monday evening—while leaving the door open for further conversation when necessary. And they came to an easy verbal agreement about time-sharing and money. Each parent was responsible for whatever expenditures were necessary during the time the children were with him or her, but not on a fifty-fifty basis. "When we first separated, our negotiations took into account the fact that his earning power was greater than mine and would likely remain so, so he chipped in extra for things like summer camps," said Carole. "This flexibility has been a crucial factor in our ability to co-parent. Really, money has never been a divisive issue between us."

In that respect, Neil and Carole were the exception rather than the rule. Their conscious decision not to use money as a weapon to establish a power base or to manipulate the children was a further indication of the maturity of mind and the self-control that made joint custody an option for this couple in the first place. There was, however, one area where their rationality and control broke down. Madeleine's appearance on the scene was not something Carole had actually foreseen, although she certainly might have. "I had thought about the possibility abstractly, but I hadn't really anticipated it," she said slowly.

Madeleine's presence forced Carole to make changes she hadn't planned on. Her access to Neil had been relatively free, but Madeleine was jealously protective of her new household and resented Carole's "role" there. Carole was the ghost from her husband's past who insisted on materializing on the telephone, at the front door, and in her husband's conversation. Madeleine wanted to delineate the boundaries of her new family in the familiar traditional ways and shove the ghost back into the attic where she thought it belonged. But ghosts in remarriage families don't inhabit attics, and in co-parenting situations they frequently *do* talk on telephones and walk in front doors. They are alive and very well and the children actually live with them half the time. They must be accommodated or they will spread tentacles into every nook and cranny, as ghosts are wont to do.

If Madeleine saw Carole as an intruder, her feelings were more than reciprocated. Carole thought Madeleine threatened the co-parenting arrangement. She feared the influence of this unknown woman on the children and on Neil as well. What if Neil began to make major parenting decisions with Madeleine? What would happen to her? To the children?

"I was very threatened," Carole said, practically whispering. "I'm a person who likes to be in control of my children's lives, not in the sense of exercising force but of knowing where they are going and what is happening in their lives. Madeleine was an unknown to me. I didn't know what she would do, and I was threatened, because it was clear that she didn't want me around in any shape or form.

"I felt afraid of losing the children's affection. It wasn't rational, because in my head I knew that the more people they cared for the better it was for them, but in another way I was afraid that they might love her more than they loved me or even that they might reject me. I thought that she might turn them against me or something like that. She never did try that—to her credit. It was just my fantasy.

"I thought I might have to face a double loss. I was already coping with having lost them fifty percent of the time. I had been a full-time mother, and when these kids who I had nurtured one hundred percent of the time were suddenly living somewhere else I found that hard, very hard. I talked it out with the help of friends who were very supportive. One of the things that calmed me was the fact that I knew Neil so well, and I knew that whatever he did at his house wouldn't be that different from what I did at my house. But when another woman moved into his life and into my children's lives, this fear of being separated from my children was activated again. It became very important to me to keep the co-parenting just between us so that she would know her place and Neil would know her place and the children would know her place."

Carole had just expressed the human reality of remarriage with co-parenting in a few concise sentences. There are indeed two experiences of loss involved: one at the time of separation from the children (in sole custody, only one parent experiences loss; in joint custody, both do, to a lesser degree) and another when a remarriage takes place. This is the identical fear and sense of loss that children experience when their parents separate and then when one parent remarries. The child's dread is that a new stepfather, for example, will come between him and his natural parents by demanding too much of his mother's time or by diminishing or by trying to replace his real, absent father. Carole, experiencing precisely the same threat, feared that her husband's new wife would come between her and her children by appropriating the time Neil devoted to their mutual discussions about the children, or by trying to usurp her position in her children's lives.

For a while they were at an impasse, Carole insisting that the children were none of Madeleine's business and Neil insisting that they were, since she was, in fact, "parenting" them half the time. Eventually they reached a truce. Neil discussed family affairs with Madeleine first, then took their joint conclusions to Carole for further discussion. Carole and he would reach an agreement. Their priority as co-parents was maintained, though Madeleine had a say, of sorts. This suited Carole and Neil well, Madeleine less so.

Carole and Neil were obliged to accommodate Madeleine's fears. "Now our conversation is focused only on the children, and it's important to keep it that way," said Carole. "Sometimes I ask how his mother is, or his sister, and he answers politely, but we have to be cautious. This is too bad, in a way, because I really am curious about his family; I always liked them very much. But in another way it makes the joint parenting easier."

When Neil and Madeleine married, Carole found it easier to accept Madeleine's presence. Sometimes she has trouble dealing with the children's behaviour when she sees unwelcome signs of Madeleine's influence, but then her head tells her that all children are exposed to hundreds of influences outside their homes and that they have to digest these influences for themselves. Her role is to try to ensure that the children come out of childhood as whole people, as "good, solid people." But the head does not always hold sway over the heart, and sometimes Carole aches to think of what she, and they, have lost.

As a result of living with three parents in two households, Carole thinks, her children have become closer to each other. Their sibling relationship is, after all, the one constant in their lives. When they move from one home to the other, they move together, and Carole is willing to concede that they probably know each other better than they are known by either of their parents. One difficulty has been to keep them from being overindulged. "Sometimes they seem to think I am entirely at their disposal when they're with me, and I've had to make it very clear that normal life goes on and that I do continue to see friends and go out from time to time. This is the trap, I think. In my house and in Neil's house, our lives do tend to revolve around them because they are only here half the time. Neil and I try not to compete with each other for their affection. We discuss this a lot.

"After all these years, there is still a certain tension in the structure of our lives. When they are leaving, I hate to see them go and I show my anxiety in a number of ways. I ask if they are sure they have this or that and I try to plan carefully for the period they will not be with me. After they leave I have an emptiness inside for a while, but then I'm fine, and at this point I truly enjoy the time off.

"I don't really know if they would have been happier if Neil and I had remained together unhappily. They are terrific kids, so this must be working for them. I really believe, in retrospect, that it has been a lot harder for the adults than for the children. After all, they have both their parents and an enormous amount of love.

"Not too long ago we were all watching a program on divorce where there were children who didn't see one parent, or only rarely. Ingrid turned to Joseph and said, 'I'm glad we don't have that.' In that tiny moment I felt reassured that we had done the right thing. It's been hard, it's still hard, but as far as they are concerned, I have no regrets."

The conventional wisdom about joint parenting is that it's terrific for the parents and hard on the children, but Carole Vikar came closer to the truth when she observed that the opposite is likely to be the case. Joint parenting is very hard for the parents and even harder when one or both of them remarries. It requires individuals who are able to separate their previous sexual and social relationship from their present parenting role and devote themselves to their children's well-being, in a way that not all parents do, whether they are divorced or otherwise. In other words, co-parenting takes a special kind of person.

In the Vikar family, the children seemed reasonably adjusted, by everyone's account, and happily aware that they have not had to lose a parent. The adults had the problems. Neil was caught in the middle, determined not to be disloyal either to his ex-wife, whom he continued to respect and upon whom he depended for the continuation of the joint parenting experience, or to his new wife. Madeleine came into the marriage not understanding the nature of this family with its open boundaries and tried to close things off in traditional ways. This effort was doomed to fail, because her husband's role as a parent depended on the boundaries remaining open. Carole was threatened by the presence of another woman in her children's lives. She either did not understand the nature of the remarriage family or did not want to.

What was missing in the relationships of all these people was a sense of trust. Carole needed to know she could trust Madeleine not to interfere with her parental rights and not to influence the children against her. Madeleine needed to know that her husband was emotionally separated from his first wife and that she had a right to be in the family and to play a role in the children's lives. Neil knew that Carole would not badmouth him to the children, but he needed to know that she would extend this commitment to his wife.

Much of what they did was instinctively right. Carole and Neil structured their relationship so that it focused on the children only. This was an important factor in helping Madeleine feel more secure; it also helped Carole and Neil limit their contact. Part of the necessary separation of roles after divorce can be accomplished just this way—fixed times for conversation about the children and separate lives as far as possible. Joint birthday parties for children are probably not a good idea unless everyone is absolutely comfortable with everyone else. And people should not feel free to walk in on their ex-spouses. People, like animals, are territorial, and new wives (and husbands) may feel their privacy is being intruded upon more than is necessary under the circumstances.

The Vikars were also on the right track when they sought counselling for their troubles. They might have pursued that option and found someone who was more sympathetic to the difficulties of a remarriage with joint parenting. They needed help in delineating the roles each adult would play and in setting up rules that would accommodate tolerance levels. "The remarriage family needs to understand that the former spouse has parental rights and responsibilities and that to enact these usually requires some continuing relationship between the former spouses. The focus must always be on the task of parenting," wrote Kenneth Walker and Lillian Messinger in their article "Remarriage after Divorce." In remarriage with joint-custody arrangements, this sort of relationship is even more necessary.

As for joint custody itself, the last word might be left to Judith Wallerstein's and Joan Berlin Kelly's *Surviving the Breakup*. Their findings pointed clearly to "the desirability of the child's continuing relationship with both parents during the post divorce years in an arrangement which enables each parent to be responsible for and genuinely concerned with the well-being of the children." They concluded that "for those parents who are able to reach agreement on child-related matters and are willing to give the needs of the children priority and a significant role in their decision making, regarding how and where the children reside, joint custody may provide the legal structure of choice." The authors estimated that approximately 25 percent of the divorcing couples in their study would have qualified as joint parents. They clarified, as well, that in their view physical custody does not necessitate a precise apportioning of the child's life. It is rather an understanding that two committed parents, in separate homes, care for their youngsters in a postdivorce atmosphere of civilized, respectful exchange.

Wallerstein and Kelly were deeply disturbed by the high incidence of depression in sole-custody families; indeed, five years after the actual separation, the incidence of depression was higher than eighteen months after the separation, indicating ongoing problems well after the acute response to the breakup had subsided or disappeared. They wrote: "The chronic and economic overload was frequently intolerable for the custodial parent and the cumulative effect on the children was all too visible in their unhappiness and depression . . . Our findings point to the undesirability of routinely designating one parent as 'the psychological parent' and of lodging sole legal and physical custody in that one parent. Such an arrangement has been interpreted by the courts to presume that the child does not have two psychological parents. This finding can be devastating to the child and parent when both parents are indeed committed to a continuing relationship with their children."

In conclusion, they firmly repudiated the findings of their esteemed colleagues, the authors of *Beyond the Best Interests of the Child*. Wrote Wallerstein and Kelly, ''Our findings regarding the centrality of both parents to the psychological health of children and adolescents all lead us to hold that, where possible, divorcing parents should be encouraged and helped to shape post divorce arrangements which permit and foster continuity in the children's relations with both parents.''

SUGGESTIONS

1. Avoid court custody battles like the plague. Mediation is always a better alternative.

2. Recognize that joint custody is now an option in most places. It can be fifty-fifty time sharing, sixty-forty, or whatever. The principle is continued, involved parenting from both natural parents.

3. Be prepared for the fact that marriage where there is joint custody of children may open a Pandora's box of unexpected emotional reactions. However, if trust can be established, joint custody is likely worth the effort.

4. If you think you cannot handle regular contact with an ex-spouse (yours or your new partner's) a marriage that has joint custody already built into it may not be for you. Discuss before, not after.

5. When there is joint custody and one ex-spouse remarries, the other does not have a lot of choice in the matter. It is difficult but important to recognize that the new partner does have a role to play in your children's lives. To accept this is to strengthen the shared parenting relationship. Get help if you have to.

CHAPTER SIX

Accepting Realities: A Portrait of an Integrated Stepfamily

THE GARDNER-GANS family is a success—at least for the moment. No one can predict the future of relationships in the 1980s, but there seems to be enough oil in the machinery to keep things running smoothly. The "oil" in their case means a willingness to confront problems that are endemic to blended families.

Some areas of their collective life run more smoothly than others. Not all four children seem equally happy, for example, but Peter and Cynthia both feel that what they have accomplished has been distinctly worthwhile. In spite of a few, perhaps inevitable mistakes, they have succeeded in negotiating their way through eight years of reconstituted family life and that in itself is no mean achievement.

Peter Gardner, Cynthia Gans, and their four adolescent children—Jill Gardner, Adam Gardner, Shauna Gans, and Brian Gans—live in a substantial town house on a fashionable street in west-end Montreal. Money is not a problem, instantly eliminating one source of potential conflict. Peter is a highly paid chemist in private industry. Cynthia is a less-well-paid free-lance radio writer, but her earnings are subsidized with child-support payments from her former husband and she has never felt needy. Long ago, Peter and Cynthia agreed to pay household expenses on a proportional basis, according to income, and that has worked well.

Peter Gardner

Peter Gardner was forty-six but looked ten years younger. He seemed to have a lot of energy—certainly an advantage when trying to create a new family with two sets of children.

If he was successful as a stepfather, Peter said, it was because he had directed huge amounts of this energy into developing a relationship with Cynthia's children; even, he admitted, at the expense of his own offspring. He also believed that the combination of theoretical analysis and trial-and-error experiment he used in his professional work had been useful in helping him cope with stepfamily life. But most important, perhaps, he and Cynthia had just assumed from the beginning that their relationship within the family was paramount. When they began to live together they simply told both sets of children that the new "family" was a reality. "We were very direct. We had a family meeting and we said, 'This is going to last, and you'll all have to try to get used to it.' Period."

How wise was that? one may wonder. Maybe it was a little insensitive, Peter acknowledged. He said he now had some regrets. But the technique had worked, and no one in the family was complaining about that.

Peter Gardner's ability to cope effectively with the confusion, the carried-over pain, and the initial artificiality of the stepfamily extended back into his own childhood. He was born in England in 1936, and, in a class-ridden society, his family uniquely bridged the classes. His father was a clerk in government service, just like his father before him. This side of the family spoke in quiet tones and had pretensions to culture. Peter's mother, on the other hand, came from a large, boisterous, coal-mining clan in the north of the country and had started her working career as a maid in someone else's home. This "mixed marriage" was, on the whole, more outrageous in the eyes of the neighbourhood than a religious mix from the same social class might have been.

Peter's parents didn't much mind what others said, and they managed to carve out a place for themselves in the middle from which they dutifully visited their relatives on both sides. His father's side was snobbish, with all the usual aspirations of the middle class. They liked Peter's mother personally, but patronized her, calling her "little Nell." They also criticized young Peter for his "rough" accent. Accent, of course, was the all-important indicator of social class.

His father's family never talked about anything "central," according to Peter. They murmured niceties and avoided confrontation. But Peter's mother's relatives were quite the opposite. They were "tempestuous, active, noisy, vulgar, and downtrodden." They had few pretensions and they loved to argue. They too berated Peter for his accent. They thought it was too snobby and they thought he was too reserved.

"These were totally different worlds for a child to grow up in, and I was able to recognize quite early that people one cared about might be very different from one another," said Peter as we talked quietly in the upstairs study of his home. This was an important insight for a man whose future would include remarriage and stepparenting.

Peter was the first person on either side of his family ever to attend a university, and there he became even more aware of the social and cultural split between the "two nations," as Disraeli had described the English class system in 1845. Later in life he would opt for the open emotionality of his working-class relatives, but then he felt only deep anger at the system of class snobbery that divided Britain.

As a result of his background, Peter was conditioned to the role of social outsider, which meant that when he eventually established a remarriage family, with no signposts for guidance and no traditions to fall back on, he was not overwhelmed. He had intimate knowledge of at least two social conventions from his own personal history; and he was smart enough to guess that if there were two there might just be room for a third.

During his twenties, Peter married a young woman he had

met at university. Beth's father was also a clerk, and the families looked similar in other ways. In other words, Peter was doing what might have been expected of him—an acceptable marriage to be followed by a tranquil career as a schoolteacher in a tranquil English town. Beth had also trained as a teacher, and together they looked like the usual aspiring middle-class couple.

But Peter's unorthodox background soon left him feeling bored with the inherent smugness built into the very fabric of this comfortable life, with its prejudices about the way the world was and ought to be. He began to watch the overseas teaching ads in the London *Times* and *The Manchester Guardian*. Before long, he and Beth were en route for a year in New Zealand.

As Gail Sheehy has pointed out in her book *Passages*, the twenties are often a time when we believe, or more likely *want* to believe, that we are self-governing adults making our own decisions and planning our futures. But what we may really be doing is living out our internalized identification with our parents. We cannot know just how deeply we are influenced by the unconscious pull of the past, and in any case this is usually not our main concern in our twenties. The consciously important task at this age is to determine what place we will occupy in the world out there—in a career, in a love relationship, or both.

Just how widely Sheehy's theories can be generalized may be debatable, but they did apply to what was happening to Peter Gardner as a recent university graduate, as a teacher in the local high school, and as a young husband. He was living according to his parents' expectations, even if they had never actually been verbalized. His parents had found a place between their own primary families. Peter had unconsciously chosen a wife and a career that would preserve that middle-ground position.

Peter's and Beth's marriage was a happy one, in part because Beth was fairly conventional and either agreed with or was willing to go along with her husband's shifting sense of direction. Peter soon emerged as the dominant decision-making partner. They had both been conditioned that way.

Beth expected to have children eventually and to stop work when that happened, so she was glad to go with Peter to New Zealand, even though it meant giving up her job.

By the end of their year away Peter had had another job offer, this time from Canada. He and Beth travelled to Montreal, liked it, and stayed for good. Peter was discovering that outside of Britain, his man-in-the-middle, outsider feelings were less of a problem. He made other changes, too. He left teaching and took a job in private industry. And once they had broken through the family-inspired mold of their early twenties, they both felt ready to start a family. Jill was born in 1967 and Adam in 1970.

In 1974, Beth died tragically of cancer. She was ill for only a few months, so the sequence of traumatic events was spread over a relatively short period of time; but the horror of it and the speed meant that no one had a chance to absorb the reality of her physical deterioration and then her death. Peter carried on, refusing to have help either before or after her death. He looked after Beth and the children and the house and went to his job every day. At the end of the school year he took the children to England for the summer to recover by staying with their relatives.

Although Peter and Beth had almost never argued, Peter hinted gently that in retrospect their marriage might not have lasted. During the last years before her illness, he was gaining ground in performance and confidence, he said, while Beth seemed to be growing less confident. "Who is to say where that would have led us?" he mused. And rightly so, because the working woman who turns to full-time mothering may be a prime candidate for depression. No matter how much she adores her children, her horizons in the "real" world outside her home have shrunk if not closed altogether, while her husband's continue to expand.

After the summer visit to England, Peter did something that might have ended catastrophically. He leaped into a new relationship with Cynthia and has been there ever since, although they have never married. (Cynthia has already had two divorces and thinks it a point of decency not to go through the formalities of marriage a third time.) But there were several interesting differences to the Peter-Cynthia merger that prevented it from going the way of the usual rebound disaster. For one thing, the two couples had been friends and knew each other's children. Second, and most important, Peter did not hook up with Cynthia primarily for practical, housekeeping reasons, or primarily to escape loneliness. The need to maintain a family environment for his kids played a role—he wasn't going to deny that—but he and Cynthia would have wanted to be together in spite of their children, and they had the good sense to make that clear. This was the first step they took as a couple, and it set the new family off to a positive start.

"When Cynthia and I came together I really wasn't thinking about all the things I might have been thinking about, like needing a mother for my children and stepparenting," said Peter. "Falling in love when you're thirty-seven is no different from falling in love when you're seventeen, thank God. When I think back now, it was passionate and precipitate and risky. I mean, I gave up my home! That was ludicrous, and no one in their right mind would have done it!"

He laughed, relishing this romantic, swashbuckling self-image. But he had also been lonely—another potentially dangerous reason for remarrying. "Being alone doesn't suit me," he said. "I suppose it is a compliment to my first marriage that I was used to exchange."

In reality either factor could have ruined the new relationship. Rushing into a love affair without thinking much about the effect it might have on the children, and doing it in part out of loneliness—possibly the worst reason of all. But the depth of their feelings for each other combined with a strong sexual attraction persuaded Peter to bet high stakes on the outcome. And once together, Peter and Cynthia did not hide their feelings for each other. They hugged and kissed in front of their children, who apparently did not mind, although they certainly might have. One of them said the visible affection between Peter and Cynthia made her feel secure. She felt that as long as they were so involved with each other, the new family would remain intact.

Peter was surprised to discover that although his marriage

to Beth had been happy and comfortable, he felt an undeniable sense of personal renewal after she died. At first he felt perplexed and guilty, and it took a while to figure things out. "When you've gone through the death of someone very close to you a very strange thing happens," he mused. "Amidst the pain there is a little something that comes creeping under the nail. It's a sense of triumph—that you're alive. In my case there was also a sense that my life took on another hue. I could never have just 'carried on.' I felt there had to be a new life now.

"Both my grandmothers had died when I was a child, and I saw how my grandfathers handled it. One grandfather did not remarry and he seemed to dry up. His sister moved in with him to help look after the children, and the two of them spent the rest of their lives tearing pieces off each other. The other grandfather had had a very happy life with his wife, and after she died he remarried fairly quickly and continued to be a juicy human being. I identified more with him. To remarry was my renewal, my statement that I had survived."

Peter felt an intense drive to consolidate his future and affirm the fact that he lived even though the person closest to him had died. But he also did not allow himself or his children time to grieve. The prospect of that great sadness alarmed him. He was afraid he would not be able to cope, that he might lose control.

After Beth died in February, Peter and Cynthia drew together in friendship. Cynthia's husband had only recently left her, and both of them were shocked and bereaved. In June, Peter took the children to England, promising to write, but he didn't and she didn't. In September, their friendship shifted in focus. They went on picnics with their children; they went to bed for the first time and liked each other sexually. Impulsively they decided to live together. In October, Peter sold his house and moved his children and all his worldly possessions into Cynthia's larger house.

This was a crucial transition as far as the children's lives were concerned, and the place so many couples with the best intentions and the highest hopes flounder. How did Peter handle his children? Well, he did something typically risky.

For the first while, he paid less attention to them than he did to Cynthia and to Cynthia's children.

This was an intuitive move that worked well in the short term (though there may still be a price to pay), but if anything in the brief history of his new family bothers him, this is it. He knew his children suffered from his choice of priorities, yet he also knew his decision had promoted family bonding.

"I shifted all my energy into creating a relationship with Cynthia and her kids," he acknowledged. "I know I withdrew it from my job; I effectively gave up a promotion I had been working towards. I know a lot of that energy might have gone to my own children, but I did what I did quite consciously. My priorities at the time were first Cynthia and then her children.

"Cynthia tells people that I am a difficult person to live with, but I think she is difficult to live with. That is not a negative statement, because I think that real people are always difficult to live with. Cynthia and I are both independent-minded and we have our own viewpoints that are quite well established at our age. I had to convince her that it was worth learning to live with me.

"Perhaps it was wrong to concentrate next on my relationship with her children, and sometimes I think now that it was, but I did it on instinct. Cynthia is quite obsessed with her children, like any decent mother, I guess, and therefore my relationship with those children was almost as important as my relationship with her. Had I not got on with them, her ability to absorb my varied and unruly habits would have been less. We have developed an elasticity in our relationship because we are satisfactory to each other in a wide-ranging way, and one of the ways I had to be satisfactory was in my relationship to her children."

But Peter's own children were only seven and four at the time, and they had been through their own hell. They had lost their mother; they had moved to a new house and into a new family; and they now had a stepmother and two stepsiblings whose personal style was quite different from theirs. Cynthia's children were like Cynthia, direct and inclined to speak their minds at all times. Jill and Adam reflected the more reserved ambience of their previous home. Most important, however, they had, in a sense, lost their father as well.

Only years after the fact did Peter become aware of this. "My children had twelve months, from October to October, in which every possible disaster that a child might scream about in the night happened. I was still around, that's true, but in a totally new guise. I was now the 'father' of four children, not two. I was around with someone who was not their mother. To a certain extent even I had been lost to them.

"In a way they had nothing to hang onto. I was not I. And both of them now had a sibling who was older than they were, which had a devastating effect. Jill had been the oldest child and she had already begun to assume the role of woman of the house. Then she found herself not first woman but third, after Cynthia and her daughter Shauna. Looking back, I might say that they needed far more from me than I gave, but only time will tell, really, if they were scarred irreparably by those events. I was also a strong believer that children are people in their own terms who, in the end, I wasn't responsible for. That may sound terrible, and I don't mean that I wasn't responsible for their well-being or any of those things, but that the person a child becomes also has a lot to do with him or her and with the hundreds of other environments they move in. Had I kept them alone with me after their mother died and created a tiny enclosed support system that immersed the three of us in love, it would have been easier for them, I'm sure, but worse in the long run for Jill, who would have assumed inappropriate domestic responsibilities and maybe a not-so-healthy kind of companion relationship to me. My son would have become quite dependent, I think. Here he has been forced into his own resources, and that may be the making of him. Forget the fact that Cynthia and I come from different backgrounds and that all the children are not our children. I see that as less important than the reality of our living an experimental life together. The fact that they have had a supportive home, a rich, warm, interesting, and challenging home, may turn out to be the cornerstone of their lives. But none of this would have been possible if Cynthia and I hadn't been willing to risk a lot and if I had not been prepared to commit that massive energy to creating a good relationship with her and her children.''

How much of what Peter said was mere rationalization and a belated attempt to justify rather insensitive treatment of his own children? The realization that he had neglected them for a while clearly pained him. But eight years later this family was intact, functioning well, and all of its members were reasonably happy. That was a feat in any family with four teenagers.

Peter and Cynthia were right to focus their attention on each other at first, for without that strong base nothing else would have been possible. Even angry children are more likely to accept a remarriage if they understand that any strategy they may be hatching to break it up will fail. And if the new stepparent reinforces his or her commitment to the new family by making an obvious effort to get to know the kids and to understand them as individuals, they will be more likely to respond positively.

Peter believed his children felt secure in his love, for they had always been a close family. They may have received less attention than they needed during the critical first months of the stepfamily, but he was sure they would never have questioned the bond that linked them to him and him to them. That special bond does not exist between stepparent and stepchild, of course, and some believable relationship must be forced between people who may barely know each other. Peter was convinced he had to win the confidence of his stepchildren to make the blended family work. ''It may sound brutal,'' he explained a little apologetically, ''but I already *had* the affection of my own children. In any case, this stage only lasted a few months. When we had established some sort of base, I was able to give equal attention to my children.''

It was also true that unlike a remarriage following divorce, Peter's children had nowhere else to go. They couldn't manipulate the stepfamily by threatening to leave and live with Mommy, for example, and that may also have influenced Peter during the initial adjustment period. He didn't really have to walk on eggs the way divorced parents sometimes feel compelled to. He felt stronger and better able to be firm.

In this regard, remarriage after a family death may be easier than after divorce. The widowed parent is free to act confidently without having to worry about possible sabotage or manipulation from an angry ex-spouse.

Peter and Cynthia think and talk a lot about their own relationship, including the way they connect with each other's children; and the willingness to acknowledge realities of blended family life has swept away some of the taboos that often cause problems. Take the issue of "love"—that overloaded and misused word. More conventionally-minded adults often approach their mate's children expecting to "love" them, but one of the realities of remarriage is that people live with and parent children whom they cannot possibly love in any real way, at least at first. How can one "love" a person one scarcely knows? The same is true for children. They cannot produce instant love any faster than adults.

Women are particularly subject to this fantasy, like Carla Renzetti, or Margaret, who was preparing to put her stepson into foster care because he could not conform to her expectations. Or it is imposed upon them, as in the case of Sandra, the young woman we met in Chapter Two who didn't want to be a stepmother at all. Raised to be the family caretakers, many women enter remarriages believing that their main task on this earth is to make the new unit work in exactly the same way the nuclear family works. They make impossible emotional demands on themselves that are not necessarily appreciated by members of the family who may prefer a little more distance in their relationships. They expect to love a needy child who has suffered a family breakup or a death—and they expect to be loved in return. Immediately. And when real emotions do not hop, skip, and jump into line, they feel guilty and resentful.

What one *can* expect to find in a successful stepfamily is mutual respect and a friendship that may flower with time and become genuine love; but even if love doesn't bloom, real friendship is, in itself, no mean achievement. However, respect and at least the beginnings of trust are essential ingredients if the stepfamily is going to function at all.

"Of course there are different levels of feeling in a stepfamily," said Peter, lowering his voice an energy decibel, "but this is only dangerous when it dominates, or worse, if one pretends it isn't there. The reason there's a difference comes from something that is not at all trivial. I have spent a lot of time on my relationship with Shauna and Brian and I still do, but when it comes to feeling pain about my four children, feeling concern, or feeling fear for them, I honestly think I feel it for my own children long before I feel it for the others. But let me add something crucial. If I don't feel it immediately, I will simulate it. I think that's very important, as long as you don't go too far.

"It's positively dangerous to pretend that there isn't a different intensity of feeling for your own children; but, having said that, I do try to treat them all the same at the level of behaviour. That doesn't mean the feeling level never shows, because it does occasionally. If it does, I try not to worry about it much."

Peter has touched on three important points. *One*: It is perfectly natural to feel closer to one's own children than to stepchildren. *Two*: At the level of behaviour, it is important to treat children fairly and without overt prejudice in favour of one's own. *Three*: If the natural bias does sometimes emerge, it's better not to worry about it excessively. Three of the four Gardner-Gans children told me they were favoured on occasion by their natural parent, and they added that they thought this was human nature. What the children did worry about was repeated and deliberate favouritism when they thought it occurred—usually from Cynthia.

Were these children exceptional in their sophisticated acceptance of a difficult reality? Yes; but only because not many stepparents are willing to be as open about anything as touchy as favouritism in the family. Even in nuclear families, children are not necessarily loved equally. Personality differences, sex differences, natural affinities—the list of what makes one child more attractive to a given parent is as endless as what attracts us to one person and not another. The same rules of behaviour apply in successful nuclear families where wise parents do not let on if they feel differently about their children. In fact, it is even less acceptable to acknowledge such differences in the nuclear family than in the stepfamily, where, at least in principle, such distinctions may be more easily understood.

Favouritism in the stepfamily is always a prickly issue, and the temptation to line up one family against the other is always present. The Renzettis, for example, had formed two camps, and when last heard from, Carla and Anthony were planning to parent only their own children—a dubious proposition. Cynthia and Peter felt the same pull, and they tended to watch each other like hawks for real or imagined bias in behaviour. They understood intellectually that they could not feel equally towards each other's children; but woe to the person who actually acted on that bias. When they fought, this is what they fought about. It was an ongoing struggle to make sure that their own kids were not losing out in the remarriage deal.

"We do tend to overlook our own children's actions," admitted Peter. "Cynthia thinks she doesn't, but she does. I guess what makes me confident about our relationship is the fact that we really don't let things go by. We may lock horns more often than people who don't care to analyze things as closely as we do, but I feel very strongly that what we do is good. I think my feelings about this come from Beth's death. If someone dies, they are withdrawn from you forever and you can't ever make it up to them. I know that sounds trite, but it's true. Everything is frozen, and all you can do is think that you didn't recognize and deal with things when they came up, the little things that are inherent in everyday life. This has made me feel that each day is important. Cynthia and I make mistakes all the time, but we talk about them. We both have a strong sense of people and their attitudes and their relationships, and this has enabled us to articulate the problems we've had in bringing these two families together and then do something about them. Cynthia challenges me in a way no one ever dared to do before. She calls me on my arrogance, if that's what she thinks, or my intolerance. Sometimes her searchlight makes me uncomfortable; but it's good, really. I do the same, and it keeps our relationship vital and pretty honest."

The particular dynamics of Cynthia and Peter in concert aren't going to work for everyone, but their policy of deliberately confronting difficulty has prevented small sores from festering. Because they talk so much about everything, they've been able to understand things a little better than some. Problems get sorted out and realities, though unpalatable, are seen for what they are. Anger is more readily diffused. It doesn't get hoarded for a future nuclear explosion.

Another reality of their family, and of the stepfamily in general, is that relationships are just a little more fragile. More delicacy is required because the steprelationship is not rooted in quite the same way. A child may speak quite rudely to his own parent, but he'll be a lot more careful with a stepparent whom he likes and respects because the steprelationship is, quite simply, not as resilient. For the same reasons, a sensitive stepparent will also tread lightly, at least at first. The most common complaint I heard from antagonistic stepchildren was that their parent's new spouse had bulldozed his or her way into the family and begun "acting like a parent." This outraged the children, who had a strong sense of what was appropriate behaviour for people in a new relationship.

"My daughter Jill is much more careful with Cynthia than she is with me," Peter confirmed. "She has twigged to the fact that her return from that relationship depends on being a little more careful, and she is working harder at it. Adam, who is only twelve, doesn't understand this yet, and he has the most problems of all the children. But this works all ways. I can be much rougher with my own children than I can with Shauna and Brian. My own kids won't like it if I'm insensitive with them, but I will not get the kind of absolute, hard rejection that I'd get from the other two. We all have much thinner boundaries when dealing with the opposite parent or child. And the children know it, too. There's just that much more give in the natural parent-child relationship."

The remarriage family may be threatened from outside as well as inside, and the most dangerous threat of all may come from a bitter ex-spouse. Children may be upset about the new marriage and struggling with conflicts of loyalty. Under these trying emotional circumstances, a former mate can wreak havoc in the new family.

When Cynthia's ex-husband realized he had lost control of his children's lives, he became enraged. Peter and Cynthia felt their relationship was threatened and decided on a risky course. It was brutal and it might have backfired on them. They cut her ex out of their lives. They did not, however, cut the father off from his children. Had they played that game (no matter how much they might have been tempted) they almost certainly would have lost their gamble. The children would have resented them profoundly and possibly retaliated in one way or another.

Still, this was a dangerous and certainly questionable action. As Judith Greif's research clearly demonstrated, fathers who are cut out often withdraw as parents, with devastating effects on their children. Indeed, there was strong evidence in the Gardner-Gans family that this event, which happened at the beginning of the marriage, was beginning to bear bitter fruit many years later and might eventually be at the root of future problems.

Sometimes, of course, remarried couples do have to take drastic action to protect themselves from a chaotic and destructive ex-spouse. Peter and Cynthia, for example, believed they had no choice.

Jack had left Cynthia for an office colleague he had been having an affair with for almost a year; and when it became apparent that Cynthia was keeping company with his old friend, Peter Gardner, he was positively delighted. Jack and Peter had been students together in England. It was through them that the wives had come to know each other, and the two couples had been friends.

"He was thrilled," said Peter sardonically. "He had already gone and then Beth died and I took Cynthia off his hands. He didn't have to worry about her bothering him anymore because his old friend had moved in, and what could be more marvellous? He thought he'd be able to come to the house freely and see the kids and be part of the family. He thought it would be just perfect. But we said, 'No, we have to build this family.' Then he changed. He went from being delighted out of his mind to being filled with hatred.''

Jack's burning anger succeeded in threatening Cynthia's and Peter's still-fragile alliance. Peter tried to talk to Jack about what his relationship to the new family might be. Jack would reply reasonably, but then he would telephone Cynthia and explode with frustration and rage. Family, even ex-family, is the place where the veil of politeness is most easily ripped away. It is the place where emotion is at its most raw.

Jack was a respected professional man, but he began to do irrational things. One night he let the air out of their tires; on another occasion he defaced the car windows with marking pencils. ''We broke it off,'' said Peter. ''We excluded him, so he didn't get consulted about plans we made for the children or anything else. His only role in this family was to threaten it, and we just wouldn't let him. He thought he was dumping Cynthia and keeping his children. He thought he might actually *get* the children, because he was sure I wouldn't want them. But he underestimated Cynthia's passion for them. He misunderstood her in every way. He thought she was the vulnerable female and my being here would just make it easier for him to get rid of her and still have his kids.''

Cynthia's children continued to see their father, but only at his new home. Jack eventually married his lover and thus became stepfather to her two children. They had a child of their own, and the focus of his attention shifted to his new family. According to Peter, the children now have a ''modicum'' of a relationship with him.

Cynthia badmouths Jack to her children (usually a major mistake) but Peter does not. ''I try to be as fair as I can,'' he said. ''Jack had a very hard time coping with his children being lost to him, as they were in a way, and I am sorry for him. There would have been a role for him here and a lot more contact. But who can forgive rages and tirades and hatred that ran that deep? Especially at a time when our situation was so new and tentative and in need of sensitivity.''

Peter Gardner's outlook has helped him place some of the common difficulties affecting stepfamilies in perspective. He and Cynthia had been together for eight years, but in his mind that was "only" eight years. "We have a long way to go," was the way he put it. "When our kids get hooked up with partners; when they have love affairs that fail or succeed; when disasters happen to them, as they will; when tragedies happen—and that's likely enough with four children—then we'll be better able to judge how well the glue actually sticks. Right now we're concerned with trivial things inside a house full of children. Children make a hell of a fuss about nothing, and so do their parents, especially parents of adolescents. But I'd like to think that in later life when we're talking about the real events, the glue between stepparent and stepchild will hold.

"I don't really know how it will end. I suppose that linked to my idea that children are independent is also a sense that our lives don't end when our children grow up. I have a lot of things I want to do, and they are important to me and I am quite unashamed about them. The kids' lives are important to them. But so is mine. And so is ours."

Some potential problems in the Gardner-Gans household would emerge in conversations with other family members, but I guessed that the glue he spoke of probably would stick. It was composed of old-fashioned commitment laced with an understanding of those realities that set life in the stepfamily apart and its members leaping over hurdles. Peter and Cynthia and their four kids were leaping hurdles all the time, and they had learned to be nimble and quick.

Cynthia Gans

Cynthia Gans spoke in a distinct, no-nonsense voice and lit one cigarette after another. Her dark shiny hair was streaked with grey and she had decided against camouflage. Cynthia clearly appreciated comfort. Her black slacks bagged at the knees and her plaid flannel shirt looked cozy. Female glamour was obviously not her style.

She steered me into her office, a book-lined refuge in the midtown house with a large window and bright light. This was where she worked and where she felt most in control.

Not that Cynthia Gans felt helpless elsewhere, I ventured to guess. If she had doubts about herself and certain of the events of her life, she had chosen not to allow them much room in her daily life. Leave the hand-wringing and the deep analysis of the past to the Freudian psychoanalysts and their disciples, was her credo. Cynthia got on a whole lot better, she said, by not probing too deep.

With Cynthia Gans, what you saw was what you got. Peter had described her lovingly as demanding, opinionated, judgemental, and as stubborn as a mule; and their relationship as an ongoing challenge.

A woman like Cynthia might have been a disaster as a stepparent. She didn't compromise much in the recommended ways. And, although she believed in fairness, her understanding of that important virtue was not entirely conventional. She had her own definitions and she lived by them.

Cynthia was successful in this remarriage family for a couple of reasons. First, she was instinctively clear and honest in her dealings with other people. When she was mad, they knew it. She liked to yell a lot, she said, but then it was over and the anger had passed. When she was pleased with others, they knew it just as quickly. People were never in the dark about where they stood with Cynthia Gans, and that was a comfort. She was warm (when she wanted to be) and emotional. She and Peter were both reflective people who also prized spontaneity.

One might account for her success, as well, with a political observation of sorts. Cynthia had refused to buy the mythology that haunts women in general, but specifically women in remarriages. She was willing to mother Peter's children—that was a natural part of their bargain—but unlike many new stepmothers, she was quite prepared to recognize that she might never love them at all. This did not make her feel guilty. With as much detached objectivity as she could muster, she had decided two things: She couldn't really expect herself to care about Peter's children the way she cared about her own kids; and, temperamentally, they were so different from herself and her offspring that she might never be spontaneously drawn to them or they to her, regardless of the family relationship.

This acknowledgement was unsentimental, but not uncaring. It was realistic; and it kept her and the rest of the family honest. It saved them from false words and empty gestures and from being eroded by guilt and anxiety. It made it possible for authentic feeling to take root slowly.

Understanding that love is a complex and elusive gift that cannot be willed did not mean, however, that she would remain aloof from Peter's children, even though she had to work at it. Her approach had worked—not perfectly, but well enough. The proof was that all the members of this household now thought of themselves as a reasonably cohesive unit.

Had Cynthia a tendency to slide into that ever-ready pool of female guilt, she'd have had plenty of conventional material to work with. Her "marriage" to Peter was her third, a circumstance that might have edged a less secure woman into self-doubt of a serious sort. But Cynthia saw things from unpredictable angles. Many women feel badly when even their bad marriages break up: They see their biological role as keepers of the hearth, and if the embers grow cold they often assume the entire burden of failure. Cynthia, on the contrary, felt deeply ashamed that she had *stayed* in her two previous marriages so long after she knew they were finished. It did not occur to her that the breakups might signal an essential flaw in her character.

Cynthia had become sexually active at a very young age—fourteen to be exact—but her attitude to herself was not self-deprecating and she certainly didn't feel guilty. On the contrary, she considered her sexuality to be one of her strengths, and the fact that it had emerged early only demonstrated how forceful the energy at her core actually was. "I've always been a highly sexual person, and part of the problem between my second husband and myself was that he was not," she told me. "I like sex for its own sake, *even* when I am in love. For him it was a chore."

She dismissed her first marriage as a youthful mistake undertaken when her boyfriend was about to be drafted into the Korean War. "We really should have shacked up for a few years instead of getting married," she said. "We had little in common, and that became obvious as we matured in different ways. But there were no children, so it really wasn't a problem in any sense."

No guilt there. Even the old female bugbear, aging, meant little to her. At the time of our meeting she was planning a large party to celebrate her upcoming fiftieth birthday. "I've never paid much attention to age," she said matter-of-factly, peering at me over the red tip of her cigarette as if to quell any latent suspicion. "I never went through any of the 'Oh migawd I'm thirty'—or, 'Oh migawd, I'm forty'—business."

Without a doubt, many of these personal characteristics had helped Cynthia cope with problems that defeat other women in stepfamilies. So how did she get that way?

Cynthia Gans was born in New York City into a family of Jewish armchair socialists. An only child, she was adored by any number of people. The family lived in a flat in the Bronx with Cynthia's uncle and her grandmother, but for the child the crowding only meant more people to love her. The apartment was always full of her parents' friends talking about the latest bulletins from the trade-union movement, or which itinerant speaker was in town.

Her mother's background was a little different. She too came from an immigrant family, but one that had longer roots in America. In her youth Cynthia's mother had wanted desperately to become a doctor, and from the time she was a teen-ager she had worked after school at whatever she could—waitressing, clerking, doing any job that was available until she had the means to succeed. She personified the archetypal Horatio Alger success story, with even more barriers to overcome; she was female and these were the 1930s. Mother didn't earn much, but her spunk and independence made a profound impression on her daughter.

Cynthia was only twenty-two when she married Marty, her first husband, but in 1954 girls were practically old maids if they were still unmarried at twenty-two, so the marriage didn't seem premature to anyone, including the bride. It lasted five years, during which Cynthia grew progressively more bored. She liked to repeat a little aphorism she had evolved that skimmed the surface of the truth: "Marty was an artist and not intellectual enough for me, so I married Jack because he was an intellectual, but he wasn't artistic enough for me." In reality, she was trying out men, the way young women often do while deciding who they are and the sort of person they are drawn to.

Cynthia was already thirty when she married Jack, her second husband, and she wanted this marriage to work—to be perfect, to be gorgeous, to be ideal. She accentuated the positive and overlooked characteristics in her husband that seemed imcompatible with her own personality. He was the successful publisher of a special-interest trade magazine, and she endowed him with heroic qualities. She ignored the fact that he neither understood nor appreciated her anarchism or her raucous sensuality. She ignored the fact that he never laughed openly and apparently did not care about the social concerns she had inherited from her family. On the other hand, she did not appreciate his strengths either. It was enough that he was considered knowledgeable and shrewd by his peers in the publishing world. She was proud to be the wife of such a man.

They moved from New York to Montreal and they had a child. Cynthia became more dependent and her husband grew resentful. He did not want emotional demands placed on him. To Cynthia this felt like a rejection. She wanted a depth of intimacy he mistrusted.

After their second child was born the sexual side of their life dwindled to nothing. Cynthia liked sex as a regular diet, but her husband liked to save it for special occasions, like a birthday cake with icing on top. "I'll never catch up with you," he once told her.

"This isn't a competition," she replied.

He became depressed and resentful. Why hadn't she done a doctorate and become an academic? Why hadn't she developed as a writer? Why, in other words, didn't she stop making demands on him?

Cynthia held on. She was approaching forty and there were now two children in tow. Jack began an affair with an office colleague. On their tenth anniversary they talked about divorce. "I did understand his wanting to leave," Cynthia said. "I understand that you don't necessarily love one person until you're old and grey and that sometimes you meet someone and you want to start over again. But I couldn't bring myself to leave him and he wouldn't leave me. I couldn't stand the shilly-shallying and the ambivalence. I would yell at him, then twenty-four hours later I would be reduced to tears."

Several weeks after their twelfth anniversary, Cynthia went away to do a radio interview in another city. Jack saw her off and cried and said they would buy a new house and start again, but when Cynthia came back a week later there was a letter waiting for her on the kitchen table. "There were smudgy tear stains on the paper," she recalled. "What a phony. I felt utterly betrayed."

Jack had moved in with his lover, but he never talked to his children about where he had gone or why. The woman turned up and the children met her and still Jack said nothing. So Cynthia told them what had happened. "I went through the 'Mommy loves you, Daddy loves you' bit and I tried to make sure they didn't feel responsible or guilty. I told them everything within reason. I thought I couldn't protect them with a lot of evasion or a lot of bullshit.

"As far as my own emotional health was concerned, I saved myself a lot of money in psychiatrists' fees over the next months by talking to my friends. Poor guys. I'm sure when they saw me coming they said, 'Oh my God, here's two hours with Cynthia,' but that kind of talking did me good. I didn't know what I would do. I toyed with the idea of running off to Montana. Don't ask why. I like the west, there's good air there. I ride. I thought I'd be a cowgirl on a ranch.

"But when I thought more rationally, I began to prepare myself for a single life. I looked around me, and the men I saw were all married or they were awful, or they were married and awful. I found myself in a difficult position. Women didn't want me around. They saw me as a threat, and that hurt the most. Some old friends became wary and rejecting just when I needed them most."

Peter and Beth Gardner had been her closest friends during the breakdown of the marriage. Beth had died recently, so it was to Peter that Cynthia turned for solace. They sat side by side during long soulless days darkened by mutual pain. They comforted each other. Eventually the chaste friendship turned sexual and they talked about moving in together. Cynthia acknowledged it might have been a catastrophe. "When the idea came up we would back off. We knew it would be hard for both sets of kids. Peter's had recently lost their mother to death and mine were going through a divorce, and we were loath to add to the turmoil in their lives should our relationship also break down. But one morning in bed I said, 'Let's live together,' and he said, 'Yes.' It was that simple because we had both been giving it lots of thought. It was an educated guess that it would work. We took a chance.

"The first thing we did was to tell the children that we were having a serious relationship and we wanted to be together. We told them we knew it would be hard for them and that they were caught up in it because they were children, but we were getting together because we, the adults, wanted to and not because of them. So if they didn't like the relationship they would just have to try to make the best out of it. I also told my kids a little later on that I would not tolerate being blackmailed with threats about going to live with Daddy. I told them never to say that unless they meant it. Then we could talk seriously about it."

But her former husband also wanted the kids. "He asked me to give him reasons why a father shouldn't have his kids. He said if I was such a feminist I ought to appreciate his point of view. I said, 'Over my dead body, because I have raised them and I am close to them, and you did not raise them and you are not close to them.'

"I guess it would have been reasonable to be afraid they would go to live with him, but I felt so close to my children that I just made the assumption that they also felt close to me. After a while, the noises from Jack subsided. I think he did consider going to court, but I didn't believe he'd be able to prove anything damaging about my competence as a parent. I had too many character references and I figured that living with someone wouldn't be grounds for grabbing custody in this day and age. And then Peter and I talked a lot with the kids and I was reassured. They gave no sign of wanting to live with their father.

"One thing that did make the kids nervous at first was the fact that Peter and I weren't planning to get married. So one day I cornered the girls in the bathroom and I asked them whether they really thought the relationships in the house would alter if we were married, and they were candid enough as children to admit they didn't think they would. But a couple of years down the road they began to feel quite proud that the family was different. Now they're convinced that no one should get married just for the sake of form. They understand our point of view, which is that I've already been married twice and that didn't guarantee permanence. Even with a real commitment to children, the existence of a marriage certificate didn't guarantee the relationship would last. Frankly, I feel that a common-law relationship is really a stronger commitment, because there's no legal basis to make it more difficult to disentangle. Peter and I stay together because we want to. The children know that and the very strength of our commitment to each other makes them secure. They have said so."

Like all stepparents, Cynthia had to confront some unexpected feelings about her partner's children, but since she hadn't expected to feel a gush of instant maternal love, she wasn't disappointed. Her only expectation was that she would help them. She felt sorry for these kids whose mother had died; but although she had been acquainted with them for years, she knew she really wasn't attached to them in any serious way. "I guess I have found myself more attached to other children I know than to Jill and Adam, even now," she said with an honesty many stepparents might want to sidestep. "It's really a question of temperament and personality—plus the fact that I'm living intimately with them. I like a friend of my daughter very much, but I don't have to live with her, and that certainly helps.

"I think Peter and I worried most about how the kids would get along and not about how we would relate to them. That may have been a mistake, but you can't really know that until you get into it. We went through the business of what people would call each other. I thought they should call me Cynthia the way they always had, but the kids themselves decided they would try to call us Mom and Dad. It didn't work. They kept slipping back to our names. So we didn't make a fuss.''

The idea of social justice Cynthia had imbibed in her childhood home was transformed into a sense of fairness; and it was this adult stance that contributed to her success as a stepparent. But it was fairness interpreted according to her own lights and conditioned by the limits of her own tolerance. Cynthia believed fairness was possible, but that perfect equality in the stepfamily was not. Children had different personalities and they came from original families where differing values were stressed. There was, for example, the issue of rewards offered for work done around the house. ''I'll reward anyone with twenty-five cents if they do something that deserves it, but they won't necessarily get a smile. That's the intangible that can never be equal,'' she said. ''If a child does a job sullenly, I'm likely not to say anything at all, although I'll still give the twenty-five cents. But if it's done willingly, naturally I'll respond more warmly. That response is very important to a child, or to anyone, for that matter, and if one person gets praised and the other doesn't, that may feel like real inequality. But I don't know what you do about it. My response to someone who is being sullen is negative. Period.''

In theory, the sullen child who gets the unequal treatment could come from either side of a blended family, or from an intact family, for that matter; but in the Cynthia-Peter merger, Peter's children did seem marginally less happy. They were more reserved by nature than either Cynthia or her children, and Cynthia did not relate to them in quite the same way. Peter's children felt the difference, too, and they did not especially like it. But they did not appear unhappy nor were they insecure. They knew Cynthia—she was so clear and forthright about everything they couldn't *help* but know her—and perhaps because of this, they accepted her. They were also quite aware themselves of the vicissitudes of stepfamily life, as will become apparent later.

''Our main focus has been on fairness as far as that is possible, but this is still the subject Peter and I fight about," said Cynthia. "He is very sensitive to the way I treat his children. I've explained that I cannot treat them exactly the same as I treat my own children, because they don't respond the same way. It's that simple. They were not responsive to me, but they weren't especially responsive to him, either. Maybe they were frozen with grief over their mother's death; I'm sure that was a part of it. But temperamentally, they're just very different. They are English children. Their mother was reserved and undemonstrative, even though Peter is quite affectionate. Since I'm fairly overt emotionally, and so are my kids, there was a difference in style that made it impossible for me to relate in exactly the same way. It wasn't natural, and you can't force these things. I'm as fair as possible, but I'm not sure how far we can control the other things that spring from personality differences, and I'm not sure it's wise to try."

The personal differences between the sets of children were visible early. Cynthia's son Brian soon realized that Peter was the sort of man who was willing to hug a boy and have him sit on his lap. So during meals Brian began to disappear without anyone noticing and reappear on Peter's lap. The conversation would continue without interruption.

Peter's children, however, would not follow suit. Cynthia would sit apprehensively at her place, wondering what they were feeling and whether they would try to displace Brian from their father's lap; but they never did and they never showed any overt signs of wanting to be there themselves.

As the years passed, Peter's children became more comfortable, but the personality differences remained, of course. Natural reserve and the trauma of having lost a parent to death seemed to have taken a permanent toll.

"Frankly, I'm not very motherly," Cynthia said, blowing out a column of blue smoke. "I don't melt around children. They irritate the hell out of me. The fact that my own kids irritate me so little seems quite a wonder to me, and I attribute a lot of that to them, to their personalities. They were always pretty happy-go-lucky kids. They didn't have food hang-ups, they smiled a lot. Some of it may have been the way I approached them, but a lot was what they were born with.

"But Peter's kids are coming along. Jill actually defends me now when there's a conflict, and even Adam, who's entering adolescence and is quite hostile, is willing to be open about it instead of complaining indirectly about everything to Brian.

"But I have to say that what keeps things going around here is the love between Peter and me. In spite of our differences we have a superb relationship. And the kids know that. They know they are cared about, but also that we adore each other and that that is completely independent of them.

"Perhaps there will always be a sadness in Peter's kids; I can't say. I give them what I can, and I think they have used it as best as they can. They've been through a lot, but so have we all. We can't change the past and I don't even try."

The secret of Cynthia's success in the remarriage lay in her honesty—that and a personal strength that enabled her to be consistently herself in a situation where many women feel pressured to adopt stereotyped roles. Where she was weakest—for example, in her tendency to be dogmatic and somewhat inflexible—Peter was able to take up the slack. The two worked in tandem. They loved each other independently of their parenting roles. They were committed to their relationship. Finally, they were determined to keep the lines of communication open.

Their personal relationship had had a definite and positive effect on all their children.

Shauna Gans

Shauna had just turned seventeen. She was the oldest child in the Gardner-Gans household, and eight years of living in this family were beginning to show. She was a fast talker and clearly at home in thinking about relationships. Just like Cynthia and Peter. They obviously had not been kidding when they said things got talked about in their home. Shauna wasn't fazed for a moment.

Shauna was surprisingly mature for her age in that she was able to see difficult situations from the point of view of the other person. "Why should anyone love their stepbrother or stepsister?" she asked rhetorically. "Everyone knows that real brothers and sisters don't necessarily love each other, though they often do. They also tend to fight a lot when they're kids. So why should things be any different in a step-family?" Asked whether children feel displaced when the new kids move in, she wrinkled her nose and replied, "They've had to give up *their* home and move into *your* house!" What about kids who feel angry at a stepparent who has assumed a role they want reserved for the natural parent? "Well," said Shauna, pondering the question, "I would tell them not to think that the stepmother or stepfather was trying to take their real parent away. Once kids are in·their teens they should be able to understand that their parents aren't living just for them, no matter how much they love them, and that their mother isn't going to live the rest of her life alone because she doesn't want to upset them by having a new man in the house. I mean, they might not love this man, but they should give it time and get to know him. The silliest thing is saying, 'I'm not going to like him because he's not my real fa-ther.' That has no basis at all, because if he's a nice person he's not going to try to be your real father, especially if he comes into a house where there's a teen-ager. Kids should give it time and try to see him as a person who's doing his best, even if it's hard at first."

If all this sounds idealized or unusually mature, both sup-positions are probably correct. Shauna had thought about these things, it is true, but she had also adopted the attitudes of her family, as most children do. Recently, though, some of her attitudes had been undergoing reevaluation.

Cynthia and Peter had succeeded in fashioning a family that worked, but there were hints in Shauna's conversation that some of their methods might eventually backfire. Cyn-thia, for example, never hesitated to badmouth her former husband, because she believed it was important to set up her new family in ideological opposition to his. So she described herself and Peter as "warm and expressive," while Jack and his wife were called "cold and repressed." She and Peter were "spontaneous and emotional" in their responses, while Jack and his wife were "remote and overly intellectual."

Shauna had adopted her mother's attitudes early on, for at an unconscious level she knew where security lay. If she were to survive in the new blended family, she had to identify with its point of view; and if that point of view meant she had to reject her father, well, *c'est la vie.*

Shauna adored her mother. She admired her, she needed her, and in no way would she risk confronting her in argument, even for the sake of defending her father. So she pleased her mother by squeezing Jack out of her heart and crowning Peter in his place—just as Cynthia had done.

Shauna had no memory at all of having lived with her mother and her natural father, although she was already nine years old when they separated. For her, memory began when Peter and his children moved in. She felt uneasy about this odd blanking-out of her past. "I know it's crazy, but I have only snatches of memory," she said, shaking her head in confusion. "I feel as though this whole block of time has been lost. It just isn't in my memory."

To remember happiness with her dad would have threatened her present family life. The unspoken credo of the new family had been clearly communicated. Dad was a rat, and to think otherwise was to betray Mom, Peter, Brian, Jill, and Adam—the entire unit on which everything now depended. "I always side with my mother against my father," Shauna acknowledged. "*He* left us. *He* broke up our family."

But chinks were beginning to appear in the armour. Shauna appeared to be edging into a new understanding of what Jack's role in her life had been and would become in the future. This change was very recent—just a few months old— and it had begun after her return from a year abroad in France, where she had found herself examining other beliefs and assumptions she had previously taken for granted. Before leaving for France her father had occupied a slightly distasteful, shadowy place in her life. "I didn't really like him," she said. "I didn't like his wife, I didn't like his stepkids, and I didn't like going to his place. The house was cold and there was no openness."

He came to visit her in France, and before his arrival Shauna felt compelled to explain to the school director that although Jack was her "real" father, he wasn't the man who parented her on a day-to-day basis. Shauna needed to diminish Jack in her mind to maintain the priorities of the new family, and she needed to make his second-class status equally clear to others.

But since her return she had begun to feel a little differently. Visits to her father's home were less tense. She liked to talk to him about different things. In fact, Shauna now realized with pleasure that she could talk with Jack about any subject that interested her, from international affairs to religion to the books she was reading. Cynthia told her that Jack related best on an intellectual level, and for that reason he connected better now that Shauna was growing older. Shauna accepted this explanation.

Although these minor changes in their relationship were taking place, Shauna still felt obliged to diminish her father and the way he lived. Long habits die slowly, and of course it still remained unacceptable to defend him openly in her mother's home. So she talked at length about how her father had never understood her. Most of all, she said, he did not really "know" her. This made her angry, contemptuous, and sad, all at the same time. "When I go there I give him a hug and kiss and I can talk to him about school and even about my boyfriend. He can talk about any subject for hours. If he calls that a good relationship, I guess it's okay, but really I hope he's sad that he has missed so much, like knowing what I really think and feel about things."

Shauna's father and stepmother sounded like caring parents to me (after speaking to children who were truly suffering from neglect) and Shauna agreed; but again she belittled them. "I guess they're nice parents, but compared to what I know, it doesn't seem like much," she sniffed.

The family credo always had to assume priority. Cynthia Gans hated her ex-husband. He had disappointed her by being unwilling or unable to understand the peculiar tenor of her personality, and then by deserting her in a despicable, cowardly way. She was intent on creating a new family that would succeed by excluding him. Her children had been "asked" to reject him; and they had concurred.

"I have the best relationship in the world with my mom," Shauna confided, a warm smile spreading across her face. "I can't think of anything in the world I wouldn't talk to her about, about my life, about guys, about anything that was bothering me. Some kids say they can talk to their moms and joke around and all that, but I don't know anyone else who can tell their parents if they've been drinking or thinking about taking dope, or what they feel about sex. At this age they are really the biggest things going on.

"My mom is a really open person and really with it, too. She is aware of changes and she doesn't have that old-fashioned point of view. My father tries in a surface way, but he really doesn't understand children of our age, and underneath he really is old-fashioned. But I was just lucky that I got a mom who really knows how to bring kids up."

Not every mother of a teen-age girl is the recipient of such an accolade. Cynthia's loving yet powerful influence over her daughter had had positive results for the unity of the family, but seemingly at the expense of Shauna's natural feelings for her father.

Shauna, however, was beginning to feel a tiny bit resentful when Cynthia ran her father down. It hadn't bothered her in the past, but now for some reason it did. Especially when Cynthia did it in front of Jill and Adam. "After all, he *is* my father," she said resentfully, voicing a rather new sentiment. But she could not openly articulate her nascent disapproval. Although she claimed to be able to discuss absolutely everything with Cynthia, her reviving love for her dad was true taboo.

When Peter and his children moved into her house, Shauna was in grade two. She didn't remember the actual move—in her conscious memory they had always been there—but she did recall writing a letter to a friend in which she said that her parents were getting a divorce and that an uncle whose wife had died was moving in with his kids. Shauna remembered not wanting to admit that some strange guy was moving into the family, and she thought it sounded better if she turned them into relatives.

Now she approved unconditionally of Cynthia's and Peter's living arrangements. "I think it's just great," she said. "I think it's fantastic that they don't have to go and sign a piece of paper to make them stay together. Mom once told us that if any of us really wanted them to get married they would do it, because it wasn't going to hurt them if it meant something special to one of us. But the older I get, the more fantastic I think it is. For sure, signing a piece of paper isn't going to make a relationship last any longer."

Shauna liked Peter from the beginning. He wasn't really a stranger. She had known him as her parents' friend, and from the beginning she felt that he liked her, too. Peter was scrupulously fair. Shauna admired that.

Yet she continued to feel some uncertainty about the perennial trouble spots that plagued the various relationships in the household. "We're one family now," she asserted. "I don't think any of us thinks of Mom and her two kids as one unit or Peter and his two kids as another. And none of the kids could ever say, 'He or she isn't my parent so they can't tell me what to do.' " But at the same time she was prepared to acknowledge that there were difficulties that hadn't been resolved. She hesitated a long thirty seconds or so as if deciding how much to say. Then she whispered, "The biggest problem in the house is with the other two kids. Don't ever tell my mother this, but I really think she is often unfair in the way she deals with them. I know there's a certain something you feel for your own children that you can't have for others no matter how close you are, but I think part of it is simply that she brought us up herself, so she likes the way we've been brought up!

"Frankly, there are moments when I think she just doesn't like Jill and Adam. For instance, when I get into a fight and run upstairs, she always comes up; but when Jill runs crying to her room, Mom never follows. When we have a problem it seems to me that Mom gets mad at Jill; then Peter will defend her by saying Mom isn't being fair, which I often think is true. Or if Peter gets mad at me, then Mom defends me, perhaps more than she should. I even realize this while she's doing it, but hell, when you're upset and your mother is on your side, you're not going to say, 'Keep quiet.'

"Peter isn't like Mom. He's really good at treating all of us the same, and if he does favour his own, he really doesn't show it. But, because he is as loving to Brian and me as he is to his own children, I sometimes think Jill and Adam feel even lonelier. Maybe I'm just imagining it, but Peter seems like a real father to us, while Mom seems more like a mother figure to Jill and Adam. Geez, she'd probably kill me if she knew I was saying this!"

Shauna was perceptive enough to be aware of her mother's foibles, but not yet brave enough to challenge them, for to take sides against her mother might disturb the fragile structures of the family. This stepfamily, like all stepfamilies, was just that much less resilient than the nuclear family might be. Shauna knew this.

Shauna also knew and accepted that her feelings for Jill and Adam were less deeply rooted than her feelings for her natural brother, Brian. "I have a stepbrother and a stepsister from Peter, a stepbrother and a stepsister from my dad's wife, and one half-sister from my dad and his wife, and one whole brother," she said, tallying up the usual odd assortment of relatives to be found in the stepfamily. "But Brian is my whole brother and I feel special about him. I don't know why. Maybe because he is most like me.

"We're all one family," she emphasized pointedly as I prepared to leave. But she was definitely reconsidering her relationship with her father, upon whom she had heaped such contempt.

Although Cynthia and Peter had created a "real" family, there was a chance they had built part of their castle on quicksand. The conflict engendered in Shauna and her brother Brian, by having to deny an identification with their father, would need to be resolved.

Brian Gans

"I have one close friend, and his father kidnapped him, then his mother got him back again, but that's the only family I know that has something strange like us."

Brian Gans was thirteen years old and, like his sister, he was very talkative and very self-aware. Life in his "strange" family was good as far as Brian was concerned—at least most of the time. The beginning hadn't been easy, though, and he remembered quite clearly just how odd it felt when Peter and his kids moved in, kids who were supposed to become his "sister" and his "brother"—and, most worrisome of all, kids who were supposed to share his mother with him. Since he had only one parent left at home, Brian wasn't at all sure how he would feel about sharing her.

As it turned out, his mom and his new stepfather, Peter, weren't much of a problem. Confirming what other children in stepfamilies had said, Brian's real hassle was the other kids. He had been the youngest in his family, but now Adam was the youngest, and Brian felt angry and displaced. Adam seemed to be getting that special attention youngest children often receive, and Brian was, quite frankly, teeth-grinding jealous. Eventually, he and Adam did become friends (there was only one year between them). Then they ganged up on the girls of the family. That felt more comfortable, somehow, more like the schoolyard: the boys against the girls.

Brian was only five when Cynthia and Peter moved in together, and he had had a strong, happy relationship with a loving mother. Over the initial months of adjustment, the connection with Cynthia did not fail, and Brian's fear of loss proved unfounded. "I never did feel bad about sharing Mom because it turned out we always got slightly more attention from her than Jill and Adam got," he said confidently, confirming the perceptions of most other family members. "I guess she really should be able to communicate with all of us the same, but I guess it's only natural for a parent to feel more for her real children."

Like his sister, Brian was deeply estranged from his dad, and like Shauna he described the estrangement in terms of differences between the two households. "Dad and his wife live in an opposite sort of household to ours. They're sort of formal and sort of traditional about things. I feel a little uncomfortable when I start talking to my real father. It's hard to communicate. I don't really know what to say. It's like if you have grandparents that live far away and you don't see them that often, well, when you meet them you don't really know what to say. But we've never talked about any of this because he keeps his emotions inside more than we do here. Here we're more open."

Brian had parachuted Peter into that special place in his heart reserved for "father." "I feel much closer to Peter," he said.

Shauna had described how Brian spent his weekends with his dad glued in front of the television set, talking to no one and in a state of obvious discomfort. Like Shauna, Brian appeared to have rejected his father in order to confirm his commitment to the family he lived in, presumably for reasons of survival. I wondered, once again, whether the need to reject one parent in order to live comfortably with the other would eventually backfire on this family.

But at age thirteen Brian had no hesitations about expressing his real happiness in having a stepfather like Peter in his life. At a profound emotional level he "knew" how much Peter and Cynthia cared about each other, and he rejoiced in their love. "If you ask me why this strange family has worked out, I can only say it's because Mom and Peter are so much alike," he said, nodding his head vigorously. "That's really why they moved in together. They're alike in their beliefs and what they feel is right and wrong. Also it was good because we all knew each other. It wasn't Peter coming over and taking Mom to a movie and us never seeing him or his kids or anything like that. Before they moved in they would come over here a lot, the whole family, and Peter would spend time with *us*, not just with Mom. I knew even then that he really liked me, and I got along with him, too."

However, no matter how much Brian liked his stepfather,

the instinctively rooted connection was with his mother. He recognized this and found it a little strange.

"There were some things that were sort of funny, because if I was hurt or if I needed a Band-Aid or something, I always went to Mom. Even now, after so many years, I find myself doing things like that. Like if I'm going to school I'll yell, 'Bye, Mom,' and forget about him. So he says, 'What about me?' Then I say 'Bye' to him. I don't do it consciously or anything. I just forget. Or if I want to sleep at a friend's house I'll phone home, and I sometimes catch myself asking Peter if I can speak to Mom, which is ludicrous and really doesn't need to be that way.

"But really, I'm better now. If I hurt myself or pull a muscle or something, I go to Peter. Now he's the one that usually looks after my cuts and stuff. I take my problems to him, too. But sometimes I find myself slipping."

The fact that Cynthia and Peter are not married has apparently not affected Brian negatively. As Dr. Steinhauer pointed out, it is the quality of the relationship between adults, and their perceived commitment to the children, that makes kids feel secure in remarriage situations, and not the existence of a marriage ceremony. A commonsensical point, of course, but one that is sometimes overlooked.

Brian had thought quite a bit about marriage—they had certainly discussed it in this talkative household—and he wasn't at all sure that he'd even like it if Cynthia and Peter got "officially" married. "If I look at marriage, I don't see why it's absolutely necessary unless you want to have kids or something," he said thoughtfully. "But my mom's already been married twice, and I don't think she wants to get married a third time. At school, though, I give the impression that they are married. This isn't because I'm ashamed or anything. It's just easier that way, and also I really think of Peter as my dad so much that there is no difference in my mind between married or not married. No one ever asks me, so I just call them Mom and Dad to make it easier.

"There is one thing I always do, though; I always make a point of wishing both Peter and Jack a happy Father's Day. That is just natural, of course."

* * *

Shauna and Brian were secure and happy in the stepfamily. Their stepsiblings, Jill and Adam Gardner, had a different set of circumstances to cope with.

Jill Gardner

During the previous six months things had changed for the better for Jill, and the change was due in part to her age. She was fifteen and in tenth grade, a time when childhood patterns begin to give way to glimmerings of new awareness and feelings.

For most of her eight years in this family, Jill had been somewhat confused and angry. She felt that Shauna and Brian were getting a lot of things she and her brother Adam didn't get. Not material things or anything obvious like that, just things that happened because *her* mother was dead, while Shauna's and Brian's father was still alive and well and living not very far away. He and his new wife went to Florida for holidays in the winter and took Shauna and Brian with them, while she and Adam didn't go anywhere or get any of the other special treats that Jack and his wife bestowed. She and Adam had only one family—this stepfamily—while Shauna and Brian had two. It wasn't fair.

Jill also resented Cynthia for not hiding her preference for her own kids, while Peter, her own dad, treated everyone the same. Shauna and Brian seemed to be getting "more," once again. And then, all the fuss that was made over Cynthia's divorce from Jack. Her dad and Cynthia would disappear behind closed doors with Shauna and Brian to discuss the divorce, and although Jill knew it was none of her business and she didn't even care that much, she did feel excluded. She thought not enough attention was paid to the fact that she and Adam had also suffered a trauma when their mother had died. "I really don't think we were comforted enough," she said sadly.

Peter himself had voiced regrets over this. So much energy had gone into building a relationship with Cynthia and her children that he felt he might have neglected his own children when they needed him most. Jill's rueful sadness suggested that her scars from that period were unhealed.

About six months earlier it had all become just too much for Jill, and she had blurted out a long list of grievances. In their tried-and-true family tradition, they all sat down and talked about them, and since that day Jill had been feeling decidedly more positive about the family. The talk had helped her understand about Shauna and Brian and to realize that her pain came from the fact that they had a real father somewhere else while her real mother was dead.

Since that talk, which had corresponded more or less with her fifteenth birthday, Jill had also been experiencing new feelings about her real mother. "It's really weird," she said. "Until then I hardly thought about her at all. When my mom was in the hospital it never occurred to me that she would die, and when she did, it sort of passed over me. I guess I was too young. And when we moved in here I just thought that my old life was finished and this was the new way. This was my family, that's all. But now, like I said, it's weird. I'm really starting to miss her.

"I can't really say what it is—just having a real mother, I guess. Cynthia and I get along better than we used to and that's fine, but there are things in a mother-daughter relationship that I wish I had. Like I do notice the way she feels towards her daughter. It's not that she's really unfair to me or anything, just certain things. It's not that I feel jealous—just that I notice I'm lacking something, something I wish for. A closeness. A special closeness."

Jill struggled to accept this sad reality. "I understand it," she assured me while trying to assure herself at the same time. "Cynthia and I have talked about it a bit. Cynthia tries hard and it's pretty good. It's just, well, that's the way it is and I have to accept it. My mother is dead."

There was, however, no question in Jill's mind that the Gardner-Gans family was a "real" family. She had privately compared her situation to that of her friends and decided that she wasn't that badly off or even that much different from some of them. She knew plenty of girls her age who didn't get along with their natural mothers at all. Perhaps that might have happened between her and her real mother? Jill was realistic enough to consider that possibility. She also knew kids who came from very large families, much larger than the blended concoction she lived in, and got even less attention from their parents than she did. "Yeah, I'd say this is definitely a real family," she reflected.

For Jill, as well as for Brian, the most difficult adjustment had been loss of status in the age hierarchy. Brian had been the youngest in his family and had enjoyed the attention youngest children get, but Jill had been the *oldest* in her family. The thing about being an oldest child is that no one except your parents gets to boss you around. Jill felt that keenly. "I didn't want to take orders from Shauna," she said, still bristling with remembered humiliation. "I think all the kids took out their anger about the new stepfamily on each other," she added with considerable insight.

"Now we all get along. Except for Adam. He's still confused. I remember how he felt, and I think he just has to grow up a bit. I just tell him not to worry about things. The rest of us have grown up now and we understand better."

Jill didn't care, either, that her dad and Cynthia weren't married; she even claimed to enjoy the variety of shocked responses she got from some of her teachers. If a teacher called Cynthia "Mrs. Gardner," Jill would correct her. "No, she didn't keep her name when they married," she would inform the questioning teacher. "They're not married."

"I get a kick out of that." She laughed. "The nice thing about not being married is that you're together only because you want to be. I know Dad and Cynthia want to be together and care a lot about each other, and that means a lot to me, too."

Like the other children, Jill got a good start in the family because she already knew Cynthia and her children quite well. "That was a good thing," she said. "If I hadn't known them I think things would have been a lot more hostile. I sort of accepted Cynthia because she was like a family friend. I even remember the night I just knew this would happen. When we came back from England after my mother had died, Dad and Cynthia and all the kids went away for a vacation to a cottage. Shauna and I were sharing a bedroom, and one night we saw Dad and Cynthia kiss. We were giggling and we said, 'Wouldn't it be funny if we were stepsisters?'

"But I would never call Cynthia 'Mom,' because I've always known her as Cynthia and there would be no reason to change. It just wouldn't feel right. I have a place in my heart for my mother—I mean, it's not that big or anything like that and it's not as though I'm thinking about her all the time. It's just occasionally, and then I feel I've missed out on something and I miss her and wish for something I don't have. But otherwise it's pretty good here. I mean, if death and divorce have both hit a family and they can go through that and succeed, they're pretty lucky. I see kids who haven't had one of their parents die or who haven't had a divorce and they don't have as good a family as we do."

Only now was Jill beginning to mourn for her mother. She missed her and recognized the new sadness at the centre of her life, but she was also realistic and she knew that what she had in the stepfamily was good.

Adam Gardner

Adam Gardner was twelve and poised on the edge of puberty. In a year or so he might be six inches taller, with a voice that cracked at embarrassing moments, but for the moment he was still physically a child.

The other members of his family claimed he was having a hard time, even feeling hatred, but Adam said that *used* to be the case. He thought his negative feelings were beginning to change.

"For a long time I didn't feel so comfortable here, but now I feel better," he said, twisting around in his swivel seat with twelve-year-old kinetic energy. "At first I thought the whole thing might be temporary. I wasn't really sure about what was going to happen, but I thought we might just stay for a year or so. I didn't mind being here then, because I liked Brian, but when I saw that this was permanent it got harder. For instance, I was really jealous when Dad paid attention to

Cynthia's kids, but now I don't think like that. I think Dad gives us a little more now, and that's only right, because after all, he is our father. Cynthia gives more to Shauna and Brian. Parents like them can't really say, 'We're going to be exactly equal and like them all the same,' because of course they're going to like their own kids more. If they treat you fair I don't think they should pretend to love the other person's kids exactly the same. But some things have to be fair, like things you're allowed to do. And allowances have to be fair, too.''

Adam was the only child in the family who thought Peter gave him *special* attention. That gave him a confidence his sister seemed to lack.

''At first I didn't like Cynthia, because she would be asking me to do things all the time, and before that when my mom was sick only my dad asked me to do things. It was just a little bit weird. And now I still might do things more if Dad asks me, but it is really a joint family. It doesn't feel as though we are two families living in the same house.

''I think of Cynthia as nearly a mother. She can't be my real mother because she's not really my mother. Like, I have memories and things like that of my real mother. And even though we don't talk about her that much—just things I did when I was a baby and that sort of stuff—in my mind she is still my mother.''

Like the other children, Adam was aware of and happy about the quality of the relationship between his dad and Cynthia. And although he was only twelve he knew that honesty had kept this family together.

''People here don't pretend about feelings and they don't pretend to love everyone the same,'' he said, taking a counterclockwise spin. ''Also my Dad and Cynthia like to be together, so we like to keep the friendships going between the kids.''

In spite of his insight and his confidence in Peter's love, there was a noticeable emotional distance in Adam. Shauna and Brian and, to a slightly lesser degree, Jill, were all tightly bound to this family that now represented the emotional vortex of their lives. But Adam was more remote.

''I'm sort of happy that all this has happened, because I've gotten a lot of friends at my new school and around this house, but I do know that if I had to leave now I wouldn't really be too sad. Not that I'd want to leave or anything like that," he hastened to say, "but it wouldn't upset me too much if I did. I mean, if I had to, it just wouldn't bother me that much."

As Cynthia had suggested, the trauma of losing a parent at age four may have taken its toll. A quiet, private space in his heart was reserved, forever, for his mother. "In my mind she is still my mother," he said, although Cynthia had effectively "mothered" him for most of his life. His idealized mother, gone forever, would never yell at him or withdraw her love even for a tiny moment. In his mind's eye, her face would always smile. She would never grow old.

But Cynthia did not try to compete with the dead. That way her stepchildren were able to accept her and care about her ("She's nearly my mother," said Brian) without giving up the love bond with the mother who bore them.

What made the Gardner-Gans family different? Allowing for their varying ages, the children seemed able to analyze and verbalize attitudes that often remain submerged in other families. It was this clarity of perception combined with a willingness to acknowledge the realities of stepfamily life that underlined their present success. Confronting these realities helped them to see the reconstituted family as it is and not as they wished it were. For example:

• Peter and Cynthia wanted to be together, and they told their children that the new living arrangements were simply not negotiable. This was a reality the children may have wanted to circumvent, but the clear message they received from their parents—We care about each other, we care about you, and you had better get used to things—helped them to view the inevitable in a positive way. Cynthia was also able to head off any schemes her children may have considered by telling them straight out that she wouldn't be moved by threats about going to live with Daddy. If they were serious, she'd be prepared to discuss the issue; but they had better not use the threat to manipulate her.

• Peter's ability to accommodate himself to Cynthia and her children came largely from his gut-level understanding that the people one cares about may be very different from each other. Cynthia was less able to accept this. As a result she was slightly less successful with his kids than he was with hers.

• On the other hand, Cynthia recognized her limitations and was realistic about them. She did not love her stepchildren, although she cared about them, and she frankly wasn't able (or willing) to push herself any further in their direction. Everyone in this family accepted the reality that at a gut, instinctive level parents will care more *profoundly* for a biological child than a stepchild. But since each of the four children had one biological parent in the house, he or she could look to that parent for special attention. Only Jill felt that her father did not favour her over the others.

• Both Peter and Cynthia could acknowledge, articulate, and therefore not get upset over the fact that the stepfamily, even when it is working well, is slightly more brittle than the nuclear family. It takes many years before the stepfamily can push roots into the earth—roots that firmly anchor its members and commit them to each other at an emotional level; in the meantime, relationships are necessarily more artificial and less resilient.

• Peter, in particular, had a helpful, long-term perspective on the stepfamily that would also be useful to biological parents in nuclear families. He recognized that parents often exaggerate their worries and, secondly, that life would not end when his family of children grew up and moved away. The important task, now, was to concoct the glue that would hold them to each other long after the children had grown into adulthood, a glue that would bind them together when serious problems arose, as they do during the lives of most people. Finally, his loyalty to his family, as great as it was, was only one of his commitments. He had also made a promise to himself and to his future. Within five years the youngest of the children would probably have left home, but if he and Cynthia were lucky, they might have thirty years together. That's why their relationship was paramount in the long run.

* * *

Dr. Paul Druckman had talked about the three main functions of a family: the instrumental level where jobs get done and people get looked after physically, the emotional level, which provides a basis for emotional and intellectual growth, and the third level, which concerns how well the family prepares its members to deal with the world as they will find it.

At the instrumental level, Dr. Druckman thought the Gardner-Gans family worked very well. There were squabbles about who was and who wasn't doing their jobs, but on the whole the household was functioning. He also thought the family operated well at the emotional level, but that a price had been exacted for that success. That price, as everyone recognized, had been the early happiness of Jill and Adam. Their father had quite deliberately given them less attention in his energetic struggle to establish the family as a working unit.

"I suspect, given his background, that Peter Gardner had learned to muddle through situations using trial-and-error techniques, and that he probably felt overwhelmed with the task of creating this stepfamily so soon after the death of his wife," said Druckman. "He felt he had to devote all his energy to his wife and to the other children, but, of course, that wasn't necessarily true. It certainly would have been possible to set up the family without depriving his own children. On the other hand, I also suspect that he was attempting to deny his own grief and sadness. There wasn't time for real mourning in this situation. Now, his daughter Jill is only beginning to confront her loss. Adam will also have to deal with it at some point."

In Dr. Druckman's opinion, Peter Gardner was the linchpin of the family. It was he who was best able to accommodate his stepchildren and find positive characteristics in them to relate to. Cynthia had a much more rigid sense of what was acceptable to her, but as long as one member of the family was handling the role of nurturer, the unit would function well. Cynthia's strengths were her clarity and straightforwardness, but Druckman wondered what would happen if Peter ran out of energy and decided one day that he had had enough of filling in the emotional spaces? What would happen if he took a real stand against Cynthia's sometimes intolerant attitude to his children and to the fact that they seemed to be receiving less, emotionally, than the others?

Finally, Dr. Druckman was concerned about the third function—how well Peter and Cynthia were preparing their children for the world as they would find it. The estrangement from Jack was the major question mark.

"One of the things we hope children learn in their families is how to solve problems and how to continually take stock. It's quite possible that Jack was an S.O.B., and sometimes there really is no choice but to cut off a parent who is so disruptive that the new marriage is being threatened, but I'm not sure anything should ever be engraved in stone. Kids have to learn to reevaluate. They have to have ways of finding out about people in an ongoing way and of working at understanding them. Shauna seemed to be beginning to do that, and that was healthy, but one wasn't sure what the consequences would be for her, because to start caring about her father would be to question whether her mother's way was really the best way to be. Cynthia was a very good, strong role model for her daughter, a mother who encouraged her to be a modern woman, and if Shauna welcomed her father into her life in any real way she'd be put into a position of having to question her mother. Hopefully people start to see that they can't judge everybody all the time. If we make predeterminations of people and never revise them, we're in trouble."

Dr. Druckman had similar reservations about Brian. Brian's passive anger at his father—when he was visiting he would sit and watch television all weekend without talking to anyone—did not indicate that he was learning to solve his problems, either. "I think one has to be concerned with what being allowed to continue in a passive, resentful state does to a personality," Druckman said. "Some people become passive-aggressive, or just passive, or they have rage reactions. Brian was also caught in the conflict of having to take a position against his father so he could preserve the family he lived in.

"But, having said all this, I do think that for the time being they have worked things out quite well. If accepting reality and being flexible are characteristics that help families to reach the three objectives I spoke about earlier, they certainly did well in presenting realities clearly and unequivocally. Peter seemed the most flexible. The danger, if there is any, lies ahead, and it may come from the conflict the children feel about their father. But if Peter and Cynthia can revise their original point of view and encourage a more positive attitude, they will help Shauna and Brian enormously and teach them that these reevaluations have to go on all the time in our lives if we are to successfully resolve the human problems we encounter."

Peter Gardner and Cynthia Gans had made some mistakes like any couple—married, remarried, or living together—like any human beings. But when it came to negotiating the difficult paths remarried people are called upon to travel, they and their children were as agile and resilient as any family I encountered.

SUGGESTIONS

1. Be clear with children about the central importance of the couple relationship. Children, because they are children, are brought into their parent's new marriage without anyone asking their approval. This is a reality they need to accept at the outset.

2. Try to acknowledge differences in people and families as a positive or, at the least, neutral characteristic. Peter's ability to accept his stepchildren as they were helped solidify the new family.

3. Be prepared to make the family adjustment a priority. At first Peter took time and energy from his work. Not everyone can do that, but the need for serious attention remains.

4. Be honest (in a gentle way) about the reality of feelings, but at the same time be fair and even-handed.

5. Keep communication lines open. Very little was allowed to fester in the Gardner-Gans household, because they talked about things constantly.

6. Negotiate difficulties as in any partnership. The ability

to negotiate is one of the most important characteristics of any successful relationship, especially in complex situations like stepfamilies.

7. Recognize that children who have lost a parent through death may have a slightly different set of problems than children who have had a divorce in their lives. Cynthia's children had a parent who lived elsewhere in the vicinity, while Peter's children did not. This caused a certain amount of envy. It is also easy for children who have lost a parent to invest him or her with idealized characteristics. A dead mother may become quite perfect in her children's eyes, and the reality of a flesh-and-blood stepmother who applies discipline, gets annoyed on occasion, and otherwise makes demands may be hard to bear. Such children may also feel that the remarriage itself is a betrayal of the dead parent and the happy marriage that produced them.

8. Do not try to compete with a ghost. Cynthia did not, and as a result her stepchildren were able to retain a living memory of their mother while fitting Cynthia into another space altogether.

9. Carefully examine the consequences of cutting an ex-spouse out of the family. They *never* become ex-parents. The children may eventually pay a price, emotionally, if they go along with the amputation.

10. Maintain a positive perspective. Peter Gardner knew, or hoped, that he and Cynthia would have much longer together than the time they spent raising their children to adulthood. He also thought that the different backgrounds and the history of death and divorce in the family were less important than the fact that he and Cynthia were providing a solid, rich, multifaceted, and stimulating environment that might well turn out to be the cornerstone of their children's lives.

Epilogue

WHAT, THEN, ARE the essential components of a successful remarriage? In my view there are two, and they are absolutely basic.

First is the understanding that the stepfamily is neither an abnormal condition nor a second-class version of the nuclear family. Structurally, the stepfamily is different. It contains what Lillian Messinger has called "permeable boundaries."

An acceptance of the differences between first and subsequent marriages is fundamental. To try to force the new unit into the nuclear mould by shutting out absent parents, grandparents, and other reminders of past history, or by adopting inappropriate roles, only leads to misery.

The second basic element is the couple itself. The second-marriage couple who married principally because they wanted to (and not to provide a substitute parent, housekeeper/babysitter, or meal ticket) will more likely survive the almost inevitable disruption that such family reorganization brings in its wake. The couple creates the framework. It is they who root the tree in the earth, and from that base, other relationships become less difficult. The strong couple at the centre will give a clear message to upset, angry children that they have every intention of making this marriage work. They will also be less vulnerable to the disruptions of ex-spouses and more able (and willing) to cooperate for the children's sake. Cooperation between the two family units benefits the children, whose own increased happiness will, in turn, benefit the remarriage family.

Although the stepfamily is necessarily more complex, it is

helpful for people to remember that in the course of raising children all parents encounter problems, that siblings in all families fight and are competitive, and that the emotions of love and hate, happiness and sorrow, are found wherever there are human beings.

The best engagement present a couple planning remarriage might offer each other might be a before-the-fact counselling session with someone who understands the unique circumstances of remarriage. Trained counsellors can help people separate themselves emotionally, from an ex-spouse and complete the mourning process that will then permit an important new, child-oriented interaction to evolve. Counselling can help children understand that to cherish a stepparent does not mean they are being disloyal to a biological parent of the same sex and that the more people we care about, the better off we are. Counselling can stress the negotiating skills that every successful blended family must develop to cope with the different styles and ways of being each spouse (and his or her children) brings to the marriage. And most important, counselling can help reaffirm the essential couple relationship upon which everything else will ultimately depend.

Although many second marriages fail, a majority do succeed. Through their courage and their perseverance, these families demonstrate that it is possible to reshape, successfully, a life that was once in shambles. In the long run, their children, who also have suffered loss and pain, receive the greatest gift of all: the visible and palpable proof that through the most trying of circumstances, love and dedication remain possible.

Selected Bibliography

THE FOLLOWING BOOKS and articles were of most help to me in my research.

BOOKS

Atkin, Edith and Rubin, Estelle. *Part-Time Father*. Signet, 1977

Bowlby, John. *Attachment and Loss*. Vol I. *Attachment*. Hogarth Press, 1969

Duberman, Lucille. *The Reconstituted Family: A Study of Remarried Couples and Their Children*. Nelson-Hall, 1975

Gardner, Richard A. *The Boys and Girls Book about Divorce*. Bantam, 1971

_____, *The Boys and Girls Book about Stepfamilies*. Bantam, 1982

Goldstein, Joseph; Solnit, Albert; Freud, Anna. *Beyond the Best Interests of the Child*. Free Press, 1973

Irving, Howard H. *Divorce Mediation*. Personal Library, 1980

Maddox, Brenda. *The Half-Parent*. Evans, 1975

Messinger, Lillian (volume editor) and Hansen, James (editor). *Therapy with Remarriage Families*. Family Therapy Collection. Aspen Publications, 1982

Noble, June and Noble, William. *How to Live with Other People's Children*. Hawthorne Books, 1977

Roosevelt, Ruth and Lofas, Jeannette. *Living in Step*. Stein and Day, 1976

Scarf, Maggie. *Unfinished Business: Pressure Points in the Lives of Women*. Random House, 1980

Sheehy, Gail. *Passages*. Dutton, 1974

Simon, Anne W. *Stepchild in the Family: A View of Children in Remarriage*. Odyssey Press, 1964

Visher, Emily and Visher, John S. *Stepfamilies: A Guide to Working with Stepparents and Children*. Brunner/Mazel, 1979

Wallerstein, Judith S. and Kelly, Joan Berlin. *Surviving the Breakup: How Parents and Children Cope with Divorce*. Basic Books, 1980

Wylie, Philip. *Generation of Vipers*. Larlin Corp (Georgia), 1979 (orig. pub. in 1942)

ARTICLES

Ahrons, Constance R. and Perlmutter, Morton S. "The Relationship between Former Spouses: A Fundamental Subsystem in the Remarriage Family." From *Therapy with Remarriage Families*. Aspen Publications, 1982. pp. 31–46

Fast, Irene and Cain, Albert. "The Stepparent Role-Potential for Disturbance in Family Functioning." From *American Journal of Orthopsychiatry*. 36:489–96. 1966

Garfield, Robert. "Mourning and Its Resolution for Spouses in Marital Separation." From *Therapy with Remarriage Families*. Aspen Publications, 1982. pp. 1–16

Goldner, Virginia. "Remarriage Families: Structure, System and Future." ibid. pp. 187–206

Greif, Judith Brown. "The Father-Child Relationship Subsequent to Divorce." ibid. pp. 47–57

Gross, Penny. "Kinship Structure in the Remarriage Family." 1981 (unpub.)

Hollender, M. H. "Women's Wish to Be Held: Sexual and Non-sexual Aspects." From *Medical Aspects of Human Sexuality*. 5:10:12–26. 1971

Lyall, Alan. "The Carryover Effects from First to Second Marriage." Given at conference on Remarriage and the Family, Clarke Institute, Toronto, 1978 (unpub.)

Messinger, Lillian. "Remarriage between Divorced People with Children from Previous Marriages: A Proposal for Preparation for Remarriage." From *Journal of Marriage and Family Counseling*. 2:193–200. 1976

_____, Walker, Kenneth N., Freeman, Stanley. "Preparation for Remarriage Following Divorce: The Use of Group Techniques." From *American Journal of Orthopsychiatry*. 48:263–272. 1978

Robson, Bonnine. "A Developmental Approach to the Treatment of Children of Divorcing Parents." From *Therapy with Remarriage Families*. Aspen Publications, 1982. pp. 59–78

Sager, Clifford J.; Walker, Elizabeth; Brown, Hollis Steer; Crohn, Helen M.; Rodstein, Evelyn. "Improving Functioning of the Remarried Family System." From *Journal of Marital and Family Therapy*. Jan. 1981. pp. 3–12

Schlesinger, Benjamin. "Remarriage in Canada." Guidance Centre, Faculty of Education. University of Toronto, 1978

Steinhauer, Paul. "The Child with Four Parents: Some Common Problems Faced by Children Whose Parents Have Divorced." Given at conference on Remarriage and the Family, Clarke Institute, Toronto, 1978 (unpub.)

Visher, Emily B. and Visher, John S. "Stepfamilies in the 1980s." From *Therapy with Remarriage Families*. Aspen Publications, 1982. pp. 105–119

Walker, Kenneth N. and Messinger, Lillian. "Remarriage after Divorce: Dissolution and Reconstruction of Family Boundaries." From *Family Process*. 18: 185–192. 1979